# THE
# TRIALS
## OF A
# SCOLD

# THE
# TRIALS
## OF A
# SCOLD

## THE INCREDIBLE TRUE STORY
## OF WRITER ANNE ROYALL

# JEFF BIGGERS

Thomas Dunne Books

St. Martin's Press ⚹ New York

THOMAS DUNNE BOOKS.

An imprint of St. Martin's Press.

THE TRIALS OF A SCOLD. Copyright © 2017 by Jeff Biggers. All rights reserved. Printed in
the United States of America. For information, address St. Martin's Press, 175 Fifth Avenue,
New York, N.Y. 10010.

www.thomasdunnebooks.com

www.stmartins.com

Designed by Michelle McMillian

Library of Congress Cataloging-in-Publication Data

Names: Biggers, Jeff, 1963– author.
Title: The trials of a scold : the incredible true story of writer Anne
    Royall / Jeff Biggers.
Description: First edition. | New York : Thomas Dunne Books, 2017. |
    Includes bibliographical references.
Identifiers: LCCN 2017024840 | ISBN 9781250065124 (hardcover) |
    ISBN 9781466871595 (ebook)
Subjects: LCSH: Royall, Anne Newport, 1769–1854. | Women travelers—
    United States—Biography. | Travel writers—United States—Biography. |
    Women journalists—United States—Biography.
Classification: LCC E340.R88 B55 2017 | DDC 910.4092 [B]—dc23
LC record available at https://lccn.loc.gov/2017024840

Our books may be purchased in bulk for promotional, educational,
or business use. Please contact your local bookseller or the Macmillan Corporate and
Premium Sales Department at 1-800-221-7945, extension 5442, or by email
at MacmillanSpecialMarkets@macmillan.com.

First Edition: November 2017

10  9  8  7  6  5  4  3  2  1

*In memory of Elizabeth "Libby" Harris,*
*my high school librarian*


*For Barbara Welter,*
*my Hunter College history professor*

# Contents

*Acknowledgments* ix

*Introduction* 1

ONE
## Her Mother's Daughter
*8*

TWO
## Flaying the Saucy Rogues
*28*

THREE
## A Female of Respectability
*52*

FOUR
## The Black Book
*80*

FIVE
**The Last American Witch Trial**
*111*

———

SIX
**The Huntress in the Den of Vipers**
*168*

———

EPILOGUE
**The Trial of Public Opinion**
*215*

*Notes 231*
*Bibliography 253*

# Acknowledgments

Inanzittutto, grazie, come sempre, a Carla, Diego e Massimo per aver condiviso le prove i tribolazioni di questo libro.

Special thanks to my editor, Marcia Markland, for her insights in shaping and guiding the literary journey of Anne Royall, and to Amanda Finn and the stalwarts at Thomas Dunne Books at St. Martin's Press, who have wonderfully moved along this project, many years in the making. Copyeditor Ryan Masteller did an excellent job in the margins.

The writing of this book was made possible by a Calumet Artist Residency, thanks to Corey Hagelberg and Kate Land in the Miller Beach community of Gary, Indiana—just up the bluff from the spirit of another muckraker, Nelson Algren.

My folks, Jean and John, have always been my first readers, and with their own octogenarian wisdom provided deeply appreciated remarks on the first drafts of this book.

Thanks, as well, to all the librarians and clerks who assisted my haunts along the trail of archives and special collections. My colleagues at the University of Iowa library, in particular, did a lot of heavy lifting of inter-library loans and retrieval of nineteenth-century newspapers. I consider librarians to be the great keepers of our stories and hence the oracles of our past and future, forever waiting for us to discover the next row of treasures. In terms of public libraries, I still define a town's worth on the quality of its library.

In this respect, I wanted to express my gratitude to Barbara Welter, my advisor in the history department at Hunter College in New York City back in the 1980s, who encouraged me to pursue my incorrigible pursuit of oral history, and whose own pioneering work on American women in the nineteenth century has informed much of my research on Anne Royall.

And finally, eternal thanks to Elizabeth "Libby" Harris, my high school librarian, who rescued my education and piled me down with novels and poetry collections and magazines that served as my real classes. I'll never forget her; she became my mentor and confidant. I've dedicated this book in her memory.

# THE
# TRIALS
## OF A
# SCOLD

# Introduction

*Bloody feet, sisters, have worn smooth the path by which you have come hither.*

—ABBY KELLEY FOSTER, NATIONAL WOMEN'S RIGHTS CONVENTION, 1851

I n the summer of 1829, more than a century after Grace Sherwood had been plunged into the Lynnhaven River in Virginia in what is generally considered the last American witch trial, a bedraggled Anne Royall took the stand at the Circuit Court of the District of Columbia to face charges of being an "evil disposed person" and a "common scold."

The US district attorney had conjured the charges from an ancient English common law that had long been dismissed in England as a "sport for the mob in ducking women," especially for older women, as a precursor in trials for witchcraft.

The 60-year-old Royall, godmother of the muckrakers, grinned in the seat of the accused for defending free speech and freedom of the press. According to the court's research, England had curtailed the conviction of "common scolds" in the late 1770s at the same time it ceased hanging women and gypsies as witches.

Not so in our nation's capital. For the throng of reporters that crowded the suffocating courthouse that summer, the *United States v. Anne Royall*—and the "vituperative powers of this giantess of literature," according to the *New York Observer*—would become one of the most bizarre trials in Washington, DC.

Anne Royall was no stranger to trials. One of the most notorious writers of her time, she had shattered the ceiling of participation for politicized women a generation before Elizabeth Cady Stanton and Susan B. Anthony entered the suffrage ranks and issued the "voice of woman" into the backroom male bastions of banking and politics nearly two centuries before Hillary Clinton and Elizabeth Warren.

She had paid dearly for her groundbreaking role as a satirist and muckraker.

Nearly half a century after Royall's death in 1854, the *Washington Post* would stretch a headline across its pages with a reminder of her still haunting and relevant legacy: "She was a Holy Terror: Her Pen was as Venomous as a Rattlesnake's Fangs; Former Washington Editress: How Ann Royall Made Life a Burden to the Public Men of Her Day."

The *Post*'s backhanded compliment of Royal's pioneering muckraking journalism, however, missed her defining element in the art of exposé nearly a century before President Teddy Roosevelt in 1906 famously decried "the man with the muck rake": her take-no-prisoners humor in defense of the freedom of the press—at any cost.

"She could always say something," declared a New England editor, "which would set the ungodly in a roar of laughter."

Anne Royall knew how to make her readers laugh, and laugh at men—a dangerous talent, especially for a freethinking woman who rattled the bones of Capitol Hill and made Congress "bow down in fear of her" as the whistleblower of political corruption, fraudulent land schemes, and banking scandals, and as the thorn in the side of a powerful evangelical movement sweeping across the country.

She didn't simply have a second act in life; she had three or four or five. Born in Maryland in 1769, her freethinking politics had been shaped in the Virginia backwoods library of her Freemason and Revolutionary War–hero husband, William Royall. Rejected by his family as a lower-class concubine, Royall was left penniless when her husband's estate was finally adjudicated in the courts in 1823.

In debt but defiant as ever, Royall reinvented herself and launched a literary career at the age of 57. She announced her intention to publish a book on her recent sojourn in Alabama as a "serpent-tongued" traveling writer in the 1820s, introducing the term "redneck" to our American lexicon and a Southern and frontier view to an emerging national identity, and challenged the prevailing mores of "respectable" Christian women through one avenue suddenly available: the printing press.

Traipsing across the rough country as a single woman, she quickly published a series of "Black Books" that provided informative but sardonic portraits of the elite and their denizens from Mississippi to Maine. Her *Black Books* became prized possessions, if only for the delight of devastatingly funny descriptions of her "pen portraits." Power brokers sought out her company—or locked their doors. President John Quincy Adams called her the "virago errant in enchanted armor."

The anti-Mason religious fervor sweeping the Atlantic Coast and across the frontier infuriated Royall and prodded her to sharpen her witty pen in a self-appointed role as journalist and judge. The Second Great Awakening had provided the nation with one of its most critical opponents: dour and reactionary Presbyterians intent on establishing a Christian Party and transforming American politics—and

Royall took them on. "The missionaries have thrown off the mask," she warned. "Their object and their interest is to plunge mankind into ignorance, to make him a bigot, a fanatic, a hypocrite, a heathen, to hate every sect but his own, to shut his eyes against the truth, harden his heart against the distress of his fellowman and purchase heaven with money."

Royall may have limped after a brutal attack in New England, been scarred from a horsewhipping in Pittsburgh, and lamented being chased out of taverns on the Atlantic Coast, but she relished the attention in the nation's capital. Andrew Jackson's secretary of war, John Eaton, would soon testify on her behalf.

The Jacksonian era's most outlandish trial underscored an alarming witch hunt in the press, singling out Royall's "unruly" boldness as a funny, foul-mouthed, politically charged, and outspoken woman in a volatile period of religious fervor. Tossed to the heap of "hysterical" women, Royall was brandished by the federal court and subsequent historians with the shame of drunkards, prostitutes, cranks—and witches.

Royall dismissed the carnivalesque proceedings as an American inquisition—they had less to do with her "respectable" behavior and were instead aimed at her journalistic right to free speech as a woman. Why had no man, among many other equally abrasive journalists, ever been put on such a trial?

For journalism historian Patricia Bradley, in her survey of women in the early years of the press, Royall's branding as a "virago" diminished "her travels around the new nation as its storyteller," which could "easily have been framed heroically, and that her accounts of the new nation, appearing at the same time as Alexis de Tocqueville's vaulted accounts, may have become equally celebrated." But they never were.

In fact, her story is far more complicated than has ever been told.

Her role as a pioneering woman satirist in a suffocating age of religious orthodoxy has been overlooked by a century of moralizing critics. The successful and enduring tenacity of her enterprising literary strategies—maintaining an independent newspaper for decades, while publishing ten books as a social critic and agitator—rarely receives as much attention as her beggarly attire of an impoverished lifestyle.

Defiant to the "bitter end," a nautical term she helped introduce into the American vocabulary, Royall roasted the wags on the Washington scene for three decades and, hence, remained an unavoidable female symbol—and target—in an era when women were "gross counterparts" in American humor. Her larger-than-life figure grew even more worrisome for critics when Royall targeted elite women in the religious and reform movements. Such audacious tampering with the "cult of true womanhood" in that period, as historian Barbara Welter notably wrote, damned such a person—especially another woman on the fringe of society—as an "enemy of God, civilization and of the Republic." To the defining traits of respectable womanhood—piety, purity, submissiveness, and domesticity—Royall overturned every rule as an itinerant iconoclast who had cohabitated with her husband before marriage and took a vow to expose the hypocrisy of the "church and state" forces.

To this end, as novelist Shirley Du Bois declared in her own harrowing period of political witch hunts in the 1950s, Royall's role as a pioneering woman politico should have also distinguished her as a de facto feminist. A generation before the suffrage movement launched its call for women's rights at the historic convention in Seneca Falls in 1848, Royall breached the accepted place of women in the halls of Congress, elbowed her way into the back rooms of political deals at the White House, and dominated the discussion of the latest news among her peers in the corridors of the national press. But her refusal to attend to the suffrage cause, above all else—especially her campaign for universal education as an entryway to public participation—set her on the margins of women's history. Royall's quick trigger in expressing her disgust of ignorance, especially among the elite social reformers, regardless of gender, won her few friends. Few women of her time, on the other hand, expressed such a concern for reversing the tide of anti-intellectualism and its fallout in political corruption.

Royall has been largely ignored or minimized by most histories on women in her era and conversely lionized by historians of the Masonic brotherhood, which had banned women from their covens.

In truth, the enduring issues that she challenged in her time—the stranglehold of financial and religious interests in the polarization of politics, the fragmentation of national unity, the unending debates over the freedom of the press and freedom of speech, the role of anti-intellectual mediums to disenfranchise the powerless from public participation, and the shifting and historic roles of women in the public arena and media—make Royall's complex story worth reconsideration today.

Her life serves as a cautionary tale of the price paid by one woman for the right to dissent; of the historical use of ridicule and satire in leveling the patriarchal claims of frightened men in power; of the small wonder of reinvention in a state of desperation; of an older woman who repeatedly rose from mishaps and refused to be silenced.

Anne Royall was warned, tried, and convicted. Nevertheless, she persisted—for decades.

Here's the coda: Anne Royall took her revenge after her witch trial. At the age of 62, she launched her own newspaper in Washington, DC, with a gaggle of orphans and carried out two decades of investigative reporting and often hilarious commentary in an increasingly divided nation as a pioneering woman journalist, editor, and publisher—effectively, the nation's first blogger.

As a witness to the historic demonstration by Samuel Morse of his telegraph in the Capitol room on May 24, 1844, Royall recognized the first "information highway" for the nation's communication expansion as its grid was laid along the very horse trails and rutted stagecoach lines that she had already traveled as a pioneering writer. Morse would be immortalized that day at the Capitol. Royall would be forgotten.

Nonetheless, the playful Royall couldn't resist edging to the elbow of Morse's tapper, insisting on her own rendezvous with history. Anne Royall was present, she informed the assistant at the key. He nodded and tapped a series of strokes, as a small wheel on his right slowly turned. Royall smiled. She didn't bother to look around. Within seconds, the assistant reached over and retrieved a narrow slip of paper that had issued from the telegraph machine, tore it off, and then handed it to the singular newspaper editor. Royall took it into her worn hands.

"Mr. Rogers respects to Mrs. Anne Royall."

# ONE

## Her Mother's Daughter

*Mrs. Royall has again appeared before the public, in her character of authoress. We know of no American lady of the present day, whose writings attract so great attention, or evince so close an observance of men and manners. The mother and a brother of Mrs. Royall live near us, with whom we have been acquainted several years—with the brother very intimately so. They are both persons of intelligence, and the old lady, apparently 90 years of age, retains a distinct recollection of the principal characters of the Revolution—particularly those of Virginia, her native state.*

—CENTREVILLE (INDIANA) WESTERN TIMES, JUNE 27, 1829

In the spring of 1772, departing with the tides of migrants crossing the Allegheny Mountains into southwestern Pennsylvania for new land opportunities, Mary and William Newport packed up a three-year-old Anne and her baby sister, Mary, and left their native Baltimore, Maryland.

"I am genuine backwoods," Anne declared upon her return to southwestern Pennsylvania in her late fifties. "A literary wild-cat from the backwoods," a newspaper had responded. Anne shrugged at the lack of an available carriage or stagecoach to take her to her childhood home on Mount Pisgah in Westmoreland County and saddled up an old family friend's horse, Fly, before setting off with great excitement into the rugged country for a rendezvous with her past.

Much that we know of Anne Royall's early life, in fact, is based on her insightful yet often contradictory notes—written when she revisited an area or encountered a member of the family or an old friend—that peppered various books.

Ye who have been torn from the haunts of your childhood, and after a separation of half a century to enjoy the felicity of seeing those sacred spots, endeared by innocence and a thousand recollections, will know what I felt! To be borne on the stormy sea of life almost an age, far from the scenes of youthful innocence, to which your heart was wended, and would give worlds to see! Thus, on a sudden, to hail those dear and "long between" but never forgotten shades, where often I used to sit and weave the many colored leaves, and stray after a Mayapple, was joy unutterable!

While the joys of nature on the Newports' family farm on the slopes of Mount Pisgah didn't last long, they provided the background in Royall's writings of some of the earliest American descriptions of the area. Anne recalled witnessing wolves and other predators trotting by her well; she penned portraits of traders who emerged from the forest, writing about her first look at a cube of sugar; she chronicled the life of a German hermit, draped in gourds, who lived peacefully among the various indigenous tribes that had continued to push back against the encroachment of the unyielding settlers.

Such experiences in nature, and her place in it, shaped much of Anne's literary form and identity as a self-described "backwoods westerner." The imprint of this backwoods upbringing defined much of

Anne's relationship with the rest of the world: at once in denial and defensive, and also haughty and defiant. Years later, feeling snubbed by the famed Noah Webster, the eminent Federalist editor and author of *An American Dictionary of the English Language*, who once eyed Anne with "ineffable scorn," she quipped to her readers that "we backwoods folks are not learned ourselves," but "we have a warm liking for learned people."

Anne, of course, wasn't the first to invoke the backwoods badge of courage. In 1827, Tennessee pioneer Davy Crockett had already taken Washington by storm, "fresh from the backwoods, half horse, half alligator, a little touched with the snapping turtle."

Nor did literary endeavors take it on the lam in the backwoods. Anne excitedly pointed out where the log cabin schoolhouse once stood. Describing how her father taught her to read at an early age, Anne recalled sitting alone on a stump before the cabin door and reading until nightfall, in the backdrop of nature's immense arena.

But the beauty inimitable of the scenery arises from a happy combination of images: like a well woven wreath, every thing is in its place—every shade and attitude is happily matched. The Loyalhannah, rough and foaming, but straight, the Connemaugh, winding in a smooth serpentine; the Kiskaminitas, flowing in a broad, smooth stream; the symmetry of the canal; the rural village; the sealike meadows, all intermingled with a towering foliage in nature's richest dress. Imagine yourself raised to the sudden height of from three to four hundred feet, and embracing an extent of three counties, in harmonious stillness, while you are seated aloft upon an even green, which seems to sit smiling at the rolling streams, and all the airy gems of polished nature. Such is the view from Mount Pisgah: but

THE TRIALS OF A SCOLD

chiefly I loved to dwell upon the Loyalhannah. It was the only image of the whole I recollected. . . .

When I took my last look of this, I seemed to leave my soul behind! The spring, where the wolves passed the dim path, where lay the snake—the slope, up which the hermit Stephen used to come. But how shall I bring my swelling heart—yes, how—to touch the tender string which, and forever, binds me to the small tranquil spot, where waves a small sugartree, as if to perpetuate the day, when surrounded by the lords of the forest, I sat upon the low stump at the cabin-door and learned to read.

The so-called lords of the forest did not accept the infringement of Anne's settlers. Requiring more protection from indigenous attacks, the family moved from Mount Pisgah to the far western margins of Pennsylvania, near the Hanna's Town settlement, where the first English court had been founded west of the Allegheny mountain chain. By 1775, Anne's father vanished from the narrative, and her mother remarried another settler named Butler, had a son, and soon lost her second husband. The worst tragedy, however, took place on July 13, 1782.

Despite the surrender of the British in the fall of 1781 and the authorization of peace treaty negotiations by the British crown in the spring of 1782, battles of vendetta continued to rage across the Ohio River Valley and into southwestern Pennsylvania.

Considered by some historians as one of the last acts of the American Revolution, British troops joined Seneca leader Sayenqueraghta in a full-scale attack on the settlement of Hanna's Town in the summer of 1782. Given its historic importance as the county seat and courthouse for Westmoreland County, a rival to Pittsburgh, and in retribution for the earlier Patriot burning of Sayenqueraghta's village, the community was leveled by the joint forces, who torched 30 cabins and all the buildings with the exception of the fort, where town residents, including Anne Royall and her mother and siblings, took refuge. Only two people were killed. The attack, though, left nothing but charred ruins, which nature soon reclaimed. Hanna's Town disappeared from the map.

Anne never forgot the traumatic experience; it informed her sense of survival and, strangely enough, provided a context for much of her longtime defense of Native American rights. "The present generation have scarcely any idea of the privations and trouble of settling the country," she wrote in her chronicles. She saw the American flag for the first time in Hanna's Town, she noted in a letter, and forever returned to that moment when she viewed the flag in other places. "And with it all the sufferings of those trying times. I suffered all that human nature could bear, both with cold and hunger. Oh, ye wealthy of those times, little idea had ye of what the poor frontier settlers suffered."

Perhaps that last line could have been aimed at her future husband, William Royall, and the sneering Sweet Springs inhabitants in western Virginia who doubted her pedigree. "On that day," she added, referring to the attack on Hanna's Town, "my heart first learned the nature of care."

Later in her life, newspapers and historical accounts went off the edge of romance in recasting Anne's fate in the frontier attack with her eventual rendezvous with William Royall. Placing her into the pages of the novel *The Last of the Mohicans*, which was published in 1826—the same year as her first book—one writer described Anne as a larger-than-life "Indian captive" who "remained with the savage tribe until she reached womanhood." Another magazine finished the story: "Captain Royal [*sic*], an officer in the Continental Army and one of the heroes of Valley Forge, hearing that a young white girl was a prisoner of the Indians on the banks of the Ohio River, resolved to rescue her." The dashing young soldier married the girl, who, "save in color and the Anglo-Saxon mold of her features, was of Indian blood."

In reality, Anne and her mother and her half-brother James packed up their few belongings and joined a wagon party to Staunton, Virginia, in 1782, where a family relative resided. A single woman who hired herself off as a laborer, Anne's mother fell from the status of a pioneer farmer to the indigent lower class, taking her children down with her. Anne's first biographer, Sarah Harvey Porter, wrote that Anne winced at the fact that she had to sit in a different place in church on Sunday, separate from her upper-class school friends. However, in visiting Staunton in her later writings, Anne noted the "mingled emotions" of joy and sorrow, pleasure and regret, and the "thousand (nay, ten thousand) vicissitudes [that] rendered those objects melancholy pleasing." Her most painful memory of their short residence in Staunton, though, involved another woman, who had sought to cross a river by ferry. "She looked tired, hungry, miserable," Anne wrote, perhaps recalling her mother's desperation or foreshadowing her future as a penniless traveler. The ferryman, who Anne identified as a local Presbyterian, refused to accept the woman's few coins as payment, despite her cries that she urgently needed to cross the river. As he readied to leave without her, the desperate woman tore a handkerchief from around her neck and offered it. The ferryman took her coins and scarf and departed, leaving her in tears.

Such brutality and contempt for aggrieved women should have hardened Anne's heart for her introduction to Sweet Springs, in western Virginia, her next stop on the road. Despite the kind entreaties to stay from family friends in the Staunton area, Anne and her mother understood their bottom rung in society.

Perched alone on a plantation on Peters Mountain in Sweet Springs, the eccentric William Royall adhered to a different order.

In the mid-1700s, Royall carried the mantle of one of the most aristocratic families in the Tidewater. The first Royall had arrived in Jamestown, Virginia, aboard the *Charitie* from England in 1622, when European inhabitants numbered in the thousands on the eastern shores of North America. A Powhatan uprising that year added to the precariousness of the unrelenting colonists' survival. Within a generation, the Royall family possessed a prime thousand-acre plantation along the James River. The settlements grew and continued to push further west.

The second son of the county court justice, sheriff, and vestry for the local Anglican church, William Royall spent more time with his dogs and guns along the confluence of the Appomattox and James Rivers than among the circles of the wealthy planters.

Failing to finish his legal studies, Royall preferred the beguiling works of writers from the French Enlightenment, especially Voltaire, another aristocrat who had spurned his father's career plans and dedicated himself to the defense of reason, religious tolerance, and civil liberties in an age of an absolute monarchy. Shipped off to run a tobacco plantation in Amelia County in western Virginia, the 20-something Royall suddenly found himself heir to the family fortune when his older brother and father both died in 1774.

Far from settling among the idle rich, Royall set out to use his wealth to provide supplies to Massachusetts after the English blockade of the Port of Boston cut off provisions under the Intolerable Acts. The young heir joined the Virginia militia, serving as both an officer and donor to the revolutionary cause, often outfitting his soldiers and con-

THE TRIALS OF A SCOLD

tributing horses. By 1776, Royall rose to the rank of captain of the 2nd Virginia Regiment in the Continental Army, heading forays into some of the worst battles in the Carolinas. In a memorial filed right before his death, Royall chronicled his seven years of service in the revolutionary forces, from which he declined any pay or reimbursement of his expenses. Surrounded at one point by the British army, Royall barely escaped his death, fleeing on a horse as he assisted the Marquis de Lafayette against Lord Cornwallis in Virginia in the final days of the American Revolution. The tide turned, of course, and the Patriots, thanks to their French allies, rebounded in Virginia.

In the aftermath of Cornwallis's surrender to George Washington at Yorktown in the fall of 1781, Royall took his rightful place as a House delegate from Amelia County in the Virginia General Assembly. But the allure of political power and its intrigues had little sway over his passions, and he disappeared without a word. One of his French Enlightenment heroes, Jean-Jacques Rousseau, had earlier admonished his fellow human beings in his "Discourse on Inequality" to be true to one's "state of nature."

Now in his early thirties, William Royall removed himself to the far reaches of Appalachia, crossing the Blue Ridge Mountains, slowly fording a succession of saddled ridges toward a small valley settlement near the mineral waters of Sweet Springs. He secured a plantation along Peters Mountain in today's West Virginia. The hemlock, white pine, and red oak, the drapes of spring flowers, the basins of streams inhabited by ruffed grouse, black bear, and bobcats—these would have all fascinated a naturalist like Royall, though he was hardly a stranger to the mountains.

Anne loved to recount the story of why her husband had abandoned the Tidewater elite for the rugged hill folk of her "Grison Republic," which she nicknamed after the independent canton in

Switzerland. Back in the summer of 1781, when the British forces moved across Virginia with little pushback, the General Assembly fled across the Blue Ridge to establish their temporary capital in the town of Staunton. Receiving word of the quick advance by the notorious British commander Banastre Tarleton, who carried out the infamous Waxhaw massacre of American Patriots, the General Assembly and militia members scattered from Staunton in all directions—with the exception of William Royall and, according to his wife, a gaggle of "old gray-headed men, and little boys, with their guns and shot-pouches on their shoulders, marching cheerfully on to meet the foe." Tarleton's attack never came, though, as the British leader returned to Yorktown. Outraged by the lack of courage by the elite legislators, Royall declared to the mountain folk, "You are fine fellows—I will disown my country, (meaning East Virginia) and come and live among you."

Staking out his libertarian claim on Peters Mountain, Royall mingled among the constant influx of travelers to the valley, which was well known among the indigenous and colonists as a curative station, and earned the respect of the small community, including the Lewis family, who had designs on fashioning Sweet Springs into a resort town and area courthouse. He kept his door open to visitors, especially to his brethren in the Masonic Lodge. When a temporary courthouse was finally appointed in Sweet Springs, Royall served on the juries for the first few years before stepping away.

Author Van Wyck Brooks, in *The World of Washington Irving*, referred to the fledgling mountain resort as the "marriage market of the South," where old men discussed politics as "invalids rejoiced in the breeze and healing waters," and "young men and girls danced and flirted."

While far from being a hermit, Royall clearly retreated from post–American Revolution society, which was undergirded by the rising merchant class and land speculators; instead, he wanted to replant the benevolent seeds of his eighteenth-century Enlightenment philosophers among the nature-bound mountaineers. He brought his library from Amelia County, and it included works by political radicals like Thomas Paine, the volumes of natural history by French writer Georges-Louis Leclerc Buffon, the satires and plays by Voltaire, and the works of English philosopher John Locke, who stressed the separation of church and state.

William Royall remained a bachelor for the next several years, emancipating some of his enslaved workers—though not all—who tended a farm that amounted to little more than a few head of cattle, and engaging in notable bouts of heavy drinking. Sarah Harvey Porter uncovered a fascinating detail on Royall during this time in an oral history that had been passed down by neighbors: the "eccentric" farmer, as he was considered, kept "cattle and horses in their natural state; there were neither geldings or steers to be found in the herd."

The "quiet country" neighbors raised their eyebrows more than once at Royall's affairs, especially when an ailing woman named Mary Newport Butler, afflicted by "nerves," blood poisoning, and eczema, and her teenage daughter Anne and young son James appeared in Sweet Springs in 1787. Encouraged to visit the curative springs by the Lewis family, who had met the travelers a few years earlier in Staunton, the 18-year-old Anne—then Anne Newport—along with her sick mother and half-brother, found work at Royall's plantation as servants. Whether he hired her out of pity or need, Royall's employment of Anne's mother as a maid caught the attention of the neighboring community as well. The same oral history passed along to Porter by relatives in the area recognized the disturbing role—at least for some—of Mary as a "wash-woman and menial—a subject of reproach of course to the slave-owning aristocratic neighbors; for few white women on our frontier had to be menials, and those only of the lowest class."

William appreciated the inquisitiveness of the servant's daughter at the door of his library. Her mother had always made sure Anne had access to books, purchasing a series of "little histories" that included classic stories like *Moll Flanders*, *Seven Wise Masters*, and *Paddy from Cork* when Anne was in her early teens. Now William opened the doors to Shakespeare; his beloved Voltaire; the French, German, and English thinkers in the Enlightenment; Paine's "Age of Reason"; and a century of classics. "Had I not fortunately fallen in with a person of learning," Anne wrote later, "I should have delved at 'little histories' all my life."

As their relationship grew beyond the rapport of plantation owner and servant's daughter, Anne soon spent more time in the library than at work, memorizing the lines from John Dryden's *Palamon and Arcite* translation of *The Canterbury Tales*: "Some pray for riches— riches they obtain." William invited Anne for walks; they toured the valleys on horseback. She became his confidant as much as his co-conspirator in his freethinking salons. She joined William in the evenings around the fireplace, and he beguiled her with stories of the American Revolution, lectures on Locke's theory of natural law and natural rights, and tales of his hunting exploits with his dog, Spad. He invoked his role in the secret society of the Masonic Lodge.

William's role as the master dominated their relationship; she was 18 years old, he was 40. She became his common-law wife. She openly took a seat aside William in the parlor rooms when visitors arrived. Anne variably recalled either a 20- or 23-year age difference.

The Lewis family refused to visit Royall once the relationship between master and servant's daughter became clear. How dare Anne become the host of the plantation when Masonic brothers or outside visitors appeared there? William Royall treated her as an equal at the dinner table. They shared knowing winks one evening, Anne recalled, when William allowed a visiting lawyer to pontificate erratically on the historical roles of Cicero and Demosthenes. The Royalls remained quiet throughout the lecture, trading only raised eyebrows, until William could take it no more and blasted the aristocratic lawyer for being a "laughingstock" and knowing less than the family dog, Citizen. "What a pity this gentleman had not chosen the profession of a preacher," Royall quipped.

While Anne was out sowing seeds one day "when dogwood was in bloom," a servant with a "saddle horse" came for her and told her it was time to get married; a circuit-riding preacher had crossed over Peters Mountain on November 18, 1797. Anne and William married that day—she was in her late twenties, Royall in his late forties—though their certificate would not be officially registered until the spring.

Their marriage may have become official, but it remained tenuous to some. Anne wrote of her fear, especially in the presence of others, of laughing at or mocking her husband in any way. "My husband never laughed," she wrote years later in a letter. "And [he] had a fashion of leaning forward, when displeased" that always made Anne tremble. "Nor did I rise from the table till he made the signal."

Moments of tenderness did exist, Anne wrote, in what she described as a happy marriage, especially when she struggled through the "pouts," a cryptic reference she made several times to lingering bouts of depression and "splenetic fits" of melancholy in the harder months of winter. The elder Royall always managed to restore her to "good humor," often by using pet names.

For Elizabeth Roane and her husband, James, Royall's anxious niece and nephew, the official announcement of matrimony was devastating. The interference of a wife into William Royall's holdings only spelled trouble for them. Nonetheless, they remained in touch with their uncle through letters. In 1806, adding to their fears over inheritance, they learned that Anne's young niece (from her sister who had remained in Pennsylvania) had come to live on Peters Mountain, introducing the first and only child at the plantation.

During their 16 years of marriage, the Royalls operated the small farm and added a lumber mill; they invested in land schemes near today's Charleston, West Virginia. As William Royall's addiction to alcohol became more apparent, even to outsiders, Anne began to oversee more and more of the daily operations. In a rare admission during a later dispute over a land deal, Anne noted the fraudulent nature of a transaction by William, given that he was "much intoxicated at the time." Her duties, therefore, included handling a drunk and occasionally belligerent husband by any means necessary, though Anne claimed in court she had never performed an "intentional act of cruelty." Stories began to circulate in Sweet Springs of strange sightings on Peters Mountain: Anne and her enslaved workers holding down the master, pouring cold water or even ashes to sober him up; William, running from the manor. Other friends, though, testified that William Royall typically ended up in a "fitt of frenzy" by the night's end.

After William Royall's ceremonial visit in 1808 to his family's Tidewater homeplace, including a less than pleasant visit with the Roanes, it was clear that he had no intention of leaving his fortune behind for his niece Elizabeth Roane and her son, named after William. In an act of desperation, the Roanes sent young William, then a teenager, to visit Royall on Peters Mountain in 1811. The encounter didn't go well. Young William made the rounds of the Sweet Springs taverns and collected stories about Anne, her nefarious reputation, and her mistreatment of his uncle. Roane sent a follow-up letter to his uncle, detailing his findings, including gossip that Anne had become intimately close with a young law student named Matthew Dunbar, a family friend who often visited the Royalls in the evenings and shared the family's intellectual interests.

William dismissed the young Roane as a dilettante, especially compared to the curious Dunbar, one of the few young men in the Sweet Springs area that valued Royall's library. Roane's letter resulted in an unforeseen backlash. Most likely with Dunbar's assistance, Anne took him to court for defamation of character and libel in his letters and actually won. Worse yet, Roane didn't even know he had already been removed from William's final will, which designated a distant relative and former Revolutionary War comrade, William Archer, as the new heir. Anne, in fact, was only to receive a typical dower and use of the plantation; her niece was granted a modest section of land.

The Tidewater relatives, emerging from their decaying plantations along the faraway coast, sought to diminish Anne's presence and demand their rightful inheritance. As the only niece of the childless William, Elizabeth Roane and her debt-ridden husband had always been reliant on the benevolent uncle, who had gifted them estates and enslaved workers from the Royall family's vast landholdings in the Charles City area, and had even waived $2,000 in a bond when one of their debts ended up in the Supreme Court of Appeals in Virginia.

The Roanes had effectively planned their future—and that of their son, William Roane—on their uncle's assumed wealth and landholdings. Until 1808, in fact, William Roane had been the designated heir, at which time William Royall had made his last trip back to the Tidewater. Everyone noticed, especially the Roanes, that his health was in decline, and William Royall was a changed man. Something had happened back at his plantation in the mountains.

Within a year of William's death on Peters Mountain in 1812, the Roanes filed their objection to the will in the southwestern Virginia county courthouse. They contended that the hastily drawn will in William's shaky handwriting did not reflect his longtime promise of inheritance to the Roane family and was thus a forgery engineered by Anne. More so, Anne's questionable character became the focal point of their petition: "William Royall never did intend to give his property" to Anne Royall, "a woman with whom he at first cohabitated without marriage, but whom he was afterwards induced to marry." They pointed out possible errors in the will, including the date of the signatures by the witnesses.

The grand scope of William's wealth, however, was misleading. Most of his eastern land holdings had been sold or given away. His remote Peters Mountain estate tended more toward nature than plantation; very little of the grounds could be cultivated. Only days before his death in the winter of 1812, Royall, aided by Anne, filed a petition with the Virginia House of Delegates for long-deferred compensation for his revolutionary service, nearly half a century late. "Untoward circumstances in this his grand climacteric of life, has in some measure already," the Royalls wrote, "and may without the timely interposition of your honorable house reduce him to abject penury and want."

Nearly seven years later, in the summer of 1819, Anne stood before Judge James Allen in a small courtroom in Fincastle, Virginia, with only two windows to one side and a chimney in the back, for the last hearing of a seemingly never-ending legal battle. Compared to the overflowing crowd of curious bystanders Anne would one day face in Washington, the Virginian courtroom was hauntingly empty, with no fans and a divided family. Only Anne, the two attorneys, and a handful of witnesses took seats; Elizabeth and James Roane were also in attendance. The Roanes had been challenging William Royall's will since they received word of his death in the early winter of 1813.

At this point, of course, Anne had no public relations platform to defend herself; she was a distraught widow whose marriage of 16 years—after ten years of a quiet courtship—had seemingly disintegrated the minute the master left the house. In the words of a Revolutionary War friend of William's, whose family had known Anne since she was in her teens, the master had simply kept her as a "concubine."

All eyes turned to the evil woman who had dared to enter the house of Royall. William's purported last will was a forgery, they charged, pointing at Anne as the perpetrator.

By the time of the 1819 trial, in fact, there was very little left of Royall's assumed wealth. William's death triggered an avalanche of creditors as early as 1813, all of whom had deferred payment on various transactions during the elder man's lifetime. Anne sought to relieve some debts through the sale of enslaved workers, including a young man who had grown up on the plantation, along with exchanges of land. Once the wintry clinch broke on Peters Mountain in 1813, the widow Anne packed up her niece, now promised to be married, and two remaining enslaved servants and moved to Charleston, where she claimed they had been planning to relocate for years. She left the sale of the Peters Mountain plantation in the hands of a local auctioneer; without her presence or any advocates, the remote mountain holdings and manor brought in less than $500, a fraction of what she had expected. The marriage of her niece siphoned off more of her finances and engaged her in more debt. Within four years, a series of investments in the Charleston area, including the construction of a tavern and a foray into the booming salt trade, had all failed to materialize in any successful way, further draining Anne's assets.

It all came to a halt in 1817 when a local court ruled in her favor on the will. Anne took what was left of her dower and holdings, including the last enslaved black worker named Davy, and saddled up a horse to leave the state. She declared her intent to join the wave of migrants pouring into the newly created territory of Alabama. Anne wanted to head even further west. Her sojourn in Alabama, though it would figure prominently in her development as a writer, did not last long. The court summoned her back to the mountains in 1819.

After 48 years of her life in the Appalachian Mountains, Anne had endured the cloistered valleys long enough. "One learns more in a day by mixing with mankind," she wrote, "than he can in an age shut up in a closet." Years later, passing through the region, she would reflect on her "Grison Republic" after hearing a fellow passenger in the stagecoach rave over the beauty she had left behind: "I have little partiality for the mountains," Royall wrote. "I have suffered too much amongst mountains; they are splendid objects to look at, and sound well in theories, but nothing wears worse than mountains when you take up your abode amongst them."

Anne's lament, of course, went beyond the rugged realities of a mountain farm. "Confined to their everlasting hills of freezing cold," the mountaineers lacked the enterprise and industry of westerners, as well as the "energy of mind, politeness of manners." Their close-minded Appalachian ways, Royall declared in a dismal fashion, "presented a distinct republic of their own."

On the last day of the 1819 trial, Anne approached the bench in the Fincastle courtroom, the persistent Roanes on the opposite side, and heard a veritable breakdown of her character, her womanhood, even her youth. The Roanes and their witnesses, all of whom had objected to Anne's entry into high society, reduced her to an evil woman who had manipulated an elderly man. This narrative would be reclaimed years later, after the publication of her first book, when a Charleston editor, offended by her comment that no geniuses had ever emerged out of West Virginia, stated that "Mrs. Royall was for several years a resident of our (Kanawha) county (in Charleston) . . . for when she was resident among us her fortunes were humble and that, far from having attained the celebrity which now enables her to command a handsome subsistence by the prostitution of her pen, she then found it a convenient mode of adding to her pecuniary resources by other questionable methods."

The identification of Anne as a prostitute, first launched when she was still a teenager at the home of William Royall, clung to her for the rest of her life whenever the discourse over decency appeared. While she never denied or responded to the allegations of cohabitation, Anne complained bitterly to her young lawyer friend Matthew Dunbar, whom she had been writing from Alabama during the winter of 1817, in a cryptic reference over the prostitution charge: "Were you not present when the news of the unfortunate _____ was announced?" The space for the word remained blank. She added: "The whole posse, with rage (instead of pity for the frailty of the sex) in their looks, hunted down their prey, more like blood hounds than human beings, and the forlorn sufferer was spurned from society."

Judge Allen read the jury's verdict, reversing the earlier ruling, and ended the six years of litigation. William Royall's last will was declared "cancelled and annulled" given that the ailing Royall "died intestate." Anne had to relinquish her "slaves, goods, chattels," and even her books; her small dower went toward restitution of the legal proceedings and other debts. Granting the Roanes possession of the Peters Mountain plantation, which had already been liquidated, among other holdings, the ruling unleashed a series of complicated legal suits over a mound of debts and transactions Anne had incurred over the past few years.

Most biographers then place Anne back on the road to Alabama, where she would reside until 1823. Yet there is a critical gap in her *Letters from Alabama*, which would be published as a book years later, from the trial in 1819 until the spring of 1821. As biographer Bessie James noted from courthouse files, the Kanawha County court issued orders for the sheriff to seize Royall's "goods and chattels," as well as "her body." James concluded, without any details or speculation, that "at this time, debtors went to prison. Anne could not pay, if she had wished to." In 1934, West Virginia state historian Phil Conley wrote that Royall "was next heard of as being confined in the jail of Greenbrier County for debt." Without any reference or documentation, Conley added, "Through the indulgence of a creditor, she was released about a year later."

No records of imprisonment have survived, nor did Anne ever mention such an episode in all of her writings. At the same time, her insistent inspections of debtor prisons in virtually every town and city might suggest a lingering experience she had never quite resolved.

Years later, Royall would look back at the trial in 1819 with her dark gallows humor. Judge Allen, a towering figure, had the "handsomest face in the world for his age." Nonetheless, "he ought to have been impeached" for her treatment.

Anne's final visit to her mother in Indiana in 1830, recorded in one of her *Black Book* travelogues, would bring her many trials and her family's journey full circle.

Having migrated with her son James Butler in 1809 to Kentucky and Indiana, Royall's frail mother never knew of her daughter's humiliating treatment in the various courtrooms—or the court of public opinion. Mary Newport Butler received little news from her "evil" daughter over the years; Anne remained the young woman, in her mind, she had naively brought to Sweet Springs in search of a cure for her ailments.

At the age of 78, Mary awaited her daughter's arrival in a log cabin, not far from the Wabash River in Indiana. Once the "handsomest of her day," Royall narrated, her mother now stooped over with a curved spine, shaking violently from a "palsy" that had affected her for years. She drank from a tube. Still, Anne captured her eyes, "as brilliant as ever," and leaned in closely to hear only one audible line: "Well, never, never, did I expect to see you again."

Royall saw her mother in a different light that day. Mary's role as an herbalist and natural medicine expert, which Anne once mocked, now appeared to be legendary among the community; despite experiencing "every vicissitude of fortune," she could sit back and have the pleasure of seeing her family "respectable, wealthy and flourishing." Except, perhaps, for her famous daughter.

Anne couldn't bear to bring her mother up to date on the trials and turmoil of her last years—from the fallout over William Royall's will to her debts and misfortune, her flight from the mountains, and, even now, her trial as a "common scold."

"I had met with a sad reverse of my fortune since I last saw my mother," Royall wrote. "But it is one upon which I have never been able to converse, and she dropt it."

# TWO

# Flaying the Saucy Rogues

*I have some notion of turning author some of these days, for though I know you are only indulging your irony (you saucy rogue, is that the way to treat your betters,) let me tell you I would not make the worst in the worst. You, and Joe Fry, may laugh again; I was never blind to your winks and nods; and if ever I do take up my pen, I mean to write a book, and I will flay you two saucy rogues.*

—ANNE ROYALL, *LETTERS FROM ALABAMA*

The seeds of Anne Royall's literary career may have been planted in the hills of West Virginia, under the guidance of the elder William Royall and his vast library of enlightenment and reason, but the catalyst for its labor took place in Alabama.

After she fled West Virginia, Anne returned to Alabama in the spring of 1821, somehow managing to avoid the last of her creditors and subsisting on the measly remains of her dower and sales of her personal items. It remains a mystery, in fact, how Royall managed to pay for her lodging and cover the itinerant pace she maintained, hopscotching from town to village in the emerging state of Alabama.

Anne eased into the role of an intrepid widow with assumed resources, unfettered from domestic duties, seeking to clear her mind on an extended vacation; she wrote letters without a hint of concern over her clearly disastrous financial situation. In effect, Anne had already begun the process of reinventing herself in the relatively anonymous and transient quarters of Alabama, where a constant stream of pioneers provided the cover—if not the color—for her new identity.

Nonetheless, Anne never allowed herself to fall into the rut of dilettantes. As early as her first trip in 1817, on the eve of Alabama's designation as a territory and throughout the "Alabama Fever" days of the land rush, Royall had already set out an ambitious plan to chronicle the new settlements in the land of the vanquished Creeks. Driven by the possibilities of the global cotton market, an estimated 127,000 immigrants and their enslaved workers had made their journey across the newly cut military roads by 1820, settling their squatter claims among the sparse cabins and former indigenous communities.

Addressing Matthew Dunbar, the young attorney now based in Charleston who had attended to her legal affairs and often visited her Sweet Springs home, Royall fashioned herself into a serious letter writer from the very first entry. Her letters are personal, at times flirty and at other times motherly, but they are clearly written in a self-conscious way to be read as informative and narrative-driven tales, as if she assumed "Matt" would share them. Or perhaps she had already envisioned publishing them in some form in the future.

"Mr. L. and myself are both sitting at one table, and trying to write," her first letter begins, though a drinking party had invaded their lodge and soon turned to arguing over religion. "I never knew any good, but on the contrary much harm, flow from these disputes," Royall went on. "As there is no sure mark of an evil disposed female, or want of virtue, than to hear her defame her own sex; so there can be no stronger evidence of a hypocrite than to hear him rail at other sects than that to which he belong; and I should want no better proof of his being every thing but a Christian."

From her first letter, long before her prose moved into book form, Anne had found her niche; a raucous, hard-drinking tavern or lodge, a debate over religion and politics in the background, the dialogue of intransigence by Christian women against any other women who dared to veer from their path, the daily inventory of the flora and fauna and most recent encounters, and generous portraits of the often larger-than-life characters filling the room with their death-defying travel stories.

A letter in the summer of 1821 from Courtland, Alabama, contained its usual updates on the local characters, and attention to the natural details; the "Colomba root has several broad leaves near the ground, in this shape like the hound's tongue," she noted on a journey through the woods. She described the "jointed snake," which, if struck with a stick, "flies to pieces with a jingling noise." The "great curiosity" for Royall was the "sensitive brier," a part of a plant that shrank when touched.

Anne delighted in the descriptions. She mused that she followed the "inimitable" Voltaire's notion that for writers to "convey a just idea of the characteristics of men, you must strictly observe the expressions which accompany their actions." Her portraits of encounters with various characters often read like stage instructions for actors. The famed Appalachian missionary and educator Reverend Gideon Blackburn was "a stout, coarse-featured man, of middle age, and very distant in his manners; but has great expression of countenance, and every mark of a sensible man." She understood her letters entertained Matt, and she wrote them accordingly. "Am I not a good old lady to send you such amusement?" she declared. But an undercurrent of irony, which bent toward sarcasm—a satirical twist to the

tavern scenes and players—was never far off. Nor was Anne unaware that her mannerisms or such literary devices could be
misread—or worse, mocked.

"I have some notion of turning author some of these days," Royall wrote that summer. Matt's reply was never referenced. Playfully
warning him that she was aware of his "winks and nods," Royall vowed
to slay the two "saucy rogues," fully aware of the assumed absurdity
of her declaration to become an author.

Royall's letters to her confidant portrayed more than landscapes
and local color. Her reading tastes were prodigious and eclectic; she
wrote book reviews with the unforgiving pen of a veteran critic.
Like many of her contemporary readers and writers, she railed against
the "insipid, frothy, nauseous" offerings of romance novels on one
hand and the Bible tracts and sermons that lined the bookshops
as the best sellers of the day. Accusing popular authors of lacking
any sense of history and philosophical understanding, Anne wrote,
"These silly novel writers must show their learning." But their
popularity among women, in particular, was indisputable. "Let blockheads read what blockheads write."

Anne was hardly alone. More than a generation later, literary ti-
tan Nathaniel Hawthorne famously echoed such criticism in 1855 in
a letter to his editor: "America is now wholly given over to a damned
mob of scribbling women, and I should have no chance of success
while the public is occupied with their trash." Hawthorne's lament
came at a dip in his career, when he was serving abroad in England
as a diplomat. When women "throw off the restraints of decency," he
wrote later, "and come before the public stark naked as it were—then
their books are sure to possess character and value."

Yet Anne's concern did not reflect envy, as some critics contend.
As early as 1818, writing letters to Matt from her temporary repose

near Andrew Jackson's plantation in Melton Bluff, Alabama, Anne pointed out the bane of romance novels in distancing readers from real-life issues. She crafted a discerning and insightful critique of the literature of escapism already afoot in early American history: such novels "corrupt the morals of our females, and engender hardness of heart to real distress."

Anne continued:

> Those most pleased with fictitious distress, have hearts as hard as iron. If they are pleased with one who relieves ficti-tious distress, the reality out to please much more, and every one may be real hero, or heroine, with less trouble than writ-ing or reading a romance. Let them just step into the streets, the highways, or the novel of the widow or orphan, heaven knows they may find enough there; they need not look in books for distress. I have seen pictures of real distress, which greatly exceeded the pen of any novel writers, and yet none heeds it.

She devoured the speeches of Irish barrister Charles Phillips, famed for his spirit of exaggeration. She mocked booksellers who offered her romance novels and Bible tracts, while she rescued the lampooning stories of Washington Irving's *Salmagundi*—or "The Whim-whams and Opinions of Launcelot Langstaff"—from the bins.

Lady "Sydney" Morgan stood out in distinction for Anne, though not for her celebrated Irish novels such as *The Wild Irish Girl*, a rol-licking tale of political nationalism. Anne preferred Morgan's travel books, especially on France, which had also gained the praise of fel-low writers like Lord Byron.

Anne gushed in a letter to Matt about Morgan's *France*:

This work will long remain a standing evidence of that towering
genius which knows no sex. Her delineation of men and manners are well drawn. Her style is classical, nervous, glowing, and
pure, and discovers a perfect knowledge of mankind. She is the
best portrayer I have met with, except Voltaire. She descends to
the bottom, and searches the lowest depths of society. She re-
ascends amongst the nobility and gentry, and unlocks the cabi-
nets of kings and ministers. She examines for herself. She bursts
the chains of prejudice, and comes forth arrayed in honors all her
own. This female, an honor to her sex, and the brightest ornament of literature, was once, it seems, an actress, and on the stage.

The critics, as a cautionary tale for Anne, tended to be less kind to
Morgan. One historian referred to Morgan as the author critics loved
to hate. One lengthy review of her book on France had its own sub-
headings: "Bad taste, Bombast and Nonsense, Blunders, Ignorance of
the French Language and Manners, General Ignorance, Jacobinism,
Falsehood, Licentiousness and Impiety." Echoing the same kind of
criticism that Anne would face in the future, another reviewer referred
to the "humpback old woman, absurdly attired, rouged and wigged;
vivacious and somewhat silly; vain, gossiping and ostentatious."

Strangely enough, Anne mentioned only once the work of author
and freethinker Frances Wright, whose travelogue, *Views of Society
and Manners in America*, appeared in 1821 to great acclaim. Her work
widened the small opening for women in travel literature. The Scottish iconoclast found much to admire in the United States, especially
among Anne's intrepid frontier settlements west of the Alleghenies.

Dismissing the "vulgar belief" of the Europeans that the American wilderness had been settled by the "worst members of the community," Wright found something visionary, "a liberality of sentiment," and a profound belief in civil liberties.

While their mutual obsession over the protection of free speech and the separation of church and state would entangle their lives over the next two decades, the itinerant Anne and Wright never met in person. "Mrs. Wright goes farther than I do," Anne wrote with a wink, referring to Wright's lectures on birth control. Years later, arriving in Wheeling, West Virginia, a day after Wright had spoken to a packed lecture hall, Anne challenged another travel writer—the Duke of Saxe-Weimar—who questioned Wright's ability as an independent woman traveler and claimed she was "very little respected by a certain class" for her writing "against religion." Anne shot back, shredding his double standard, clearly interpreting the criticism as her own: "And what if Miss Wright did travel alone. . . . Suppose Miss Wright had travelled in the company with a gentleman; would this have silenced their slanderous tongues? I fancy not; this is one sure mark of the hypocrisy of these people."

Such attacks on Wright only emboldened Anne to keep traveling— and writing. The mark of "vileness" resulted in accentuating the "merit of the other." The bitterness and envy against Wright had only confirmed Anne's "exalted" opinion of the Scottish author and activist.

Much to the dismay of a bookseller in Alabama, though, Anne championed James Paulding as her favorite writer, a detail few observers ever noted. Years later, on her first visit to New York City in 1824, Anne raced to meet the "celebrated man" with the passion of a fan. "If I admired him as a writer, I was charmed with his appearance and manners, which perfectly correspond with the idea we are led to form of him from his writings."

A co-conspirator with Washington Irving on the *Salmagundi* stories, Paulding published his masterful *Letters from the South* the same year that Anne first visited Alabama. The New York author had nearly generated a genre by himself, driven by the epistolary narrative, combative lawyers, and a "waggoner and a batteauxman" duo and their adventures among the new frontier. According to literary critic James Justus, Paulding shaped a generation of writers, whose works included "frontier fights" that were "heavily verbal affairs." Not everyone appreciated Paulding's satire, though. One critic gently noted his humor "is not always of the most refined nature, and his satirical attacks are perhaps more vigorous than witty."

After publishing a long poem, *The Backwoodsmen*, its narrative drawn with the "battle-axe of satire," Paulding drew national and international attention for his raucous lampoon of the English travelogue in America, which he aptly named *John Bull in America*. Inventing a pompous narrator who embarks on a journey to understand the inhabitants of the rising country, Paulding's protagonist reveals his "non-prejudiced" views of the "barbarous" Americans. "I also fully believed that the people were a bundling, gouging, drinking, spitting, impious race, without either morals, literature, religion, or refinement."

Anne devoured the embellished language, the smirking sense of aggrandizement, the thumping put-downs of those who claimed the freedom to chat about their private affairs, the scowling Englishman in the face of American rusticity, even the outrageous tales of cannibalism. She identified the narrative possibilities from stretching the familiar scenes of rural transport, navigated by whiskey-driven stagecoaches, into storylines of social and political satire. In her own contradictory way, the backwoods-proud Anne embraced many of the stereotypes and caricatures from Paulding's work, much in the same way that Davy Crockett loved the role of the future "Nimrod Wildfire" in Paulding's play *The Lion of the West*, in which Nimrod serves as a sort of comical cultural broker between the savage and the tender. Paulding's narrator in *John Bull* delighted with these contradictions:

> But there is one thing which puzzled me at first. Notwithstanding the disappointments of these poor people, their being gouged, dirked, roasted, and having their pigs stolen by the judges; their being regulated and rowdied, and obliged to cut down trees as big round as a hogshead—notwithstanding there is neither law, gospel, decency, or morality in the whole country, and that no honest person can possibly live in it; notwithstanding that every emigrant, without exception is sighing ready to break his heart, to get home; notwithstanding all this, I say it is a remarkable fact, that not one in a thousand ever goes home again!

Paulding's ridiculous narrator entertained the budding writer, his style clearly affecting Anne's outlook on the emerging American literature. She absorbed the power in self-deprecating and even distasteful humor to strip the masquerade of so-called cultural progress. Her letters to Matt, in fact, became increasingly more colorful, ramping up the descriptions beyond the real to the imagined; she infused her daily adventures with tart comments on the manners of her hosts or settlements, often with the biting and self-reverential language of a detached narrator like Paulding's own Bull.

Departing from Melton's Bluff one day for a trip to a temporary Cherokee camp where she encountered those who had been forced off their lands, Anne shifted to a more flippant tone than when she had earlier lamented the unjust situation of the native inhabitants. She framed her story as a clash of cultures, starting first with a comic description of her own travel party, as if the absurdity of their attire underscored the disconnection of white people to the local surroundings—and the natives. "A more ill-looking, frightened, chagrined, fatigued, be-drabbled, and be-drown set of miserables," she wrote, "than our party exhibited after being rocked and tossed about." Though the day had started well, "all the curls, crimps, and flourishing of gay gowns, new shoes, silk stockings, pantaloons and petticoats, shawls and other flaunting finery humbled." Once among the indigenous encampment, whose residents resisted the entreaties of the tour group, Anne set out alone to engage with the Cherokee women. She squatted to the ground and attempted to grind corn with them—they drank a mush of the fine roasted powder mixed with water—and asked them questions about their habits, even trying at one point to smoke a pipe with an elderly woman. The Cherokees tolerated Anne's imposition, though most refused to speak despite their knowledge of English. Anne understood: "It is very probable that the most effective means have been resorted to by our government to overcome their prejudices," she quipped. "I mean our rifles."

In some respects, Anne viewed Paulding's malevolent travelers and social critics as informative prototypes; and the writer himself emerged as an exemplar who had successfully chronicled the absurdities of his times—beyond the insipid romances that lined the shelves of the quickly forming American parlor rooms. Instead, Paulding frequented the domain of the solitary wanderer, like Anne, who also shared the raucous stagecoach with "banditti" and sought out the unusual in the American outback. Paulding's narrator couldn't resist issuing another declaration, which could have easily come from the future pen of Anne: "I came to recollect that considerably more than three-fourths of the people of this puissant republic were themselves rogues and banditti," which means, of course, that he had a "three to one favour" of being robbed by his fellow passengers.

The precarious, whiskey-fueled, and crime-laced stagecoaches would also figure prominently in Anne's travel writings. One broken-spoke adventure in particular stands out with a Paulding-like narrative that virtually all reviewers—and biographers—interpreted as real, and therefore a comment on Anne's lack of sanity, while they somehow missed the intentional embellishment of the tale for the sake of entertainment.

Climbing into a stagecoach bound for central Pennsylvania, Anne joined a cadre of Irish travelers "and the poor, penniless, Teague; shabby, friendly, disconsolate, and thinly clad . . . with a red face and shivering with cold. He was by far the gentlest man in the stage." Anne noted the role of two Americans, "depraved and dangerous, which will appear in the end."

Weaving the tale with whiskey pit stops along the Allegheny mountain road, Anne cast her story as a variation of "Billy Potts," that ubiquitous legend of backwoods crime.

As we stopped at the door [of an inn], a gang of robber-looking men, to the number of eight or ten, rushed out of the house to view the passengers, who all descended from the coach but myself, to take a fresh priming of whiskey. While they were in the house, those ruffians, who were impudence itself, surrounded the coach. Some would come up to the door and peep in; others would walk round to look at the boot, as if examining the baggage. At length, one of them addressed me with insufferable impudence. I assumed an air of courage, and ordered him to begone. The new driver, who was little better, by this time had come out of the stable with the horses, and hearing what passed, resented the affront bestowed upon his companion, with a volley of oaths, and said, "if I did not mind he would break my neck." Meantime, the Teague with the pewter-dish face, came to the door, and grinned from ear to ear.

. . . At length the passengers entered the coach, all more than half drunk; but imagine my feelings at seeing one of the ruffians, after whispering to the Pats, mount the seat with the driver, for which, he (the driver) ought to have been sent to the state-prison. This ruffian, as well as most of those at the house, were discarded drivers; and being drunken, vicious, and lazy, gathered about these Inns in the mountains, with a view of robbing and murdering passengers, and riding in the stage from one stage to another, free of cost.

. . . It was dark, raining, the road very deep, and we were without light, consequently were in danger of upsetting every moment from the steepness and winding of the road. We arrived safe however, at the Inn on the top of the mountain, where I got out and ordered out my trunks; but the ruffians had laid their plan too well to let me have my trunks. . . . But imagine my surprise, when the landlord informed me, he could not let me stay at his house nor would he take out my baggage, saying he kept no tavern, and as no stage office was kept there, he would not, nor dared not, take out my baggage. I saw through the tiling at once; the Teague, with his fellow ruffian, had put the landlord up to this, to carry their plot into execution, whatever it might be.

Spurned by various taverns along the road, Anne decided to take her stand for the night, no matter the cost.

Whatever they told the people of the house, I neither knew nor cared, as I was determined not to move from the house at the point of the sword. I began to perceive—in fact had some time—it was but death, and I might as well meet it in one place as another. Upon entering the house, I met another appalling sight, another gang of ill-looking men, and here I must remark, that nothing but my courage saved my life. "What, another band of robbers here too!" I exclaimed. I heard one of the ruffians whispering to somebody as I entered the house, of which I only distinguished the word crazy.

After an extensive argument with the landlord of the tavern, who finally recognized that Anne had no plans to climb back onto the dangerous stagecoach for the night, the author was led by a woman with a candle to a room with two doors, both without locks. "I saw the drift, but was perfectly undaunted."

Refusing to undress, Anne prepared herself for the night's denouncement.

One door was at the foot of my bed, and one at my head. I watched both, and had also put out my candle. About eleven o'clock, I heard footsteps approaching up the kitchen stairs, at the foot of my bed; and presently the door opened softly, and the landlord entered with a candle in his hand. . . . He passed round my bed softly, and walked to a pile of apples that lay in a corner, and picking up one of the apples, stood and listened, and walked back again, close to the side of my bed, and seemed to be ascertaining whether I was asleep or not. Just as he was opposite my bed, walking on tip-toe, I sprung up, and accosted him with "You ruffian, how dare you come into my room at this time of night? begone this instant, or I will shoot you." But never did a fellow run down stairs faster, while I had neither gun nor pistol.

As wily as her fellow backwoodsman Davy Crockett, Anne delighted in showing her readers the underbelly of the western trails in a self-mocking fashion, unconcerned about the caricature of her gun-toting backwoods origins. She inhabited a world still unfit for honest women, a place she happily called home as an itinerant storyteller.

Anne reveled in these tales, pitting her female David against the masculine Goliaths, using her wit as a weapon in the face of death-defying circumstances. Another story in Virginia, published years later, kept up this farcical element of Anne's writing that many critics once again deemed as proof of her deranged mind. A closer reconsideration of the story, however, suggests otherwise; a provocative Anne embellished one of her travel tales with a crafted narrative arc and outrageous dialogue, clearly to get a rise out of the institutional ranks of men she loved to skewer with derision.

Preparing to depart from Staunton, Virginia, one early morning, Anne noticed a loud commotion outside the stagecoach. She hustled down, only to be informed that her paid picket on the coach had been canceled due to the needs of government leaders, including the "Commandant of the Western Army" and the governor of Arkansas, who had suddenly arrived. Anne wouldn't have it: "I will not give up my seat to the President of the United States."

A friendly major worked out a compromise after Anne "delivered a speech to these men of war, to teach them the difference between defending our rights, and invading them." As a sneaky aside, Anne admitted she would have gladly given up her seat had she been "solicited in a gentlemanly manner." She climbed into the coach with a general and a few other selected dignitaries. All went well, Anne wrote, and added a few hilarious descriptions of the crew—"until the assassin's hour, when the war commenced" by one of the passengers, "his holiness Burnet."

His face had assumed all the colors of the rainbow, during the day, and when shrouded by darkness, he began by saying, "I was a dangerous woman, (to hypocrites, I am) and I ought not to be allowed to travel over the country, abusing every body, I ought to be taken up, and a stop put to my writings. I was deranged." Then it was useless to argue with me, I replied, and for that matter, the whole of the United States seemed to be deranged, or such hypocritical knaves as he and the whole of his sect would not have plundered them of such vast sums of money, under the cloak of religion . . . "I never broke any bones, or drew any blood, which is more than I can say of your Presbyterians, and if you are offended, I have a friend at your service."

The general intervened, Anne wrote, "calling me sundry ungentlemanly names, and finally expressed the same opinion of his ally, and hinted (for he was too great a coward to speak plain,) something about throwing me out of the stage—this would have been a bold act, if not to say a soldierly one." The tiny Anne could hardly keep herself from laughing aloud. "Thus the battle waxed warm—this is what I like, close fighting." She couldn't resist goading the general, pointing at his sword and its "terrifying broad gilt belt, and gold handle." No one but a coward would assault an aged woman in the dead of night, she declared, adding "that the stage was a common highway, of equal rights." Then Anne unleashed a zinger: "I thought it was time he should have his sword taken from him—'you wear a sword, sir, but you have not the courage to use it.'"

He was outrageous, and to convince me he had courage, he clapped his hand on the hilt of the sword—I sprang forward, and putting my face close to his, and my finger almost in his eyes, said to him, "Now, Sir, draw your sword, if you dare, you assassin, none but an assassin would assault a defenceless man, much less a woman!"

Anne recited a few lines of poetry from the ancient Greek songs of Alcaeus: "Dropped, alas! the inglorious shield. Where valor's self was forced to yield!"

But the best is yet to come, the little Penny Doctor. You have remarked that when dogs fight, if there are a dozen, they all united against one, while the little Pennies, too cowardly to take hold, yelp, and skip round and round, with bristles up. Just so did our little Penny, tonight—his bristles were up in a moment, and he continued to yelp, while the big dogs held on. I asked what raised the wind with him; I thought there were enough against me already. "I'm not going to sit here and hear my General abused!"

"This was a hard cut," Anne admitted, but she "amused" herself with the general on the subject of courage. She asked him how many battles he had ever fought and where he distinguished himself in the late war. "I had never heard of his valor or his name, till the present time, but the world should not have this to say hereafter."

With the general vanquished, the rest of the stagecoach journey passed quietly into the night. Anne smiled, as if the whole episode had been a lark. By morning, she returned to her portraits of the landscape emerging from the gap beyond the Blue Ridge. "The beauty arises from the sudden, yet steep descent to both vallies, the presence of the mountains beyond them, their changing figures, the distinctness which mark the farm on the east, and the deep green, waning fields and meadows," she wrote. "It was at that moment, the most heart-reviving sight that fell in my way on my journey."

Within time, Anne would evolve as a forerunner of other more popular mid-nineteenth-century women satirists like Frances Whitcher and Sara Willis Parton, who filled *Godey's Lady's Book* and *Neal's Saturday Gazette* with mocking tales of small-town avarice, hypocritical churchgoers, and social backbiting. In one *Godey's* story, Whitcher's character revels in the muck of the sewing society at the local church, discussing her nemesis Miss Sampson Savage, "a coarse, boisterous, high-tempered critter, and when her husband grow'd rich, she grow'd pompous and overbearin'."

Anne, though, preferred to go outside these accepted circles of women. She wanted to go beyond main street; she didn't just try to take off the veil of conformity and expose the hypocritical mores of daily life, but she also sought to sharpen the edges of her social critique to rip apart the elite conventions and religious dogma that had shaped such aggravating ways. It wasn't enough to criticize the bonnet and the sanctimonious sneer hidden behind it. Anne soon went after the institutions and their leaders who had created such monsters, in her mind.

Ironically, the readers who best understood this lampooning narrative approach resided a thousand miles away—at Harvard University. In the late 1820s, the Harvard Med Faculty Society, a secret society dedicated to lampooning dignitaries, granted Anne one of their fake honorary degrees; with it she joined the heady company of Andrew Jackson. As a follow-up, whether it was a spoof or not, Anne received a sensational letter from Harvard students in advance of one of her appearances:

Dear Madam:

Hearing of your arrival in Cambridge but a few hours since we, humble admirers of your talents and literary acquirements, hasten to pay our respects to one whose labors (laying flattery aside) in the cause of truth and science, cannot fail of rendering her one of the brightest spots in the literary horizon, to which the youthful devotee may offer his humble homage, without the fear of being either insincere or: disrespectful.

It has heretofore been a matter of astonishment to the literary world that females have contributed in so small a degree to the advancement of knowledge and science, and indeed so much so that men had begun to think that they were deficient in point of intellect. It was reserved for Anne Royall (we say it with unsophisticated pleasure) to remove this unjust impression from the minds of men, and I to show that the female character, however useless and incapable of literary exertion it may have been thought to be, can rank with the Newtons and Lockes of other days, and Scotts and Coopers of the present. It would be useless for us, humble individuals, to attempt to do justice to the works with which you have favored the world, but we sincerely hope we may not be deemed impertinent if we express with classic enthusiasm, our admiration of works which are admirable beyond the diamond's splendor or the ruby's brilliancy. God grant that your future exertions in the good cause you have undertaken may render your fame and popularity greater, if possible, than that gained by your former productions. We have heard with pleasure of your intention of visiting the vile and unprincipled system of Anti-Masonry with the severity of your powerful pen. No wonder that its intolerant principles should excite the indignation of a virtuous and fearless female whose great spirit will not brook to be fettered by any narrow minded blood-suckers. Let us hope that, with justice and divine Providence on your side, you cannot fail of success and as incentive to exert your gigantic powers your name will hereafter be enrolled on the tablet of fame as one who, while her country-men were tamely submitting to unjust oppression, casting aside in the hour of peril, the garb of womanish bashfulness and timidity, opposed the lowering storm and restored her countrymen to peace and liberty.

We have viewed with heartfelt sorrow the blackguard manner in which you have been treated in many parts of this country, and have also admired the spirited manner in which you have resented those insults alike against common decorum and female delicacy. Were it not that modesty forbids it we would not hesitate to say that our hands and our powers will at all times be devoted to the cause of one persecuted as you have been.

It may seem, respected Madam, that our addressing you in this manner, is impolite as well as uncalled for, and insulting to the delicate feelings of a woman, but may we venture to hope that the enthusiasm of youth, and a devoted admiration of your superior worth, will excuse this abrupt expression of our feelings and remove any disagreeable impressions which may have at first arisen in your mind.

Hoping this communication may meet with your approbation, permit us to subscribe ourselves, Your Devoted Admirers, Many Students. Cambridge.

Funny enough, Anne's first effort at authorship did not immediately pursue the path of the satirical travelogue. Writing Matt one spring day in 1819, after a horse ride through the countryside near Moulton, Alabama, Anne confessed that she had met an elderly gentleman, "the incidents of whose life is a complete novel." His name was Burlinson, a native of New Jersey, who had joined the rebellious

Watauga settlement that had defied the British on the Tennessee–North Carolina border before the American Revolution.

"I spend most of my time with the Tennessean," Anne wrote in a subsequent letter. She recounted how she often read to him in the evenings, the stories of which served as a departure for his own personal adventures, which Anne jotted down on paper. In her letters to Matt, Anne became so caught up with Burlinson's story that she occasionally shifted from reporting to assuming his role in a first-person narrative. "I thought I had seen all strange sights that were to be seen in the world, but never saw the equal of this."

"Mr. Burlinson is equal to the best library," Anne gushed. "I love to hear his anecdotes of General Jackson's struggles and difficulties in various campaigns, and the incidents of those brave men who suffered with him."

Imbued with this element of the romantic hero, Anne quietly began to write her first book, *The Tennessean*, a novel "founded on facts," a style that had been in vogue since the success of *The Coquette* (1797) by Hannah Webster Foster. Anne added: "Founded upon a well-known fact—a secret expedition undertaken by a number of enterprising young men (principally Tennesseans) to the Spanish dominion some fifteen years since. The novel is little more than the narrative of the sufferings and difficulties encountered by the party." Anne slyly nodded to Burlinson as she named her protagonist: "Burlington."

As if to verify her own bona fides, Anne even interrupted the novel in parts to ascertain the truthfulness of her story, especially in describing characters: "This is no fiction. The author lived in the neighborhood of a female, who was a native of the north of Ireland, and who was never known to wash her face or hands, so that the dirt had actually become a part of her."

For literary historian Van Wyck Brooks, as he mentioned in his biography of Anne's contemporary author Washington Irving, her novel rose from the dingy inns, "the common room, the jollity, the fire, the grog, the fiddling and the gossip" as she turned into a "garrulous, rambling and untidy" chronicler, the "female Parson Weems" of her times. The comparison to Weems would not have been lost on Anne. Considered one of the most uniquely successful American authors of his time—in terms of book sales, not literary skill—Mason Locke "Parson" Weems didn't just break ground with his horse on the back trails; he gave birth to the book tour, the shameless self-promoting author saddling up his "flying library" and traveling from town to town to hawk his books. His works included the classic *Life of Washington*, which originated the "I can not tell a lie" legend with the fateful cherry tree in 1806. Like Anne, Weems favored showmanship over reliability in the pursuit of good storytelling, while he still considered himself a defining historian of the nation.

An advertisement for his arrival in a small Georgia town proclaimed his extraordinary role as a pied piper for literacy: "In a happy republic, like ours, where for the prize of Fame and Fortune, all start fair and fair alike; where everything depends on merit, and that merit is all dependent on Education, it is hoped that wife and generous parents will need no persuasion to give their children those very great advantages which Books afford." Weems made good on his promise. When he died in 1825, a North Carolina newspaper noted that Weems had sold over a million copies of his books and others, though many of them were Bibles. "His very eccentricities, for failings they could not be called, were the eccentricities of genius and benevolence."

Wrapping up her manuscript in burlap, Anne sent *The Tennessean* to Mathew Carey, Weems's publisher in Philadelphia, in the winter of 1823. Within a short time she would ask her friend Matt to return her letters, which she subsequently repackaged into a collection titled *Letters from Alabama*, one of the first epistolary surveys of the new territory and state and its people. Having not heard back from the publisher about *The Tennessean*, Anne wrote a fairly desperate letter to Carey just after New Year's in 1824. She admitted that the novel had its problems—"I made a bungling hand of the shipwreck"—and now considered *Letters from Alabama* to be the most marketable, especially for the burgeoning western readers. But she still urged the publisher not to overlook "The Tennesseans."

Regardless of the publisher's response, Anne understood she had crossed a line of no return in her literary career. She had become a writer—an author—in her mind. Years later, she would reflect during a visit to her brother's home in Indiana: "All this I liked—it was novel, it was rural, it was wild—was what I had once been used to, and what I had long mourned for. But how was I to write? For you might stop my breath if you stop my pen."

In the meantime, another letter from Matt in West Virginia brought bad news: the court had not ruled in her favor regarding her last debts and properties. The husband of her niece, James Roane, had even broken into a storage area in Charleston and appropriated the rest of her belongings, including the last pieces of furniture. The dower had been completely drained. How Anne managed to cover her outstanding lodging expenses in Alabama remains unclear. How she avoided another stay in the debtor's prison is another question.

In the last entry in her letters, the incorrigible Anne beguiled Matt with the great possibilities in Alabama's agricultural future. "There is a country for you," she affirmed, detailing the receipts for cotton, the growing market for vegetables, and even the varieties of grapes. Alabama flourished, rich with blessings; the only curse, Anne said, was slavery.

Her last letter also recorded her experience of attending her first revival. "This was the first Missionary I ever heard," Anne noted. The preacher collected a large sum, "several hundred dollars, to convert the Heathen." She called it "a burlesque."

Anne quietly abandoned her Alabama dream. One final option remained, according to her attorney: travel to Washington, DC, to plead her case for her husband's Revolutionary War pension, which he had never collected.

Whether Anne and Matt continued their correspondence after her departure from Alabama is unknown. She never mentioned him again. Matt married during Anne's last year in Alabama, and he eventually became a well-respected judge in Charleston, West Virginia—and, surely to the chagrin of Anne had they remained in contact, an elder in the Presbyterian Church.

In a clever endeavor that bankrolled, however tenuously, her next years, Anne announced her intent to write a new travel book, *Sketches of History, Life and Manners in the United States*, based on her journeys across the emerging nation. Borrowing a page from Parson Weems, she rolled out a scroll to collect subscriptions in advance— paid in full—for her forthcoming book. In effect, she mastered the art of crowd-funding two centuries before its time.

The endeavor was audacious as much as it was absurd: a threadbare woman in an impoverished state, without any friends or connections or standing in societal circles, daring to request interviews with the leading social and political figures of the day while cajoling everyone she met for a subscription and contribution. Not to mention Anne had no publisher—only two other unpublished manuscripts.

In a letter to Thomas Jefferson, Anne revealed the desperate circumstances she faced, and her depiction of her literary career as a last resort:

A poor and friendless female asks of you to patronise her works as named in the enclosed prospectus. I am a Virginian, the widow of one of your revolutionary worthys, Maj Wm Royall once of Augusta County in your State and no doubt known to you. Since his death I have been stripped of everything by his relatives even to the last change of Rayment—a wanderer in the streets of this city without house or home or other comfort I have no resource, no prospect of relief but in the sale of these writings.

Anne saddled up a horse and headed to Virginia. Along the way, the 54-year-old self-proclaimed author decided to conjure a new version of her story. She left behind the impecunious past, the flight from debt and its collectors, the years of suffering in the mountains, and now the Alabama low country. "It will be asked then, what encouragement I have to write?" Anne recalled later, "and how I am able to publish at all. To the first, I answer, I do not write for profit or for fame. I write for the benefit of my country, and to please my friends."

Anne reinvented herself again as an American author on the road to great adventure. "Having been advised to try the mineral waters in Virginia for my health," she began her new book, adopting her mother's affliction for her own, "I set out on horse back from St. Stephens, in Alabama, July 1, 1823, intending to take the stage at Huntsville. With a view to divert my mind from melancholy reflections, to which it was disposed from ill health, I resolved to note everything during my journey, worthy of remark, and commit it to writing, and to draw amusement and instruction from every source. In doing so, I shall not imitate most journalists, in such remarks as 'cloudy, or fair morning,' and where we stop, dates, etc. This is all the preface I deem necessary."

# THREE

### ⟨⟩⟨⟩⟨⟩

# A Female of Respectability

*The author is a female of respectability . . . the widow of . . . an officer of the revolution. This Lady, by one of those unforeseen misfortunes common in the human family, has fallen into distress, and appeals to the humane and benevolent citizens of this great and patriotic city for their patronage. These Works, we find, are patronized by the most distinguished men of the United States.*

—Advertisement, *Albany Daily Advertiser*, February 12, 1825

In her early letters from Alabama to her attorney friend Matt, Anne actually described attending a witchcraft trial in 1818. The whole town, even the "respectable physicians," was ready to testify that the woman "was afflicted with some supernatural disease, over which medicine had no control. Finally, they carried on the farce so far, as to have the supposed witch apprehended and brought before the magistrate, and hundreds (likewise bewitched) attended to hear the trial. But the magistrate happened not to be bewitched, and the woman, producing proof of a fair character, was acquitted." Unconvinced by the ruling, local men stormed the woman's house, only to find that the source of her sorcery was a barrel of brandy.

"When I first began to write," Royall said, years later, "I

imperceptibly fell into this manner of writing—I mean that of personal description, and had been told (for I am no judge, of course) that this and scenery was my forte." Before too long, though, the portraits and stories resulted in a "sameness" for Royall, and she found herself more interested in local travails more than travels. "I might die myself in the meantime, and many a good and bad man would be consigned to oblivion." That need to become a social critic, a muckraker, a cultural broker—whatever her chosen entre into the day's events—suddenly shifted the direction of Royall's writing.

A lingering despair still underscored Anne's first trip to Washington, DC, in the winter of 1823. She had departed on horseback from Alabama to petition for her husband's Revolutionary War pension, embarking at the same time on her book project, *Sketches of History, Life and Manners in the United States*. She grappled with "splenetic" attacks and bouts of depression.

The unavoidable affront of poverty tugged at her single dress, but she managed to charm or cajole her way onto stagecoaches and into taverns for meals and lodging. Living by her wits, she quickly perfected the art of the scrounge, and she turned her daily needs into an assignment of her writing.

After making it through the Appalachian Mountains, Royall somehow found the resources to continue her journey to Alexandria, Virginia, just across the river from Washington. Since "grog shops abound" on the road, Anne teased the last of the stage drivers by concluding that her safe passage only occurred because the "horses were sober." When the stagecoach finally came to a halt in front of Alexandria's City Tavern, a penniless Royall invoked her husband's Masonic connection to ingratiate herself with the tavern owner, Horatio Clagett. A dedicated Mason, Clagett was the "friend of the friendless and pride of mankind," Anne would write many years later. "At ten o'clock, one cold December night, I arrived at his house without one cent in my pocket, a single change of raiment and badly dressed. I had not a friend on earth." Clagett offered Anne an "elegant parlor and bed-chamber" and even provided "a servant to wait on me the whole winter." She had promised to repay him from the proceeds of her future books.

Not that such a desperate predicament or self-portrait entered the pages of *Sketches*. Reimaging herself in the narrative as a celebrated visitor of Alexandria, Anne never once mentioned Clagett's charity until years later. She produced extensive notes on the history and design of the city, its municipal institutions, and some hair-raising descriptions of ethnic demographics that were at once stupefyingly racist and uncompromising in their depiction of slave owners' brutal behavior. Chronicling her adventures in the town market, Anne carefully deferred any expenses under the guise of being "a traveler, I only call from curiosity."

"After spending some months in Alexandria," she casually wrote, as if completing the assignment for a commissioned story, "I took my departure for Richmond, in the steam boat, 'Mount Vernon,' intending on my return to visit Washington city." In truth, having been turned down by the pension board for lack of documentation on her husband's service, the distressed Royall was forced to travel to Richmond to collect statements from her husband's Revolutionary companions. Sadly, the records had apparently been lost in a fire. Anne would also learn that a statute of limitations on pensions for Revolutionary War widows capped out at 1794; any marriages after that date, such as hers in 1797, required a congressional petition.

Again, the day-to-day reality of her burdensome journey to Richmond was revealed years later in a subsequent book, when fame, notoriety, or adversity allowed her to divulge a rare moment of nostalgia. Such episodes, in fact, often came during Anne's encounters with other older women.

Years later, Royall's visit with the former first lady Dolley Madison in Richmond during a Southern book tour offered a flashback to her first visit in the region.

Offended by a carriage driver's fee, and most likely with little money in her pocket, Anne wrote that she had walked three miles to reach Madison's front door in Richmond. The White House's former first hostess had celebrated better days, too. Her famed dinner parties had often fed hundreds, but after a decade of isolation at the Montpelier plantation on the edge of the Blue Ridge Mountains in Virginia, Dolley now complained privately that she had been forgotten. Her son's mounting debts had landed him in prison and left her heartbroken. Her husband, former president James Madison, had even been forced to mortgage half his family's declining estate.

When Royall was spurned entrance to the boardinghouse in Richmond where Dolley and her husband were spending the winter of 1829, the former first lady clamored down the stairs to meet the notorious author.

Dolley wore a plain black silk dress with her iconic "silk checked" turban. The buoyant greeting from the 61-year-old Madison immediately dismissed any murmurs that Royall had overheard in Washington; Dolley was far from the "little dried up old woman" the author had been told to expect. "She was the self-same lady of whom I had heard more anecdotes than any family in Europe or America." Anne gushed: This "tall, young, active, elegant woman stood before me."

The banter over aging must have stung Royall; she was only a year younger than Madison. She had already penned her portrait of James Madison, who moved with "a vigorous countenance" at the state's

Constitutional Convention in defiance of his 78 years. Anne found him the "most diffident man in the world."

Only days earlier, in Petersburg, Virginia, Anne had joined a "pleasant party of ladies" for cake and wine as they mockingly toasted a new "temperate society" in town. "She was all life and spirits," Royall said of her older host, whom she described as a wealthy woman in "advanced" age. "She would join none of their societies—indeed, she liked a glass of wine as well as any one—they are exactly what you call them Mrs. R, a parcel of wolves in sheep's clothing."

Such comments delighted Anne. The ladies of the "old school," she wrote, describing them as "whole soul folks." They laughed at the "missionaries" and swapped stories of their encounters with the "priestcraft." She noted their "fascinating" manners.

Dolley Madison conjured the same fascination. The "irresistible grace of her every movement," Royall wrote, "sheds such a charm over all she says and does." Upon Anne's arrival at Madison's house, the former first lady brought Anne a glass of water and wiped mud from her shoes, a burst of activity that stunned the author who had only three months earlier been trotted into federal court as a social pariah and notoriously hailed in Washington as a "common scold."

"No wonder she is the idol of Washington," Anne noted. "At once in possession of everything that could ennoble woman."

Anne had not always enjoyed such a reception from the elites of Richmond. She quietly divulged years later in the publication of her third *Black Book* a life-changing experience in the Virginia capital that happened after her meeting with Madison.

It had taken place in 1824, on her first trip to Richmond. She had arrived on a steamboat with a single dress, a few thin rags, and nary a "handkerchief round my neck." Anne didn't even have enough money to afford supper in the ladies' cabin. "A pennyless stranger,"

she wrote. She journeyed out of misery, to obtain the affidavits of her
husband's military service.

Shunned by other "ladies," Royall earned the pity of only one
woman on the steamboat: an African American chambermaid, "who
spoke with much feeling" and retrieved a cold piece of pie for her. Royall never forgot the kindness of "Emma," she wrote, "the only human
being, at the time, that seemed to have the least friendship or feelings
towards me."

Rising from her seat in the cabin years later, still moved by the
memory, Anne emerged onto the boat deck for air, carrying such grief
in her heart, and stumbled onto several large containers of religious
tracts and booklets. She looked around the deck, empty of other passengers. Then, reaching into the containers, she gathered a bundle of
religious tracts with the delicacy of handling eggs from a henhouse.
How the northern "hypocrites are making a great row about Indians
and slavery," she wrote. But the Indians and slaves possessed too much
honesty to "rob the poor and call it gospel."

Anne moved to the steamboat's edge and held up an armload of
tracts. "So much money thrown away," she declared. "This money
would have fed the poor in the large towns, from whom it's been
filched."

With the impish joy of an outlaw, Royall tossed the tracts into the
water and watched as they disappeared into the black water of night.

"I would have given worlds to have met with this dear creature in
the cabin again," she wrote about her friend Emma. "But, to my grief,
she was not [there]."

In this back-and-forth narrative style, draping glimpses of the
past onto her present-day adventures, searching out face-to-face
encounters with the renowned and the nameless, and taking metic-
ulous notes on her visits among the town's back warrens and

locked-up institutions, Royall's *Sketches* began to take shape. From her journaling, in effect, Anne became a de facto *journalist*; while she kept her focus on her books, her peripatetic presence at many events lent itself to coverage of breaking news items, or even historic occasions—or, at the very least, insights into the evolving American culture of the day.

While she dedicated most of her time in Richmond to the pursuit of her husband's affidavits, Anne received little encouragement from his associates. The town itself disappointed her: the capitol was "not half so large or splendid" as she had anticipated, and the people lacked the celebrated hospitality that had been attached to their name. "I saw very little of it," she mused. Beyond her inventory of the town streets and businesses, she gleaned more from her interactions with the shop-keepers; she noted their dialects and accents and recorded their con-versations. A chat with a carriage driver, for example, about the upcoming presidential election in 1824 granted Royall and her read-ers insight into a surprising study of political attitudes of the day. The driver didn't even know or care about the candidates other than Virginia favorite William Crawford, who had suffered a stroke, and viewed the election as more of a regional battle over dividing up the spoils of government pork.

When the political leaders "descend so low," she wrote, "as to aid in blinding and misleading the honest and unsuspecting yeoman of his country, by fashioning him into a tool to vote as they please, to help a set of needy unprincipled men into office, it is time for the people to think for themselves—no matter what party rules."

Returning north, Anne's entry into Washington came by sea. After arriving at a dock on Potomac Creek by ferry one evening, she boarded a stagecoach and put aside her own personal misfortunes in favor of a traveler's starry view of the city. The "backwoods" scribe couldn't hide her awe, mixing embellished descriptions with fact-finding notes. The Capitol dome shone in the moonlight like the "eighth wonder of the world." Captivated by the town, no more than a village on the "majestic Potomac, with its ponderous bridge, and gliding sails," Anne scanned the "swelling hills" that embraced Washington, the spacious squares and streets. "It is not in the power of imagination to conceive a scene so replete with every species of beauty."

The seeds had been sown for the writer, who would soon claim Washington as her hometown—all 13,474 inhabitants, and 2,141 houses, she would add, in her notable attention to detail.

Her survey of Washington attended to the usual attractions: the government buildings, an inventory of the various businesses, the shipyard, and even the public graveyard. With the diffidence of a veteran, she didn't hesitate to knock on doors and interview political figures, government workers, journalists, shopkeepers—always with an eye on enrolling people as subscribers for her forthcoming book. Her encounter with the sober Secretary of State John Quincy Adams was quite satisfying; despite the fact that the future president had probably never "laughed in his life," Royall found him amiable. She had always admired his writing. He listened to her stories. He paid his subscription in advance. So concerned was he about her predicament, he even wrote her a note to be delivered to his wife, who graciously gifted Anne a shawl for her winter travels.

She soon learned that the art of the interview functioned as a rare key into the heart of any city, granting her access to people and ultimately power that she would have never held in any other fashion. Anne crafted her lopsided portraits with the savvy of a street painter, carving out a role for herself in each story. Her survival skills had been sharpened over the many years of conflict; she quickly learned the ways of flattery and its disarming effect on even the most self-contained stalwarts. "Every feature in his face shows genius," Royall wrote about Adams, "every gesture is that of a great man." Tossing aside any protocol of privacy, she found that people loved to be interviewed; they gushed out their thoughts, their opinions, their prejudices, and they often shared secrets and acquaintances. Anne rarely left without a new subscriber or a letter of introduction to the next target.

Nonetheless, she admitted her star-struck moment with Adams, sitting in his chambers, wearing her oft-stitched dress, only a coin or two removed from the poorhouse herself. Royall took a deep breath and exhaled sheer amazement. "While beholding this truly great man, I was at a loss at how to reconcile such rare endowments with the meek condescension of the being before me."

Her most unique insight—unlike most of her traveling peers— took place at the "Poor House," this "wretched establishment which only exists to disgrace Washington." From there, she inspected the prison, which she found clean and stocked with food. The debtors' section was spacious and airy.

Her commitment to profiling the government's treatment of the poor set Royall apart, and it defined the rest of her travels in other cities. "Of all the institutions which ennoble human misery," she wrote, the orphanages, with their terrible treatment of abandoned children, ranked at the top of the list. She issued her final judgment: "But if you are poor you have no business in Washington, and unless you are well dressed you will have good luck if you be not kicked out of doors by the servants."

After six months of survey—and vainly begging members of Congress to petition for her husband's Revolutionary pension—Anne gave up on the immovable bureaucracy and moved on to her next destination: her birthplace of Baltimore.

The Baltimore streets "bursted upon" Anne in a barrage of wonders. While she found the city to be in the lead in fine arts, she bristled at the urban warrens clogged with formidable carts and wagons, the "massy" public buildings, the great shipyards, and the disparity between the number of well-dressed persons in the streets and the prison conditions for debtors. After Anne offered a few words of consolation to six female debtors during a visit, one burst into tears "and cast on me a look which I shall never forget." Meanwhile, the prison warden announced that Royall planned to "write their histories," which brought a round of laughter and disbelief.

Often in her writing, Anne anticipated a smile from her readers. She again declared herself in her native Baltimore to be "an awkward backwoods country person," a status that granted its own auspicious insights for someone to see anew and distinguish overlooked details in the growing cities—and then she flipped that stereotype on its head, noting her naïveté was no less than that exhibited by urban East Coast explorers issuing poetic diaries about the "solemn forests, our wild mountains and deep caverns" that had defined her upbringing.

While such details unfolded in the cityscapes of Royall's "sketches," some of the most compelling insights often came as understated asides in the thunderstruck moments of a journalist rube.

Her last day in Baltimore showcased such a moment. Anne waxed angrily after she, a self-proclaimed country person, had been swindled: "I cannot, however, depart without one more remark which forms a link in the long chain of human depravity; and proves, that as men become refined in the arts and science, they also become refined (if I may be allowed the expression) in knavery." The crime in Royall's mind: she had been sold a fraudulent silk scarf. She railed about her ridiculous barter for a long paragraph.

Yet the reader didn't have time to shrug off the silliness of such a charge. Anne followed with a rare footnote of news about the bottom chain of human depravity that truly stung: "An execution of a negro took place the next day," she wrote. The "eagerness" of so many citizens shocked and appalled Royall. "Who is said to have a soul at all," she asked, "who can calmly stand by, and view the struggles of a fellow mortal in the pangs of such an exit?"

A fellow mortal, in this instance, was a "negro" woman in the age of chattel slavery. The attention to the silk scarf disappeared, despite its earlier emphasis, as if tossed from Anne's coach. It took her days to recover from the "tragical" event.

Nonetheless, as she traveled on to Philadelphia, she stewed over a conversation she'd had earlier at a theater in Baltimore. With her usual panache, she had called on the proprietors with some "dramatic pieces" in hand that she had composed in Washington and offered to write a play; they squashed her proposal before she had finished speaking. Taken aback, Anne held her ground until another theater partner arrived. "He received me with an air worthy of Chesterfield." After she pitched her idea again, the proprietor declined, claiming the theater "plays no American pieces at all." He encouraged Royall to give up her writing and not give herself "further trouble."

The rage for British literature in this period outraged Anne. The publisher in Philadelphia who had rejected her *Tennessean* novel had expressed a similar sentiment: "American works do not pay the expense of publishing." Royall questioned them: "If we aspire to be a great nation," how could publishers turn their backs on literary genius from their own continent? "We are in effect pulling down with one hand, what we put up with the other."

By the time she visited Philadelphia and made her way toward New York City, Anne had found her voice in the *Sketches* narrative. Meeting in a shop in Philadelphia, she traded notes with author

William Darby—whose popular *Emigrant's Guide to the Western and Southwestern States and Territories* had been published in 1818—as if she already took part in the literary canons. The *North American Review*'s critique of Darby's work, however, should have been a harbinger for her. While his book had a "great deal of valuable information," the editors faulted it for lacking "great skill, and perhaps not always selected with the greatest judgment." Still, they admired Darby's work on the road, and concluded: "We ought not to complain that his education has not made him an accomplished scholar."

Darby encouraged Anne to write. Notably friendly, he had even invited her to stay at his home, an invitation she declined.

Confident, curious, jocular, and decidedly judgmental, Anne asserted her views of the local "manners," measuring not only daily interactions but also attire, speech patterns, and the relationships between free and enslaved, white and black, and men and women. On a boat traveling to New Jersey, she began to make the distinction between the South and the North, especially when it came to women. "Here, society appeared in a different light," she wrote, watching how women and men mingled together without the cloak of matrimonial protection. "Here was no silly affection among the females, no impertinent forwardness among the men." Royall raved at how mixed company could "crack their nuts and eat their apples" and simply chat without concern of judgment. In her view, such a scene presented a happy medium between the "impudent rusticity" of her experience in the South and West and the "repelling hauteur" among the elite in every community.

At her boardinghouse on Front Street in New York City, Royall's shifting perspective on women continued, though not in any moralistic fashion. If anything, her traveling began to confirm her own views, many of which had been chastised or considered outside the norm in her rural South. As the boardinghouse residents convened in the parlor room after dinner, the old men smoking pipes, the young men and women flirting through the exchanges and taking turns on the piano, Anne reveled in the "independence of manners." Liberated from the Southern protocol of class and gender that still consumed her in Washington—and, in many respects, clashed with her earlier views—she embraced the "free trade and sailor's rights." She added in an aside: "I never found myself more at home in my life."

Anne dedicated a lengthy amount of time to New York City, where she traversed the usual gamut of sights, buildings, government services, schools, and, of course, the various prisons, jails, and asylums. She walked the "far famed Broadway," which she said was "distinguished" in 1824 "for the fashionable, the gay, and the idle," and then she descended among the "throng of men" on Wall Street. Anne frolicked in an almost Whitmanesque fashion of lists, a generation before the great bard published his *Leaves of Grass*:

> Broadway, Chatham, Pearl and Division Streets, Maiden-lane and the Bowery are literally strewed with every article of ornament and use, which, with the thrice told multitude, not only fills the western stranger with amazement, but is the wonder of foreigners. Here the feminine graces meet you at every step; they thrust their lovely faces into yours, and shoulder you on all sides, without even stopping to apologize. Here the earnest merchant steps, there the gay cook and merry chamber-maid, with some scores of honest tars, hucksters, rude boys, and chimney sweeps, with the rolling coaches, and the rattling carts, may give some idea of this life-inspiring city. But all this is only a drop in the bucket compared to that on the wharves or slips (as they are called here,) the warehouses,

docks, ship-yards, and auction stores, which occupy South, Front and Water streets, pouring of human beings. Here the sound of axes, saws, and hammers, from a thousand hands; there the ringing of the blacksmith's anvil; hard by the jolly tar with his heavo; the whole city surrounded with masts; the Hudson, East river, and the bay covered with vessels, some going out and some coming in, to say nothing of the steam-boats; in short, imagine upwards of an hundred thousand people, all engaged in business; add to these some thousand strangers which swarm in the streets and public houses; such is New York. This is, however, only a running glance; the result of my first ramble through the city. I shall compose myself, and give something more like a description.

She recorded the city residents' unique use of the word "stoop" for their buildings. She inspected City Hall, the hospital, the Asylum for the Insane, and Columbia College. She toured the Asylum for the Deaf and Dumb, the fire department, and spent an afternoon in the Lyceum of Nature History before visiting three schools. "To see such a vast number of children, from four to eight hundred in one house, governed by a word, a nod, or even a glance of their teacher, is truly astonishing," Anne wrote. She wasn't quite sure if schools produced the "best disciplined army" or were "hushed by death," but she returned numerous times to observe. The young women attending schools excited Anne with their revolutionary possibilities: "If there were a few more schools, bigotry and witchcraft would soon fly New York."

Over 500 inmates populated the state prison; the city jail, though, with more than 200 "in this abode of wretchedness," affected the chronicler. "To see a friendless female in a gloomy prison, locked in with massy iron doors and grated windows, the mind that can think, and the heart that can feel, must be shocked at the sight, however just it may be, however necessary for the good of society. But never did I, till now, feel that degree of compassion for the sex, which the sight of those females called up."

More confident than ever, she made a list of the city's notable residents and then knocked on their doors, occasionally with little success at entrance. Surprisingly, however, she found more success than might be expected of an unknown woman who appeared like a mendicant, including a meeting with her literary hero, James Paulding. Visiting the author at his "princely" home, Anne quickly penned one of her portraits:

> Mr. P. is in height about five feet ten inches, his figure is light, and he moves with ease and grace, being spare, but well formed. His complexion is dark, his hair the deepest black, his eyes what is usually termed black, of the middling shade, and uncommonly brilliant. His face is oval, his features delicate, but regular, and what may be called handsome; his raven locks fall over his neck and forehead in ringlets of ineffable beauty. His countenance comprises all that can be conceived of benignity and diffidence, a little dashed with the facetious. His language is simple, his voice soft and harmonious. In his manners he is frank, generous, and gentle as the dove. He is a man of quick discernment, and is said to be humane to a fault.

To be sure, Anne invoked her husband's Masonic Lodge connections every step of the way, which often resulted in helpful collections for her travels.

Royall's best contacts took place in the city newsrooms, where, with the savvy of a publicist, she cunningly interviewed editors and journalists, as if setting the stage for her future book announcements. These sessions introduced her to Mordecai Noah, founder and editor of various newspapers, including the *National Advocate* and the *New York Enquirer*, who would become one of Anne's main defenders during her witch trial.

New York's verve affected her most. "While others are debating the questions of right and wrong," she noted, "New York is acting." She attributed its uniqueness to the extraordinary range of foreigners who had mixed into the city. To be sure, Anne visited the first house she claimed was ever constructed in Brooklyn, the Dutch "Remsen" house, which dated back to an era when the place was "inhabited by the Canarsee Indians, who were subject to the Mohawks." But times were changing in New York City in the 1820s, Royall remarked: "143 dwellings were erected" in a single year in Brooklyn.

She reluctantly left the city and moved on to Albany by steamboat. In truth, she traveled now with some means, having picked up more Masonic support. Various lodges promoted her arrival and even took out a major advertisement in Albany, touting her unpublished books. The endorsement rang clear: "The author is a female of respectability." Anne's last months of work had been busy—and productive:

The letters (from Alabama) are a miscellaneous production embracing strictures on Manners, Customs, Dialects, Religion, Education, Literature, and Females, of the United States, with Biographical sketches of the most distinguished men of Alabama and Tennessee.

The "Tennessean" is a novel founded upon a recent and well known fact, still fresh in the memory of hundreds in that

part of the United States where . . . everyone remembers a secret expedition undertaken by a number of . . . enterprising
young men (principally Tennesseans) to the Spanish domin-
ions some fifteen years since.

Sketches by a Traveller will comprise physical and moral
remarks on the Eastern and Western parts of the United States,
including the history of the principal cities and towns from their
origins.

She returned to New York from Albany and on the way turned to
the works of Lord Byron to pass the time on the steamboat: "Everything now must pass the fiery ordeal of criticism, compared with which,
walking on red-hot plowshares would be recreation," she read in an
introduction to Byron's *The Corsair*. Anne set down the book and
thought about her *Sketches* manuscript; the quote made her quake. She
continued reading: "A critic, like the tiger, attacks all whom he can
master, and kills for the dear delight of butchering." Royall set down
the book again to write her own notes. "If that be the case," she
quipped, "there will scarcely be a mouthful one of them."

As if preparing herself for future criticism, Anne occasionally confessed a sense of inadequacy with her self-taught writing. "It is understood I never have, nor am I capable of dressing out my subjects
in learned phrases or bold images or any of the elegance of style." On
the other hand, she presented her travel credentials as a justifying factor
in her observations, albeit with a little folksiness. She only wished to
bring her travel insights "as near as possible before the eyes of those
who have not an opportunity of seeing them, and that in my own homespun way without regard to style or rules of composition, which I know
nothing of, and care as little I know."

Anne turned a corner in her writing while she was in Albany. She

had deviated from her original design to fill her *Sketches* with anecdotes and detached incidents from her travels, and now found herself
engaging in actual reporting. With each new city, and interaction with
its leaders and engagement with its institutions, she took her talk
even more seriously. As her travels ranged across New York and
Massachusetts to Boston, Anne became increasingly aware of her
own prejudices—and the power travel had in forcing her to confront
them. "On my way thither I fell in with two of the citizens, whose
manners and conversations effectively dislodged the prejudice I had
imbibed since infancy against this city, that it was inhabited by sour,
bigoted, priest-ridden race—noted for nothing but psalm singing
and hanging witches and Quakers." In contrast to her mistreatment
in the city of Philadelphia, which she had been taught to admire,
Royall's opinion of Boston changed for the better as she gained a
newfound appreciation of its generosity. "One grain of reflection
might have removed this prejudice; for it is impossible that illiberal-
ity and science should exist in the same place."

This was the power of travel—and travel chronicles—for the
writer. "To cure the errors imbibed in our youth, traveling is indispensable," she wrote. "In short, to judge accurately of men and
things, they must be seen." The bias she had learned against Salem
and its witch trials, for example, "vanished the moment I came to see
and judge for myself" the city's current ways and its handling of the
"delusion of the age." She now saw the universality of such discrimination against women: "How many of those supposed witches
were burnt about the same time in England, a country famed at this
time for refinement and liberality, with as much reason as we might
adjure Paris for the massacre of St. Bartholomew?"

She had done more than shed some petty prejudices along her
thousand-mile journey. The budding author also embraced her role

as an American chronicler, a literary force of nature shaped more by the ideals and aspirations of the American Revolution and its nascent concept of national unity than any regional pride. "My country is my home," she would one day respond to a critic who had told her to "go home." Royall added, "My husband fought and bled in the cause of its freedom." Whether or not this sentiment reflected an honest assessment of her view, it provided a cloak of defense for the criticism she continually encountered as an itinerant gadfly on her own. "I am one of the sovereign people," she would muse later.

With her *Sketches* overflowing with notes at this point, Anne left Boston with the realization that she still lacked a publisher. New York editors, like those in Philadelphia, had been cordial in their visits, but frank in their rejection. It wasn't until she reached New Haven, Connecticut, that a serendipitous moment led to a breakthrough. Governor Oliver Wolcott came to town, and Royall took part in a special dinner in his honor. (An unnamed acquaintance had even purchased a dress for the raggedly Anne as a gift for the occasion.) As per her routine, she collected a letter of endorsement from the governor, which she used to arrange an agreement with the publishers of the *Connecticut Herald*, John Carrington and Thomas Green Woodward. They offered to publish Royall's *Sketches* on credit through the Durry and Peck printers in New Haven and struck a deal that allowed her to order and sell her own books.

Anne Royall's first journey as an author had come to a successful end. She did little to rest, however, as she braced for the momentous literary event of publication. The fiery ordeal of criticism noted in Lord Byron's work finally arrived when *Sketches of History, Life and Manners* rolled off the presses in 1826—the same year that the anti-Masonry movement exploded and the nation celebrated its fiftieth anniversary of Independence.

The first-time authoress, as she now referred to herself, had just turned 57 years old. Still, having committed to a life on the road, the peripatetic writer granted herself no time to celebrate. Her luggage now included a crate of books. Extending her journeys as far north as Maine, only to turn around and head toward the Gulf of Mexico in New Orleans, Anne continued her interviews and accumulated her journal entries for future books.

Strangely enough, her first book was published anonymously, as "A Traveller," but it did not take long for its real author to reveal herself in public.

As Anne's prime backers, the network of the secretive Masonic society appeared at first to be a boon for the Revolutionary widow's publishing efforts. The men paid homage to her husband; and they paid their subscriptions for her books in the process. Armed with their own newspapers and connections to higher ranks of society, the Masonic embrace of Royall also presented a precarious two-step. While Anne happily carried the banner of Masonic hagiography—"the most liberal, humane, and enlightened citizens we have," she wrote—she soon bore the brunt of the attacks on the society.

Her *Sketches* appeared in public at the same time a dismayed William Morgan famously announced in September 1826 his intentions to reveal the society's secret rituals in a book of his own. In many respects, the nation's biggest controversy of the year drew more attention to the Masonic connections in Royall's relatively mild political overtones in *Sketches* and forced her to ramp up her rhetoric or remain quiet. (The latter was never much of an option for Anne.) When Morgan suddenly disappeared in western New York, word quickly spread that he had been abducted and murdered by Masonic followers. According to historian William Vaughn, "no other crime in the period attracted as much attention in the northern press." In the process, the event ignited a "dormant hostility to Freemasonry and all secret societies, which now swept the northwest and Middle Atlantic states, taking shape first as a moral crusade, and then, after 1827, as the impetus for the nation's first or significant minor party." Within a matter of months, the anti-Mason movement managed to frame society members and their supporters as political and religious threats to the "common man and evangelical Christianity," wrote religious historian David Hackett in *That Religion in Which All Men Agree*, "spurred by an expanding print culture and democratizing ethos" that "laid bare a larger battle over Christian identity."

Anne didn't hesitate to enter the fray—nor did she have a choice. The backlash over the Morgan story, she declared, played out "precisely like the witches of Salem; nothing keeps those fanatics from cutting the throats of every Mason in New York." She mocked those "engaged in this farce" and predicted that the movement sweeping the country was nothing more than a "missionary scheme to raise money" and an aim for political power. In an attempt to defuse the situation, Anne doubled down with the intransigence of an old friend: "Was not General Washington a good man? He was a mason—was not LaFayette a good man? He was mason." As she ranked other leading stalwarts on the historical list, Royall dismissed the anti-Mason campaign as a "silly" endeavor: "Might as well attempt to pluck the sun and moon out of the heavens." Anne concluded with a personal note. "Masonry can boast of the best men, and the best Christians, since the world began." She reminded readers that her husband, "one of the most respectable men, descended from one of the most respectable families in America, uniformly told me, it was the greatest institution in the world."

Anne's loyalty notwithstanding, the anti-Mason uprising exploited the political capital of Morgan's disappearance for years, especially in Anne's main stomping grounds of New York and New England. It cost the author dearly, as those with Masonic affiliation retreated from public view. As *Forgotten Ladies* biographer Richard Wright noted, "Before the outbreak there were five hundred lodges in New York alone, with a membership of over twenty thousand; by 1830, there were only eighty-two lodges, with three thousand members."

The remaining Masons repaid Anne's courageous stand. In reviewing *Sketches*, the *American Masonic Record and Albany Saturday Magazine* proclaimed Royall to be the most "indefatigable literary being of which our country has the honor to toast. She is as volatile as ether; without being subject to evaporation. One day, with all the spirit and sanguinity of a Junius, she is writing down the Boston Lyceum; the next, she is holding a tete-a-tete with the President." The newspaper then addressed her New York newspaper friend, Mordecai Noah, who had recently attempted to establish a Jewish colony in upstate New York: "The gallant governor of Ararat says she is the Mrs. Walter Scott of America; the National Advocate insists she is the Madame da Stael." Royall only lacked for poetry, the newspaper insisted, encouraging her to pursue a volume in the tradition of Lord Byron's *Childe Harold*. Should she consider that notion of poetry, the newspaper declared, "we will engage to puff all that she has written."

The *Boston Commercial Gazette* added its own praise: "She marches on, speaking her mind freely, and unpacks her heart in words of censure or praise as she feels. Sometimes she lets fall more truths than the interested reader would wish to hear, and at others overwhelms her friends with flattery." Regardless of anyone's political difference, it concluded, "her book is more amusing than any novel we have read for years."

The *New York Commercial Advertiser*, in direct contrast to Noah's generosity and the largely positive reviews of *Sketches*, struck back.

Despite her husband's Revolutionary bona fides, "a more contemptible book was never palmed upon any community." Anne only "pretended" to draw up sketches of the country; her means of reporting were "mischievous," whereby she "grossly abused" people for the "sole reason they did not treat her with as much attention as she thought proper to demand."

Other newspapers, like the *Salem Gazette*, opted for mockery, reprinting a review that had run in the *Providence Cadet*. After spoofing her birth from descendants of the legendary Captain Smith and her rescue on the banks of a river like a "Princess Pocohontas" by the gallant William Royall, the reviewer wrote that the despondent widow seized the pen as a "worshipper of literature." Far from any dabbling, she had become the "biographer for nine-tenths of the great men of the Union," and "immortalized several of our citizens who were vain enough to hope for the jobs of immortality, or the wreath of imperishable fame."

With her eye on book sales more than the critics, Anne continued to barnstorm with her copies of *Sketches*, often sending letters to editors in advance of her arrival. Her problems lay beyond critics: "When you send me more books," Royall wrote her printers, "do, dear gentlemen, put none of those rat-eaten ones up, it is cruel to treat me in this manner." The role of the post office and its function as both the vehicle and outlet of her work also raised her ire. Something evil was at play when "the frauds of agents, insolvencies, losses by sea, and thefts by post-offices, have exceeded my credit by a hundred percent." While she had resisted attacking the Presbyterians and other religious groups to any grave extent in her first book, she now faced greater obstacles in the post office and from booksellers, which were at the forefront of her economic survival. The post offices, in particular, were "strung along the road" to serve the interests of the religious movement and deliver their tract publications, she charged, blocking her work in the process.

Despite such inventory challenges, Anne's book tour became its own road show.

"We have had the honor of a visit from Mrs. Royall," the *Northampton Post* told its readers, "and cannot permit an event of so much importance to pass without a special notice." The *Post* described Royall as "striking . . . rather below middling height, and possessing a very comfortable degree of en-bon-point." The editors found that Anne "may be taken for a personification of a Dutch Cleopatra." While she reminded them of those "London fashionables," they also noted that she "retains the rude independence of character" of Native Americans, with whom she had resided, "and their scorn for the forms and dandyisms of what we are accustomed to call civilized society." Slightly taken aback at her attacks on the anti-Mason movement, they concluded that she "is truly one of the greatest phenomena of this age of wonders."

Her friends at the *Boston Gazette* parodied the garrulous confidence that now drove her interactions. After her salutations, the paper wrote, she launched into a series of questions: "You are a lot of cut-throat scoundrels. They tell me you are missionaries. I'll leave you all in my Black Book. Who told you I was a friend of General Jackson? I am a friend of General Jackson, of Mr. Adams, and the whole human race, except the missionaries, who tried to persecute me, and hurt the sale of my volumes." The *Gazette* sent her off to another newspaper, where "in all probability," they added, a "Royall blast" will be "heard and felt beyond the mountains."

In Maine, in anticipation of her visit, the *Hallowell Gazette* reprinted reviews about this "modest and delectable lady, and a distinguished traveler, who attracts so much attention." Anne regaled them with stories about meeting General Lafayette, who presented Royall with a rose in Boston. Though she enjoyed patronage from literary men, the newspaper said, Royall had to deal with the "opposition and obloquy of the ignorant, the bigoted, and the weak-minded, but this does not dishearten her 'independent spirit' in the least degree."

"We stop the press to announce to our readers the arrival in this town of the celebrated Mrs. Royall," the *Portland Argus* wrote. They found that an interview with Royall resulted in a "highly interesting" experience. "Mrs. Royall is a little, short, snug-built, sharp-eyed lady, who looks just as if she were ready to give you place on her black list."

The *Philadelphia Album and Ladies Weekly Gazette* noted that Anne had twice visited their offices, books in hand, hoping for publicity. The editor had been out of town but couldn't help quipping, "We are exceedingly vexed at this, for from the descriptions we have received of this lady's affable demeanor, lady-like-compliance, and interesting conversation, our curiosity has been considerably excited." Not failing to overlook a chance to add to the eccentric labels increasingly fixed on Royall, the editor continued: "Mrs. Royall's outward appearance, we understand, is quite prepossessing, and the apt index of a refined and gifted mind."

While Boston gobbled up her books, New York sales surprisingly lagged, especially among women. In a city where she once only professed praise, Royall now struck back in bewilderment: "A New York lady will not look at a book, unless it has a red cover." While Royall assumed her portraits reflected an honest representation of her visits, she noted a shift in her own reception, especially in New York: "Since the appearance of my *Sketches*, I have observed that the moment I make my appearance in any town or village, one part of the community avoids me as they would a pestilence, while another part advances to meet me with demonstrations of anything but fear."

Before long she recognized that notoriety often drew better results than reviews, so she heightened the intensity of her attacks on the anti-Mason crowd, raised the level of her involvement in political issues of the day, and openly engaged the critics of her books. As she traveled to Philadelphia, for example, she wrote a typical letter to a newspaper, clearly intending it to serve as a provocation for her appearance: "I shall leave this city in the morning for Philadelphia, and blow up Walsh for his treachery in aiding the United States Bank."

Such letters, once overlooked, now drew more scrutiny: The *Philadelphia Album and Ladies Literary Port Folio* would one day wonder if Anne was "more anxious for notoriety than for pure fame." Now a national public figure, she reveled in the fact that reviews often triggered an exchange in the press; a Massachusetts paper accused a nearby competitor of being "bewitched by the flattery" of Royall's pen. The harsh tone of the exchange increased. Anne Royall was a "silly old hag," or "either an idiot or maniac," added another newspaper, which suggested she be "placed under the care of a keeper."

Years later, Anne made a confession to her readers—or rather, dispelled the rumor that she had become fabulously wealthy from her books. "Of all the works I have published, I have not been able from sales to pay for the paper, much less the printing. . . . Upon one work alone, I lost $1,000." Detailing her "humiliating" and impoverished living conditions, including a winter without furniture or even a bed during the cold nights, she praised the "specimens of female perfection" who had come to her rescue with charity. "How I am able to publish at all is answered at once by the aid of my friends, by private donations bestowed on me for food, clothing, fuels, etc., but of which comforts I deny myself, to pay my debts."

The author tended to overlook one fact about those escalating debts; unencumbered by a real publisher or bottom-line-touting agent and arranging for the publication of her books on hasty terms, she became one of the most prolific authors of her times and went broke in the process. Over the next five years, she would publish nine volumes of travel, as well as her novel, *The Tennessean*. While she met her financial obligations to her New Haven printer with the moderate sales success of *Sketches*, Royall rushed out the next book with little consideration of its value—or potential backlash.

Journalist and biographer Helen Beal Woodward called *The Tennessean* the "worst American novel of all time." Forever loyal, the *Boston Commercial Gazette* was more generous: "If it were not ungallant to apply terms of disapprobation to the production of a female, we might add, that the 'Tennessean' contains some phrases of profanity, which in our opinion give no interest to the work and had better have been omitted." One of the most entertaining reviews simply stated the facts: "The best mead of praise we can bestow upon *The Tennessean*," ran the *Boston Lyceum*, "is to say that it consists of 372 closely printed duodecimo pages, very vilely printed, at New Haven."

Whether or not Anne accepted the brutal criticism of *The Tennessean*, she returned to travel writing as the main focus of her career. An encounter with one of her old journalism heroes, William Duane, had left her disturbed and in a quandary over her direction, however. "Almost since I can remember to have read a newspaper, this gentleman interested me," Royall wrote about Duane, the radical editor of the *Philadelphia Aurora* who had served as the thorn in the side of Federalist leaders like Alexander Hamilton and John Adams. Duane wrote biting and satirical editorials that mocked the monarchic attitudes of the Federalists and rallied the Republican opposition. Credited by Thomas Jefferson with playing an instrumental role in his presidential election in 1800, Duane twice faced sedition charges, barely escaping trial. While Jefferson's influence brought Duane to

Washington, the rebellious editor and author had fallen into a desperate state when Royall knocked on his door. "After fighting with his pen gratis for most of his life, in defence of the freedom of his country," Anne remarked, "he is now in his old age forgotten, and left in struggle with poverty."

As the unrelenting pace of travel took its toll on Anne and her pocketbook, she realized she had come to the proverbial fork in the road. With religious publications suddenly abounding, gaining popularity within an evangelical revival that she detested, and the anti-Mason books on Morgan flourishing in demand, she made a calculated choice on her publishing career.

"We are informed by various papers and by a letter from Mrs. Royall," her editor friend Theophilus Gates at the Philadelphia-based *Reformer* noted, "that she is at present engaged in publishing a work entitled the Black Book, 'a great part of which,' to use her own words, 'is devoted to the rapacity, swindling, and hypocrisy of the Missionaries.' She adds, 'I have exerted all my powers to go to the bottom of the evil, (which gives name to my book), and the work is now in the press.'"

Many years earlier, in a letter from Alabama to Matt, Anne had naïvely written: "What think you, Matt, of the Christian religion? Between you and I, and the bed post, I begin to think it is all a plot of priests. I have ever marked those professors, whenever humanity demanded their attention, the veriest savages under the sun."

Now had come the time to make good on her bedpost hunch.

# FOUR

# The Black Book

*Am I black enough, think you, dressed up in a lasting suit of ink? Do I deserve my dark and pitchy title?*

—THOMAS MIDDLETON, *THE BLACK BOOK*, 1604

One evening back in Alabama, during Anne's earliest period of being alone, one unnamed woman impressed upon her an acute awareness of politics with her willingness to buck protocol and engage men in a debate. "I have always heard widows were jealous of each other," Royall wrote, "but this time I had ocular proof of the act." Unlike the other women who carefully avoided "violating those rules of politeness," this woman—a recent widow—sat among the men and "put her rivals to shame, and gained a complete victory."

The author watched closely, taking notes. When the conversation turned to Jackson's victory in New Orleans and its effect on the British government, including its costs and debts, the woman interrupted and corrected a gentleman who had overcompensated for the British losses. "She took up the subject where he left off," Royall wrote, and explained the British policy, "the measures of their ministers, and their effects upon the people at large." The rest of the women in the room "turned their eyes upon her in astonishment," Anne noted, but then returned to their whispering conversations. The woman's level of education and audacity left Royall spellbound.

Above all other characteristics, Anne valued this intellectual awareness and the ability to express it—and harbored a deep-seated hatred for any anti-intellectual response, especially among those with wealth, and especially among women.

Aghast at the lack of education she observed in her fellow tenants at one boardinghouse in Alabama, she wrote her lawyer friend Matthew Dunbar in sheer frustration: "A lady asked me one day, 'What state Virginia was in?' Another asked 'If Canada was not in Kentucky?'"

Royall didn't accept that such unawareness happened by accident. She chalked it up to the religious communities' intent on keeping their flock, especially women, uneducated—despite the fact that the Presbyterian pioneers from Scotland and their Ulster ranks from Northern Ireland who populated the South and Appalachian communities had brought one of the highest rates of literacy among any eighteenth-century immigrant group. "It appears to me, since I have had the opportunity of mixing with the world, that there is a certain class of citizens, whose interest it is to keep their fellow men in ignorance."

"Hence arises all our mistakes in religion, morals, and politics," Royall wrote in 1818. "When our reason is cultivated and our mind enlightened by education, we are enabled to strip off that disguise which knavery, bigotry, and superstition wears. It rectifies our judgments, holds the reins of our passions, in short, enables us to discover whatever tends to promote our present and eternal welfare."

Over the next ten years of traveling, Anne never veered from this opinion about the value of education and the bane of its denial and cultivation among those she referred to as "the masses." Stripped of any intellectual engagement, she argued, this mass of people became vulnerable to political corruption and a circumvention of democracy—and the calculating efforts of the rising class of evangelical elites. "This is to be the downfall of our country some day!—All republics have fallen from the same cause." The men of learning rallied on the side of liberty, according to Royall, while the common people worshipped Caesar, and "all the common people want rope enough."

Foretelling a sense of persecution years before she would ever publish, Anne continued: "Why, a person who is reputed to know any thing of geography, philosophy, or astronomy, is looked upon with as much abhorrence by the great mass of the people, as if he was in league with the devil?"

In league with the devil—or, in the opinion of powerful Presbyterian minister Ezra Styles Ely, in league with "Thomas Paine's *Age of Reason* . . . Theophilus Gates' *Reformer*, and Madam Royall's *Black Book*," which Ely listed in a satirical article in his own newspaper, the *Philadelphian*, invoking appropriately enough, "So help me, Devil."

Anne Royall had now reached a stature as one of the nation's great infidels.

Anne's editor friends at the *Boston Sentinel* called out Ely's rather bizarre spoof on Royall, and her opposition to his movement to halt Sunday mail and place Christians in political office, "for want of argument to sustain his cause." The *Christian Baptist* newspaper, edited by Alexander Campbell, joined the backlash against Ely's attack on Royall. "This attempt to caricature the expression of public opinion on a question deeply affecting its interest, ought to be reprobated by every member of the community." The paper added that Ely deserved "public abhorrence."

Ely had constructed a series of "resolutions" by his dreaded opponents, lampooning their own charges against him: "That if said

E. S. Ely, D.D. should refuse publicly to sign this reasonable recantation, he be reported as intent on the union of Church and State; be denounced as such in the legislature halls of this country . . . and finally, that he be enrolled in Madam Royall's *Black Book*."

Anne shrugged at the attention and probably appreciated Ely's attempt at humor more than she felt any sentiment of offense. She had first tried to meet Ely a year prior to her trial, during the final throes of the 1828 election. Traveling again to Pennsylvania for a new book— "give us our state by itself," she wrote self-mockingly of the demand for her books—Royall joked that she could have been of service to Ely's campaign to get sound Presbyterian voters to the polls. "But I have something else to do besides aiding Dr. Ely," she quipped, quoting the ancient scourge of evil, "unless it were to the fate of Haman." Undeterred, she eventually sought out Ely's home address, given that he was a "pious Christian," and brought her books and subscription list in hand. "I was informed how to find him, and that his house stood back from the street, in a square, and on his gate, some distance from the house, on the street I would see a large silver plate with 'Rev Dr. Stiles Ely' on it. I found the gate, and the silver plate—the big letters—the big house—and the BIG man."

As if to heighten the drama, Anne crafted this narrative with the gory details of her precarious situation, as she, penniless as ever, with her shoes literally shredding, wandered the streets of Philadelphia for her notes and interviews. The set-up of the scene prior to reaching Ely's house presented a litmus test on his level of compassion. Royall wrote:

> Next morning the shoes, stockings, and feet, were all glued fast together by the blood! But it was Sunday, and I had time to devise ways and means to get them asunder.

I had kept as much of my difficulties as possible, to myself, and was determined to finish what I had begun, lest my feet suffer as they might. I concluded (and wisely no one will dispute) that I might as well walk to death, as starve to death, and set suffering of all sorts at defiance.

After some time (though I disliked the spirits as I smarted bitterly) by bathing and soaking the wound I separated the shoes from the stockings, but to get the stocking from the raw flesh was no easy matter, and took up several hours. The bleeding, however, was, upon the whole, an advantage, as it prevented the swelling and pain. On Monday I set out again, but this day my feet swelled and became so lacerated by the tightness of the shoe, that light as my purse was I was compelled to draw upon it for the amount of a pair of shoes, for which I paid seventy-five cents to Mr. Kelly, corner of Strawberry alley and Market street. These were of course the lowest quality, and Mr. Kelly, a very good man, doubtless, remembers it well, as I left the bloody shoes in his store and pursued my labors with unshrinking perseverance. Thus I walked."

The visit at the door of the "pious Christian" by the distressed traveler did not go as planned, or perhaps it did, for the encounter provided Anne with the means to display Ely's lack of piety:

The big door was open, and in a splendid passage were a few seats very tempting to a person dropping with fatigue. I did not, however, sit down, or approach nearer than the door, at which I knocked. After sometime the doctor appeared and I briefly repeated my business, and though he saw I was sinking from fatigue, he turned off short and said he was engaged:

even one minute's rest on one of the seats would at that time have been a greater benefit to me than ten dollars; but the savage—he convert the heathen! he might cut Christians throats, or hang them! but as for heathens I would go no farther than himself if I was upon the hunt of one. This is the monster who talks so much of "kissing the Son," in his fourth of July sermon, and has the impudence to dictate to our Presidents what they must say in their messages, viz: "that they are Christians," such as he is, and that "they preferred a Christian temple, to a Socinian conventicle;" the daring traitor. The whole of this fourth of July sermon is treason from beginning to end, and the time was when any man who would utter such treason in our country would be strung up.

Anne's reference to Ely's infamous sermon on July 4, 1827, at the Seventh Presbyterian Church in Philadelphia—"The Duty of Christian Freemen to Elect Christian Rulers"—revealed her stated naïveté was a bit of ruse. Ely's sermon, which was published in various newspapers and distributed as a pamphlet around the country, had ignited a cantankerous debate on the role of religion in politics—timed brilliantly for the 1828 presidential campaign—and demonstrated the audacious actions by a powerful religious movement. His work cultivated the ground for cycles of extremely conservative Protestant involvement in party politics for the next two centuries. In effect, Ely laid the groundwork for every "moral majority" movement to come.

Ely had "thrown off the mask," Royall wrote, often referring to him as "Pope Ely." Calling for the creation of a "Christian Party," Ely spoke in both pragmatic and prophetic terms—and, at times, chilling ones: "If a ruler is not a Christian he ought to be one, in this land of evangelical light, without delay." Ely's bold plan, which set Anne on her own literary *Black Book* response, covered the very cornerstones of religious tyranny that she had long feared—and eventually used as testimony at her own trial:

> I propose, fellow-citizens, a new sort of union, or, if you please, a Christian Party in politics, which I am exceedingly desirous all good men in our country should join. God, my hearers, requires a Christian faith, a Christian profession, and a Christian practice of all our public men; and we as Christian citizens ought, by the publication of our opinions to require the same.
>
> . . . Moral character has some influence in our elections, but not that place which it deserves. The law of public opinion excludes confirmed sots, and persons judicially convicted of high crimes and misdemeanors against the State; but it ought to render the election of all profane swearers, notorious Sabbath breakers, seducers, slanderers, prodigal and riotous persons.
>
> . . . If three or four of the most numerous denominations of Christians in the United States, the Presbyterians, the Baptists, the Methodists and the Congregationalists, for instance, should act upon this principle, our country would never be dishonoured with an avowed infidel in her national cabinet or capitol. The Presbyterians alone could bring half a million of electors into the field.
>
> . . . It will be objected that my plan of a truly Christian Party in politics will make hypocrites. We are not answerable for their hypocrisy if it does. There is no natural tendency in the scheme to make men deceivers; and if real enemies of the Christian religion conceal their enmity, that concealment is for the public good. We wish all iniquity, if not exterminated, may, as if ashamed, hide its head.

The itinerant author did not stand alone against Ely's extraordinary declaration for the rule by a Protestant majority—hardly. The *Hartford Religious Inquirer*, under the headline of "Dark Ages Returning," admonished its readers to stay far from Ely's "schemes of priest-craft." It added, "Beware of those who come to you in sheeps' clothing, while they are ravening wolves in disguise." But the *Inquirer* also included an eerie warning for those who confronted the "orthodox" leaders: "All who exhibit a spirit of non-conformity, their language is—'this people which knoweth not the law is cursed.'" Royall's editor friend at the *Reformer*, Theophilus Gates, issued an immediate warning: "We may bid a final farewell to our religious liberties and the right to enjoy our own faith." Gates drew a line of distinction between Ely's Presbyterian and institutional elites and the rest of the flourishing evangelical movement rooted in the rural areas who "would soon be placed in the background." He added a historical touch aimed at Ely's colleague, Presbyterian minister Lyman Beecher in Massachusetts: "Such as the Presbyterian doctors of divinity would esteem the best and most pious, we should fear and dread much more than his 'Holiness' the Pope. Such religious rulers once had the rule in New England, and they ruled indeed with a rod of iron, imprisoning, whipping, cropping, and hanging those who dissented from them in religious matters."

Anne's objections, however, placed her in a different category, as one of only a handful of female critics—and with Fannie Wright, certainly the most unyielding—willing to intrude in the male-dominated discourse. "Had she been male," literary historian E. J. Clapp wrote in her study on the "common scold" trial, "Royall's behavior would not have stood out as extraordinary."

Strangely enough, the "missionary" movement launched by Ely and Beecher brought together an unholy alliance of critics, many of whom shared little other than their distrust of the motives of the northern and East Coast churchmen. Beyond the Unitarians in Massachusetts, freethinkers like Wright and Robert Dale Owen blasted Ely's efforts as a betrayal of the American founders and encouraged people to "seek the opinions of the great men in their works," many of whom would be considered "infidels" by the Christian extremists, and rid themselves of "the trash of the tract house and the libels of the pulpit." Baptist pamphleteer Reverend Lawrence Greatrake delighted with the rise of this "class of mankind then (and they at this time amount to an army of no small size)." Far from rejecting "deists and easier skeptics," Greatrake wrote, a lot of the evangelicals opposed to institutional titans like Ely were "combining their power and arranging their forces for entering the Mystical Babylon." Years later, he singled out Gates's *Reformer*, the editor of the *Christian Baptist*, and "other such characters, both male and female, including Miss Frances Wright and the caustic Mrs. Anne Royall," who the Baptist writer warned had been "hunted down" during her "common scold" trial in Washington, DC, due to her opposition.

"The writer bears testimony to the general correctness of her [Royall's] moral portraiture of the 'General Assembly of Presbyterian,'" Greatrake wrote, siding with Royall that Ely and his missionary allies were "all that she represents them to be, in a moral and a political point of view; and ineffably more serpent-like, and detestable in a theological point of view." He held up the woman writer as a victim of "mongering rabidness" by the various "missionary, tract and sabbath schools" and expressed his surprise "that she escaped with life."

Comparing Ely to the "kings of the east," Greatrake would eventually come to consider Royall's witch trial as a result of her castigation of Ely. "Their blackguard Sabbath school progeny, Tract and Temperance agents, tools and factotums were set upon her, to provoke her to intemperance of expression," he lectured, "and then they drag her before one of their civil tribunals as being a nuisance or a common scold. Such is their mode of operations all over the country."

Two centuries later, modern Baptist historians have been less kind to Anne. "Anti-Missionism reached its slanderous nadir in the writings of Royall," according to Byron C. Lambert, author of the *Rise of the Anti-mission Baptists*. "No charge against the clergy was too extravagant, no suspicion too base for her to entertain and circulate. Careless hyperbole abounds in those passages of her books."

"Were a foreigner, immediately upon landing, to take up a newspaper," Scottish writer Wright noted prophetically, placing such hyperbole in context, "he might suppose that the whole political machine was about to fall to pieces and he had just come in town to be crushed in its ruins." As a foreign observer who eventually settled in the States and launched her own social experiments, including a utopian community in Tennessee for freed slaves, Wright appreciated such a raucous exchange in the American newspapers. Unlike some contemporary critics, perhaps, she distinguished between the hyperbole in the press— and its jocular role in generating discussion—and the more formal social protocols in person. "The Americans are certainly a calm, rational, civil, and well-behaved people," she wrote, "not given to quarrel or to call each other names—and yet, if you were to look at their newspapers you would think them a parcel of Hessian soldiers." Such an unrestricted press, the foreigner noted, "was the safety-valve of their free constitution."

Writing in the *Journal of Southern History*, Bertram Wyatt-Brown identified two often-overlooked anti-missionary strains emerging from Royall's rural South that may have differed with her in theological terms but appreciated her writings against Ely and Beecher. Such an emergence of two seemingly different groups also highlighted an element of dissent that was clearly rooted in her upbringing. The Hard Shell Baptists, who were active in the Appalachian Mountains, rejected this "modern evangelism—protracted meetings, missionary and tract societies, and church discipline matters on liquor and other vices" as an abrupt "modification of scriptural truth." A larger opposition, according to Wyatt-Brown, "disapproved" of the "northern agency system of benevolent associations" and mission work, especially among Native Americans and enslaved blacks who viewed these practices as intrusions of societal boundaries.

In this respect, Greatrake, in a Hard Shell Baptist tirade that made Royall look like a moderate, also railed against Ely's and Beecher's auxiliary efforts to foist reform societies onto their own congregations as part of a larger missionary scheme and authored an "Anti-missionary Dissertation."

To be sure, Anne never disclaimed any religious beliefs. "I spurn the narrow mind which is attached to a sect or a part, to the exclusion of the rest of mankind," she wrote. "I am far from being among the number of those who set at naught the worship of the Deity, however much I deplore the prostitution of that religion which is pure and undefiled."

Members of Pennsylvania's state legislature, which had invited Royall to address them soon after Ely's infamous sermon, placed a printed response to the sermon on every legislator's desk, an especially timely gesture relating to a bill over the use of religious texts in schools that was scheduled for ratification. Within three years, Ely claimed the Sunday School Union had distributed over 3.5 million copies of religious materials, which meant that the "political power of our country would be in the hands of men whose character had been formed under the influence of sabbath schools."

By 1829, according to author Eric R. Schlereth, the three major evangelical organizations—the American Bible Society, the American Sunday School Union, and the American Track Society—had launched an ambitious effort to put a Bible in every American household and to publish and distribute millions of copies of religious tracts. Even the Baptist churches, among others, complained about the "tracts, magazines, religious newspapers, etc. they [Presbyterians] are sending forth and inundating the religious world with the most voluminous and discordant commentary with it, that human ingenuity can devise or human agency operate!"

In a sermon that was reprinted widely in various newspapers, Beecher reaffirmed the sabbatarian movement's plans and his prophecy of a nation led by Christian-trained leaders: "It is needless to say that under this economy the destinies of the Church and the State will soon be in the hands of those who are receiving their education. In our academic halls will be the future lawgivers and religious teachers of our great Republic."

To compound matters for Royall, the "zealots" in the anti-Mason movement, which had so brashly dismissed her work, took up Ely's call for a Christian Party. Within a couple of years, the "Antimasons felt they had translated Ely's dream into reality," according to Cornell researcher Leslie Giffen, "that in launching the Antimasonic party they had created a new sort of union, a 'Christian party in politics.'"

Anne didn't relent. "May the arms of the first member of Congress, who proposes a national religion, drop powerless from his shoulder," she wrote, upping the pitch in her writing, "his tongue cleave to the roof of his mouth and all the people say amen."

The sound of a Christian Party would have shaken the barley in the fields of William Royall's deist plantation back in western

Virginia. Anne's religious faith, to be sure, had evolved over the years. One evening in Alabama in 1821, Royall took a seat next to a "stout, jolly" woman at a boardinghouse dinner table. "A great many got religion that day," the woman said, seemingly innocent. Anne responded: "What religion did they get?" The question struck the woman as "queer." She returned that there was only "one religion," which everyone knew. Royall didn't give in: "There you are mistaken, Madam. There are many religions. There is the Christian religion; the Jewish religion; the Mahometan religion." Unaware of what Anne was referring to, the woman shook her head in puzzlement, and then she asked: "What religion are you?" Without hesitation, Royall stated her religion "was piety," to which the woman responded that "she had never heard of it." The woman added: "Is there many of the pieties where you come from?"

Folding over with laughter in her letter to Matt, Anne couldn't resist a shot at the "priests"—her term for Presbyterians and other Protestant leaders, not necessarily Catholics as typically used—who had held the revival that night. "So they can draw the women, they care for nothing else. If there is a hell, there will be more priests in it than any other description."

A decade later, with Ely's star on the rise, Royall couldn't resist praising her own righteous remnant in the literary world. "As to the *Reformer*, and other Editors and myself," she declared, "we have acted in a faithful and fearless part, in the discharge of our duty." Gates, Anne remarked, had a Shakespearean quality to him, and he had done well to "open the eyes of the people." But his reach and patronage were tiny compared to the vast operations of the major evangelical movements and their presses.

Now, Anne announced, she had resolved to "risk her talents." She introduced her new book as a continuation of her travels:

*Black Book!* (with the exclamation mark). "It is, by this time, well authenticated that alone, friendless and pennyless, I came to the Atlantic states, and succeeded, beyond example, in obtaining literary patrons," Royall began, quickly complimenting supporters who showed her generosity in New Haven, including those from Yale College. "But this is the bright side of my book," she continued.

Only a few months after Ely's controversial sermon in Philadelphia, Royall went through a life-changing experience in Burlington, Vermont. "They became more and more hostile," she wrote in a letter to a newspaper editor, referring to the anti-Masons and Presbyterians, "until (knowing I was about to expose their conduct to the world), they made an attempt on my life, and though they failed in this they succeeded in maiming me for life!"

Once again employing the narrative tendencies of a novelist, Anne put the dramatic incident in one of her *Black Books*. In a surprising move, she did not quickly sensationalize the event, and it didn't appear until page 35, as if an expected part of her journeys. After the former Vermont governor, C. P. Van Ness, met her at a tavern on a wintry afternoon, Royall visited the local newspaper editors, who confessed they didn't know what to write about her, since "so much has already been said." There in Burlington, they said, the "blueskins"— her favorite word for the anti-Mason and evangelical elite—had considerable support. They pointed at a building across the street from the tavern and announced the resident was a "good specimen of the blueskins." Anne considered it her duty to interview and obtain portraits of both sides of the political debate.

The house had high steps before the door, from which the snow had been removed; upon going in, I found a hard featured, gloomy looking man, standing outside of the counter, another was standing inside, which I took to be the proprietor. [Royall assumed the building was a store.] If the first was gloomy, the latter was fierce and savage; he was about fifty years of age, stoutly built, and wore a wig of sandy color, his face looked of iron hardness, and seemed as though it had lain out on a frosty night; of all the Jonney Saws, he had the most stern, terrific look. I asked if he was Mr. Hecock; "yes" he replied, but never raised his eye to look me in the face. As he seemed to be engaged, looking at some papers, which the other man was showing him, and which were scattered on the counter between them, I stood still (as I was not invited to sit, though there were several chairs in the store) till he was at leisure. Meantime I continued to scrutinize his countenance, in which there was a causeless, unceasing, and unappeasable savageness. Perhaps he took me for a daughter of "Baal, or Ashteroth," or one of the vain women of Tyre and Sidon, or a kind of soup meager witch, or some outlandish thing. Be that as it may, this emperor of Heroes, what we in the south would call "a bit of a blood," or a gallant "of the first water," was not for mincing the matter.

When I observed him to have got through with the papers, I informed him who I was, and that I had called on him for his patronage. "Yes," he replied, "I'll patronize you, I have heard of you before": "And now you see me." "Yes, I see you ought to be put in the workhouse, instead of being suffered to run over the country." "Is that your religion, sir? Is this the language of a Christian? And pray, sir, what have I done to consign me to the workhouse? Mind who you speak to, you hypocrite." As I said this, I laid my reticule, with some papers I held in my hand, on a chair that sat about the middle of the room, and was about to open a paper to convince the gentleman that I was not a fit subject of the workshop. I was standing near the stove, which, as well as I remember, was about the middle of the room; while I was opening the paper, Hecock walked deliberately to the door, and opening it, walked back, and passing on as though he was going behind the counter, came behind me, took hold of me, with a hand on each shoulder, and pushed me with such force that he sent me to the foot of the steps, into the street! The whole distance, including the height of the steps must have been not less than ten feet, and had it not been for the snow, which fell the preceding night, I must inevitably have been dashed to atoms on the pavement; as it was my ankle was dislocated, and one of the bones of the same leg broke, and the whole limb bruised and mangled in the most shocking manner.

The Hecock "ruffian" refused to help Royall, who screamed in pain. Another man claimed a dog had pushed her down the steps. Anne tagged the "monster" as a Presbyterian, "a contributor and supporter of the whole missionary scheme; went to church three times a day, and how many times at night, I do not know. He makes long faces and long prayers, is an Elder in the church—a hopeful convert, a pious man of the true brimstone race."

Eventually rescued by a Unitarian in a horse and carriage, Anne spent the next five weeks recovering from the incident in agonizing pain. Less than two hours after the attack, her leg in a splint, her foot dangling in warm beef brine, she insisted on being set up in front of a table in order to write. The authorities never charged her assailant. "His gospel spreading minister told him he had done a righteous act," Royall wrote. In fact, under further threat, Royall gave her manuscript to a friend for safekeeping after being told the "gospel-spreaders" had planned to destroy it.

For weeks, she recovered in the darkness of a tavern room, giggling as a young boarder named Brooks read her bawdy excerpts from the comic novel *Tristram Shandy*.

Taking five weeks to heal, she finally issued a warning: "Let this missionary scheme be called madness, or what it may, a many headed monster, as it doubtless is, or any other opprobrious name, it seems that those who advocate the scheme are determined to persevere till an army has to settle the business."

With her theatrical story recorded, Anne admitted that she should not condemn the entire Protestant sect for one villain. "I admit the truth of the maxim generally." But in her mind, the only difference between Hecock (also noted as Hickock) and the rest of the Presbyterians, ironically, was his courage to act on his convictions: "Which is the worse crime," Royall asked, prophetically, "to murder the body or the reputation. It is well known that those monsters attacked my reputation throughout the whole country, by propagating falsehoods of every color and species; charging me with being a vile imposter, a swindler, a drunkard, and every thing their malice could suggest."

Far from being a random act, Anne viewed such calumny through the lens of a bookseller: the more the "missionaries" attacked her, the more the "whole of it has recoiled upon their own wicked heads and my popularity has increased in proportion to their efforts to suppress it." Notoriety, alas, served as a great marketing tool. With the gutsy flair of a gonzo journalist, Royall clearly set out to provoke even more response. Her stories often recounted her conflicts in transit.

"We almost flayed Judge Peters of Hartford, a good sound Presbyterian whom every body knows," she wrote in one of her *Black Books*, recalling a steamboat trip back to New Haven. She set the scene at the dinner table on the boat with a doctor friend who took pleasure in sparring with the religious stalwart, as Anne peppered the story with little shots of lead. When the judge mocked one of her comments about a fellow justice in New Haven, the doctor chimed in to the conversation on her behalf. "How long has it been since you hung a witch, judge," he asked. "Not very long," replied the judge dryly. "You have very few left," the doctor replied, nodding at Royall. "When do you suppose you will get through?" The doctor "kept the table in a roar," Royall wrote, concluding her story in this edition of the *Black Books*. "Those Calvinists are certainly not made of the same materials of which other people are."

Anne's biographers and critics have overlooked this literary deftness, preferring instead to dismiss her writing as reactionary and vindictive, as if the *Black Books* simply served to settle scores with those who didn't buy them. But such an analysis misses Royall's greater ambition: to be recognized as a defining social critic and satirist of her day, and unmask much of the hypocrisy in her travels through knowing and humorous embellishments, delivered with a wink and smile. For many, her *Black Books* became prize possessions, if only for the rare honesty found in her descriptions. For those on the receiving end of her jokes, of course, her books were nothing less than slander.

Some of Anne's most faithful defenders, like biographers Sarah Harvey Porter and Bessie James, dismissed the author's *Black Books* as little more than "a compilation of extremely unflattering portraits of anti-Masons." In her insightful thesis on Royall's role as a "social critic," Linda McDonald agreed with such assessments of the *Black Books* but noted that "biting sarcasm and delightful parody were her weapons." In fact, the *Black Books*, widely panned as hackneyed invective, deserve reconsideration in the context of Anne's assumed role as a satirist and the reverberations of her writing among the male power brokers.

"Mrs. Royall's rude sketches convince us of one fact," noted New York editor Mordecai Noah, "that there is a great portion of pride and haughtiness among men of our country, whom fame and public employment have designated as prominent citizens."

Far from being a literary legerdemain, this fundamental understanding and appreciation of satire defined Royall's motives behind the *Black Books*. As Noah understood well from his roost in New York, Anne had a rare talent as a writer in her ability to strip away the shield of male privilege with a single line of biting humor. Even more surprising to fellow journalists was the fact that she chose to employ her skill during a period when women remained "cloistered," according to French observer Tocqueville.

Leaving behind her benign and idiosyncratic *Sketches*, she eased into the role of a satirical commentator who suffered no fools— expressly to make readers guffaw in their circles of friends. Anne peppered her portraits, and eventually her newspapers, with archaic phrases and words that often mocked the elite's lack of learning. She could quote Shakespeare as well as the latest parlor songs. More importantly, she wrote material that sought to inform, to entertain, and, finally, to sell—while she exposed the foibles of Ely's Christian Party, Beecher's sabbatarian crusade, political hacks in Washington and state capitols, and the emerging women's reform movements for temperance and abolition, all of which Royall viewed as disingenuous schemes for power and money.

Royall had also done her marketing homework. Reading the *Reformer* one day, she had learned about a best-selling book in England that had taken that nation by surprise. Originally published in 1820 in London, *The Black Book; or, Corruption Unmasked*, had already gone through several editions. Since the work "is very scarce in this country," the *Reformer* announced, it planned to run a series of excerpts, to give "full detail of the corruptions and abuses in the English Church." Written by John Wade, who had also in the late eighteenth century edited the *Junius Letters*, which ruthlessly satirized the prime minister for his ineptitude at governing, *The Black Book* sought to "expose that ulcerous concretion, that foul and unformed mass of rapacity, intolerance, absurdity, and wickedness, ostensibly formed on the doctrines of Jesus, but no more to do with his doctrines than with the creed of Mahomet or the maxims of Confucius." Wade's warning of the union of church and state resonated with Royall. Before long, she would be using some of his provocative terms, such as "priestcraft."

The *Black Book* tradition in England enthralled Anne. Recalling the comic jaunts of late-sixteenth-century author Thomas Nashe's "Pierce Penniless" set in the Elizabethan age, she repeatedly described her early days with the "pennyless" term in her own *Black Book*. Acerbic and wickedly funny, Nashe's "penniless" character shared Royall's ability to swap misfortune and abuse for mocking satires of their perpetrators. Pierce Penniless warns, "Write who will against me, but let him look his life be without scandal; for if he touch me never so little, I'll be as good as the Black Book to him and his kindred."

Thomas Middleton followed up Nashe's Penniless adventures in his 1604 *Black Book*, a satirical pamphlet in the age of the plague that intended to "unmask the world's shadowed villainies." In launching her own *Black Book*, Anne declared in a similar vein, "Now comes the black page, which gives name to the book, and terror to the evil doer."

Anne's literary sweep was as broad as it was damning. Issued in biannual editions over three years, the six volumes of the *Black Books*, along with Anne's Southern tours, canvassed the "virtues and vices" on the religious frontlines, town by town, state by state. Royall aimed particularly at the collusion of Ely's associates and the rise of reform societies, especially among women, for "charitable" causes:

> From Maine to Georgia—from the Atlantic to Missouri, they swarm like locusts; and, under the name of foreign missions, home missions, Bible societies, tract societies, societies for educating pious young men, to spread the gospel, pincushion societies, cent societies, mite societies, widows' societies, children's societies, rag-bag societies, and Sunday school societies, they have laid the whole country under contribution. Figures cannot calculate the amount collected by those public and private robbers; it is more than would liberate every slave in the United States; it would pay the British debt! They say, "We do not force people to give." I see no difference between forcing a man out of his money, at the mouth of a pistol, and forcing it from him by trick and cunning.

Forever committed to the imprisoned and dispossessed, Anne questioned whether the charitable motives of this host of "gospel-spreaders, those pious, godly men and women" included any movement to "redress wrongs, visit the disconsolate prisoners, console the afflicted, feed the hungry, clothe the naked." She answered her own question: "You never see them enter the house of the mourner; the orphan's woes, and the bursting tear of the widow are totally unheeded by them; you never catch them at the side of a sick bed, unless some rich man, from whom they expect to extort a legacy."

Methodically laying out her case, she attempted to stitch together the powerful inner workings of a vast network of religious fanatics under the sway of "St. Ely and St. Beecher," among others. "In all countries, and in all ages, from the Druids down to brother Beecher," Royall wrote, "priests have aimed at universal power," which included the corridors of Washington. By devising means to compel others to "think as he does," this priest or missionary figure would then be successful in "acquiring power and money," she added, resulting in an Orwellian world (long before Orwell) that made "black white, foul fair, wrong right, base noble, old young, cowards valiant, buys religion, places thieves with senators on the bench, and old foolish widows wed again."

The key, of course, was "unconditional obedience." According to Anne, this took place in the Sabbath schools and the theological seminaries, where huge waves of deracinated young men were being trained—brainwashed, in her terms—and then unleashed into communities in "brigades, battalions, regiments, companies and platoons" as priests and missionaries. Like a scourge upon mankind, the missionaries entered every city, town, village—even the smallest child did not escape them. "They go into oyster cellars, barber shops, shoe blacks, and sailors do not miss them; they creep into widows' hovels, and the orphans, shed like the frogs of Egypt." Royall warned: "They preach up Juggernaut, and draw up such pictures of heavens going to Hell by thousands, that they frighten ignorant women and children into compliance."

One of Anne's main concerns evolved into a lifetime pursuit that she would defend and expose: the exploitation of Native Americans by land swindlers and religious groups. The "atrocious acts" by religious missions among the Choctaw, involving the transfer of land deeds and "vast sums of money," she wrote, "exceeds any thing upon record, and ought to have alarmed the whole country; instead of that, perhaps there is not one in a million of our citizens knows a word of the matter, and why? Because by this very money the people are kept in ignorance. This money is employed in setting up presses over the country, and issuing papers and tracts, full of trash, to blind the people, and keep them from reading intelligent papers, which would expose the actions of those pirates."

On the other hand, Royall complimented the work of the Moravian Church among various native tribes. Still, her vitriol poured forth. "It is a fact well known that there were not a more upright, noble or virtuous people on the globe, or possessed of a higher sense of honor, than the aborigines of America," Royall wrote, "until they were contaminated by the missionaries."

Part of the missionaries' arsenal, Anne wrote, churned from their printing presses. The writer grieved at the popularity of Beecher's religious tracts over her own work; struggling to hawk her books on the road and in league with unreliable booksellers, she bristled at the extraordinary networks of dissemination developed by the Sunday Union School and tract societies. "These presses issue enough annually," she noted, "to load the largest ship in the navy." Royall objected as much to the literary styles as she did to the content of the materials.

What is it? Nothing but trash, falsehoods and slanders, against other sects; not one word of common sense in the whole of it. Their newspapers, their magazines, their heralds and tracts, are filled with nothing but stupid old wives' stories, about some old woman, little child, some fool or knave, sham revival, bitterness against neighbors; and ends with money. In every other sentence you have God, the gospel, and the blessed Sabbath. Then comes a long story about "Ann Brown," "Sally White," and Tom, Dick and Harry, "that lived a long time without God in the world" (what blasphemy! as if God did not exist everywhere) "but through God's mercy they came across a bible? If the reader wants a bible, he may get them by the bushel, in Calcutta."

It gets worse—Anne went on: "So far I have only fed my readers with skimmed milk, I am now coming to the cream of my subject, church and state."

The friends of virtue and religious liberty are divided in opinion on this business; some say it has the union of church and state for its object; others say the idea is chimerical; while all unite in denouncing it a serious and alarming evil; but the truth has at length burst upon the people. Their late attempts to establish their power by law in the Pennsylvania legislature, has at length resolved the doubting, and left no room with the most credulous to question their designs. This daring attempt upon our liberties, has however been long foreseen.

"But this world was not made for Caesar," Royall added. "They will find many, many a Brutus." Providing excepts from numerous Presbyterian sermons and documents from their General Assembly in 1827, Royall pointed out alarming quotes in church doctrine that the "day of spiritual conflict is approaching; and it becomes the church to stand ready to sustain her acquired glory." Drawing on her well-versed sense of history, Anne asked her readers to look no further than the bloody Presbyterian past in England and Scotland to gauge their intent: "Do you think we have forgotten how they put innocent men, women and children to death, in cool blood, under the pretence of witchcraft?" Her answer: "They are itching to get hold of the halter."

But Mr. Presbyterians, I know a little scripture too; we are not under the law, but under grace; and I hope I have enough left effectually to defeat your treasonable designs. I see your drift; you want to persuade government to adopt the laws of Moses, the old Jewish law, under which our Saviour suffered, the religion of peace does not suit your blood-spilling religion, if it deserves the name. Is it not astonishing that this sect, having the liberty to worship as they please, cannot be at peace, and let other sects enjoy the same liberty?

Satire inked in vitriol certainly defined much of the period's political writing. But for that ink to be in the hand of a woman, an "old woman" no less, and for it to target the hallowed institutions of Protestant stalwarts like the Presbyterians and the Congregationalists was an affront that broke new territory. Even worse, this "belligerent authoress" could celebrate a few minor victories over Ely, Beecher, and the evangelical reform movements.

When the Pennsylvania General Assembly finally threw out the "Chain Act" in 1831, which had allowed the powerful Presbyterian churches and other congregations to drape chains on the streets in front of their places of worships on Sunday, effectively shutting down the city's main traffic arteries and squares, Royall claimed a hand in the effort as a symbolic victory against religious despotism. "Glory to the Pennsylvania Legislature, we have given Dr. Ely's good sound Presbyterianism another good broadside," she wrote. "Those tyrants, not satisfied to chain the consciences of the citizens, clapt chains on the carriages, and the next step would be to chain us hand and foot. The friends of liberty must rejoice at this bold and manly stand against clerical tyranny, and as for God, any fool might know He could make money if He wanted it."

Anne's string of triumphs continued. The "Sunday Mail men and Anti-Masons entirely failed with Congress this season," she updated her readers, "and trust the people may no more disgrace themselves by electing such infamous men." In a brief stop at the Capitol in Washington, the author felt a wave of gratitude and accomplishment when she noticed a copy of her *Black Book* on the desks of so many US senators.

The newspapers took note: "The works of Madam Royall are we grant an exception," the *Boston Commercial Gazette* wrote, "for her style is so highly seasoned, her love of country so predominant, she gives so much of her local topics and applies the lash so unsparingly to her enemies, that her books like her manners are resistless."

"Mrs. Royall is traveling through the interior of the state, circulating her *Black Book*, and annoying the Missionaries," the *Reformer* noted. "She speaks of finding a nest of them and their supporters at Carlisle, where she observes, the Presbyterian clergy rule with absolute sway." On the other hand, the newspaper noted, Royall "speaks highly" of the German immigrants, and "their independence" and "superior judgment."

A letter from a Cincinnati clergyman addressed to Royall in 1830 demonstrated the undeniably commanding role her *Black Books* played in upsetting the religious community and, in effect, the broader society. "The cloth I wear is sufficient apology for addressing you," the minister wrote. "Your arrival in this city has caused a considerable sensation, even among my own little flock." He attempted to gain some sense of clarity about her motives. "That your writings and conversation have operated injuriously to the cause of good Morals, not to say of Religion, is well known to all who have bestowed a thought on the subject. Yet, that the motive influencing you is also bad I am not prepared to say." He asked Royall to explain in detail her objections to the work of the missionary societies and the prolifer-ation of the tract societies. "If to subserve the cause of religion and morals be, indeed, your motive, I pledge myself to use my feeble abilities, with divine assistance, to expose their fallacious character to the world."

Aware of her national prominence, and the number of newspapers that would reprint her letter, Anne responded to the clergyman in one of her most pointed, playful, and personal missives.

Sir: I have the honor to acknowledge the receipt of your letter of yesterday, and admit your apology as to your cloth, which I presume is that of a clergyman, though you happened not to name it. You say, sir, that my arrival in this city has caused a considerable sensation even among your own little flock. Then they do not trust in their god, it is plain, or they would not be afraid of an old woman. Permit me to assure them, through you, that I shall leave them in full possession of all the piety and goodness they ever possessed to which I may add, life and limb.

You speak of various congregations recently engaged in the good work of your Lord Jesus Christ in this city, and of a glorious harvest feast of love enjoyed by more than three thousand fellow-mortals, and that the doctrines of your Lord and Saviour, etc., were freely delivered to thousands by those who were chosen for that purpose. To these declara-tions, permit me in the first place to say, that I am entirely governed by actions, and pay no more respect to people who boast of their labors, glorious harvest, etc., etc., etc., than I would to a female who would boast of her virtue, or a man who would boast of his honesty. I would rather see one good

action, (and I presume God would too) than hear ten thousand good words. In the second place, I would merely remark
as I have seen none of your good works, I am unable to judge
of them, and that self-praise is very much like hypocrisy.
Now the essence of the foregoing is this that three thousand
righteous people, with their god on their side, and yourself at
their head, should be intimidated by a single old woman, and
one, too, who was raised in the woods among the Indians,
without the benefit of education, or any religion, save that of
the savages, demonstrates either that your god is not able to
protect you, or that you are unworthy of his protection. I do
not, I assure you, sir, say this from any other motive than a
strict regard for our mutual benefit. I am one of those heathen
you are so anxious to convert. I never read the Bible nor do I
know the tenets of any sect. I am a heathen and have come
to your door. I have saved you the trouble and expense of
traveling. I am not an infidel—that is, I do not say the Bible
or the Christian religion is untrue. All I say is that I do not
read the Bible and I will tell you why. I was raised, as I said,
among the heathen, where I learned nothing but virtue and
independence.

When introduced among civilized people the Bible was put
into my hands. But before I looked into it I watched the conduct of those who read it, and I found they committed murder,
they robbed, they got drunk, they betrayed their friends and
were guilty of all kinds of abominations, and I was afraid to
read the Bible lest I might do so too.

You say, in the next place, that my writings and conversation have operated injuriously to the cause of good morals, not
to say religion, proves that you have never read my writings,

for you will find that the main object of them is to inculcate virtue and expose vice to patronize merit of whatsoever sect, country or politics, to put down pride and arrogance; to strip the mask from hypocrisy. You speak of Christian charity, and suppose I am ignorant of your faith and practice without which it is at least unsafe to war with an established creed. To this I reply that the threat in the last sentence proves the kind of Christian charity you possess. But you are a little mistaken, sir. I am not ignorant of your practice (or at least the practice of your sect) whatever I may be of your faith. The attempt upon my life in Vermont, by one of your elders, a Mr. H, of Burlington, who left me for dead! The attempt on my liberty at Washington, last summer, proves enough. Both these parties practiced long prayers, attended Bible-Sunday-school, and other societies, which includes your practice too what the faith of such people is, is a matter of no consequence. But your object, you say, is to elicit my views on the subject of Bible, Tract and Missionary societies. I view all those schemes as vile speculations to amass money and power (for money is power) ties, which (and the Sunday mail) proves your object is to unite church and state.

I am opposed to these schemes because the money is taken from the poor and ignorant, as no man of sense would pay for the gospel, which I understand, is to be had without money and without price. I know you will say this money is to spread the gospel. What I understand of it is, that it comes from God, some of his laws. I would rather have a god of wood or stone than one who robs the poor and ignorant under a cloak. But to come to the point at once: God made the heaven, and the earth, sun, moon and stars, etc. Now I am a poor ignorant heathen, as I told you before, and would merely ask if the god who made all these things could not make money, if he wanted it? But the fact is that God has nothing to do with this swindling; the money is laid up in the bank to overturn our government. Every Bible given away last year cost the poor (see the Report) the modest sum of $17.57. This proves your practice and tracts the same. Now these tracts, you say, are to save souls. What became of the souls of all who died before tracts were invented?

You say, sir, that if I would prefer a public discussion you would not, under proper restrictions, object to it. As I did not seek the discussion so neither will I shrink from it, in any place, and assure you, sir, that I would be happy to see you at my rooms, or in public as Messrs. Campbell and Owen did heretofore. I do not know what you mean by proper restrictions but I would suppose that, armed as you are, with mountains of tracts and Bibles, to say nothing of your sex, you can be in no danger from an old woman. If you are afraid of one heathen, how are you to convert thousands, nay, millions? And who knows but (as I hear you are very pious and holy) you may convert me? This blessed event would be of infinite benefit to your cause. I am, very respectfully, yours, Anne Royall.

P. S. I am disposed to meet and part with you on friendly terms, but if you choose to war, as you say, you recollect the fate of Dr. Ely. I have a few more sky-rockets left.

The *Philadelphia Album and Ladies' Literary Port Folio*, like many newspapers, frequently alerted its readers of Royall's journeys, adding their own comments to her writing. Its editor mocked her as "the queen of literature" and described Anne as a "hatter's block on a whiskey barrel" and "her eye as a fiery orb, which glows upon you with an expression intending to denote vast condescension." The paper chided her for declaring that she was a "people's woman, (which, we suppose, means a woman for the people's money)." Comparing her to the wife of Augustus, the editor roared, "has not Mrs. Anne Royall an equal claim to be dignified with the appellation of 'Mother of the Republic?'" Done with its satire, the *Literary Port Folio* labeled Royall "a common nuisance to the country."

"A lady in New York observed to me once," Anne wrote in her first *Black Book*, "what you say of those people Mrs. R is very true, they are the greatest curse in the country, but it is a dangerous thing to meddle with." The overtones of threat appalled Royall, as they seemed a usurpation of her basic right to freedom of speech. "Has it come to this already?" she asked her readers. "If it be dangerous to speak now, what will it be in a few years?" She made her stand, foreshadowing her defense at her "common scold" trial: "The danger of the thing proves the necessity of it, and it proves more; it proves that it ought never have been countenanced; the monster ought to have been crushed in its infancy; it has now grown formidable and will require the united energy of our country to put them down."

Far from intimidated, the defiant author viewed her own showdown as a larger victory. "I am advancing on the missionaries," she wrote in her final *Black Book*. "They will now be obliged to run, fight or surrender."

Anne savored the task: "My pen cannot be better employed," she concluded, "nor am I afraid."

# FIVE

# The Last American Witch Trial

*. . . [T]he indictment, trial, and the condemnation of Mrs. Royall, upon the grounds alleged, are certainly among the most extraordinary and unwarrantable proceedings in the records of our own, or perhaps any other country. This case claims the attention and consideration of every friend to the freedom of speech and of the press in our land, as ominous of future events of the most alarming character to American citizens. The whole transaction is indeed a stain on our country.*

—REFORMER: A RELIGIOUS WORK, SEPTEMBER 1829

The clerk hadn't even spelled her name correctly on the summons for her arrest. That annoyed Royall, who had always insisted on the "e" at the end of "Anne" in tribute to England's queen of the same name. She did come from royal blood, she would add with a wink, a detail that sent critics and biographers scurrying to the genealogical charts of the Calvert family in colonial Maryland.

This deceptive sense of humor underscored so much of Anne's provocative writing—and the interpretations by her readers and fellow writers—though it did her little good when US Marshal Tench Ringgold knocked at her home on Capitol Hill on July 20, 1829. The court awaited her arrival. His official carriage had already attracted an audience outside her house.

The summons required her to report to the Circuit Court of the District of Columbia, "whereof fail not, at your peril, and have you then and there this writ." The first attempt to file a plaintiff's complaint had been thrown out after Anne noticed the date of the incident had been erroneously filed for the wrong day.

The now famous writer had anticipated this moment, prophetically writing in her last *Black Book* of a coming showdown with the powerful Presbyterian Church, Christian extremists in her eyes, enemies of the state; they had already begun their attack on her, she warned.

Escorted by Marshal Ringgold, who towered over her diminutive figure, Royall climbed into the carriage and looked back at the Bank House where she lived, a four-story brick boardinghouse built by the district's great landowner Daniel Carroll, which stood a block away from the historic Carroll Row that would be leveled half a century later to build the Library of Congress. Royall relished living in the "heart of the blackcoats," one of her pet terms for the "long-faced" Presbyterians who dominated the emerging civil servant ranks in government. Her window on the upper story overlooked their Columbia Engine House, where she could literally distinguish the individual voices funneling from their endless sermons and songs at the nightly prayer meetings.

"I had them front, rear, right and left," Anne wrote in her *Black Book*, relishing the role of a "gadfly," as historian Thomas N. Baker noted in his study on the trials of literary fame, "bent on exposing polite society's foibles as they exploited their commercial potential." Huddling in the dark corners of raucous taverns, she recorded entries of her daily encounters like a modern-day blog, far from any editorial and journalistic restraint: her observations were hastily written and unedited, unconcerned about the appearance of vulgar language or tone, unapologetic for their knee-jerk discrimination, self-aware of their take-no-prisoners punch lines. "This is what I like—close fighting."

The amassing crowds may have flocked to Washington, DC, to witness one of the last American witch trials, but Anne saw herself in a different light. "I'll be another Joan of Arc," she had once declared. "I know very well how to shoot a rifle; and if I don't drill an army of women and shoot every Presbyterian I can find, there are no snakes. My motto is 'Liberty or Death.'"

Beyond the hyperbole of Anne's satirical writing style, a closer look at the historical record would suggest that her legendary trial in 1829 took place precisely as myriad issues of church and state politics, now seemingly insignificant, nearly fractured the fledgling nation. Singled out by her religious critics as "a fit subject for the jail, if not the insane asylum," her obsession with "free thought, free speech, and a free press" set her in direct confrontation with a surge of evangelical might in the late 1820s. She took the stage during the rise and fall of the anti-Mason movement, a Christian Party campaign, and the sabbatarian Sunday mail controversy, which was proclaimed by imminent Presbyterian preacher Beecher as "perhaps the most important" cause "that ever was or will be submitted for national consideration."

At the same time, Royall had emerged as an infamous writer on the cusp of the 1828 presidential campaign, which had pitted Tennessean war hero Andrew Jackson against patrician New Englander John Quincy Adams in a rematch of their bitter 1824 election and ushered in a "new low mark for vulgarity, gimmickry, and nonsensical hijinks" in political discourse, according to historian Robert Remini.

Anne's "civil war" with her neighbors had come to a tipping point that summer of 1829, as the writer's national prominence rose to its highest level, just as the rogue ranks of Presbyterians intent on pushing a Christian Party agenda descended on Washington and Jackson's new administration.

Aware of Anne's Washington home base, Ely and his Presbyterians carried to town a chip on their shoulders from the years of suffering her sardonic jabs of endearment. Some jabs had been less than endearing: "May both their heads [Ely's and Beecher's] be severed from their shoulders, before we see the day." A year earlier in Pennsylvania, at a special banquet in her honor at a local tavern, a legislator picked up on her vulgar one-liners with a toast of his own—a quote erroneously attributed to Anne in many documents: "I will pledge you, Mrs. Royall. Blue-skins, may all their throats be cut."

Ely and his minions were outraged. Royall walked the streets of Washington with a little skip of victory.

"I fear that the time is not far distant," she wrote from her Bank House roost, "when no man who will not receive the mark of the beast, can be elected into any office."

Far from the mark of the beast, Royall experienced her own brutal initiation into political discord and its all-too-easy expression through violence. A cowhide whip, in fact, would soon tear bloody gashes on her face in front of spectators at a bookstore in Pittsburgh, the deranged attacker exonerated due to Anne's "tongue and pen" and given a small fine.

Swine, horses, and cattle paraded the muddy streets with the throng that accompanied Royall and the marshal. Her eyes scanned the little grog shops that hinged on buildings in decay, rows of crooked smiles jeering and asking for charity. The desperate poverty troubled Anne. A city in disarray. The wilted saplings planted along the rutted streets mirrored the precariousness of life for most of the residents. The ranks of those without work filled the dark alleys. The racial mesh between the enslaved, free men and women of color, immigrants, Southern transplants, and the itinerant political class crept from the ashes of a Washington that had been burned down fifteen years earlier by the British.

These "abodes of wretchedness," she wrote. What did the committees for the District of Columbia "know of this distress?" Anne answered her own question: "They do not see, and of course, they do not feel. And as to the citizens they have no plan."

The barefoot, threadbare children affected her the most. Royall had entered the city only a few years before as a penniless and "distressed" traveler, clad in rags and a 75-cent pair of shoes that eventually disintegrated into a trail of blood. While the city's orphan asylum provided adequate care to girls, Anne had found on her frequent visits that the squalid poorhouse and its beds of straw and crocus remained a "disgrace" to the capital.

While her raggedy attire still drew the raised eyebrows of high society, Royall always walked with the gait of celebrity. She wore a calico gown, white muslin ruffle, and a silk scoop or bonnet, according to one of the rare reports of her appearance, draped in a brown bombast cloak. But her dark curls, dangling on her forehead and to the side of her face, gained the attention of traveling writer Robert W. Scott. "Her countenance was humorous and pleasant," he wrote only months after this incident in Washington, "talking and laughing with anyone who would permit her. Her language was vulgar and a little profane, but indicating nothing of spleen or malignity."

"Ridicule is the only weapon which can be used against unintelligible propositions," Thomas Jefferson had written to radical Dutch scholar Francis Adrian Van der Kemp, discussing the "mangled ideas" of "pseudo-Christians." A decade earlier, Jefferson had already dueled with the divine rights–driven Presbyterian leader Ely through a series of letters. "You say you are a Calvinist," Jefferson wrote in 1819. "I am not."

Anne seized the weapon of ridicule in the form of satirical writing, and did it well—and successfully, especially when she aimed it at Presbyterians like Ely. Her "wicked" sense of humor had elevated her to a celebrity status, albeit notorious.

In truth, Anne had thrown a few stones, as well—verbal retorts at the kids and profanity-laced barbs at their parents at the nearby Presbyterian Engine House. This included local Presbyterian leaders who feared for their coveted jobs from the turnover of the incoming Jackson administration. Two of their fellow members had already lost their positions; they knew Royall had championed their demise in a letter to the *Washington Journal*, affirming her crusade to "bar Church and State men" from civil service.

Anne claimed her verbal attacks were a form of defense, both literal and literary. "Respectable" church kids had been pelting her window at regular intervals with rocks, even knocking out a pane on their way to Sunday school, like follow-up calls to the proselytizing knocks of their parents. "Flinging stones is the daily employment of the children on Capitol Hill," Royall wrote.

But these shots were nothing compared to the barrage of hilarious one-liners issued from the barrels of her series of *Black Book* travel exposés, which had brought these respected Goliaths to their knees. Her descriptions of the Engine House neighbors and Presbyterians leaped from the page like characters in a Charles Dickens novel. She was defiantly incorrigible; she published portraits with the élan of a failed novelist, and the readers (other than those profiled) loved them.

"There is Rev. Peter Post," she began, borrowing from her beloved Scottish poet and satirist Robert Burns, "and Holy Willy in front, and near him, you Mucklewrath." Meanwhile, the Sunday school teachers included "Tom Oystertongs—he came up the square from toward the city. Next came Pompey Poplarhead, in a sleek coat, big hat, quite in print." The men opened the Engine House door for "Miss Sally Smirk" and "Miss Dina Dumpling," and soon "Miss Riggle," who was attended by "Simon Sulphur—I smelt the sulphur so strong." And finally, the service could begin when "Hallelujah Holdforth" and "Preacher Thunder" arrived.

A woman's public actions in 1829, Royall would soon learn at the trial, did not include the instigation of such ridicule championed by Jefferson. Women were to be laughed at, lampooned, and satirized—not the opposite. In his nasty book of verse *The Trollopiad: Or, Travelling Gentlemen in America; a Satire*, author Frederick William Shelton mocked Royall and fellow authors Frances Wright and Frances Trollope as a "very precious trio" of "wandering scribblers who infest the land / spleen in your souls and papers in your hands."

Future Supreme Court chief justice Salmon Chase would add in a letter: "I don't like argumentative ladies. . . . They have no right to encroach upon our privileges . . . we are entitled to an exclusive monopoly of all the wit (and) sensibilities in the world."

The travel writer Trollope returned to her beloved England, leaving behind a trail of words she didn't need to defend in person: women in the United States, she concluded, "were guarded by a sevenfold shield of habitual insignificance." The Scotland-born Wright, meanwhile, defended herself from her harsh critics with her wealth, connections to power, and oratory eloquence; her fairly brief collaboration on the *New York Free Enquirer* with Robert Dale Owen provided a community of support by giving her colleagues and institutional respect, however on the radical margins, that eluded a solitary wanderer like Royall. "One enjoyed famous associates, the other fought cruelty and contempt," declared historian Louis Filler, who authored several works on muckrakers.

While Wright, as the "high priestess of infidelity," had her share of enemies, Anne unleashed the kind of cutting remarks that left men wounded and plotting their revenge—especially if that woman was successful and sold a lot of books.

The New York *Commercial Advertiser* claimed Anne had "affected a retreat" and disappeared from Washington a few days prior to her trial. "If captured, it will only be a severe conflict, and through over-powering numbers," it howled, comparing her to the last Ottoman ruler in North Africa. "Her assaulters will find her to be a Mrs. Hussein Path—she will never surrender at discretion." Royall shot back a letter to the editor, equally in jest: surrender she had, though she would never retreat from the battle. To be sure, "a scheme had been laid amongst the godly of the Capitol," she added, "but I was a hardened sinner."

Appealing to US District Attorney Thomas Swann, the Engine House congregation was rewarded when their description of Anne soon resulted in a federal indictment by a grand jury: the old witch was "an evil-disposed person and a common scold and disturber of the peace and happiness of her quiet and honest neighbors . . . in the open and public streets of the city of Washington . . . [who] did annoy and disturb the good people of the United States residing in the County aforesaid, by her open, public, and common scolding to the common nuisance of the good citizens . . . of all others in like cases offending against the peace and government of the United States."

The court immediately dropped two of the three counts against Royall, asserting the charges were too general for her to be tried as a common slanderer or brawler. It left the District Attorney with a single count: of being a common scold, an ancient common-law crime applicable only to women. *Communis rixatrix*, the Judge would explain, "for our law-latin confines it to the feminine gender." The law stemmed from medieval times, when England was in a "barbaric state."

Paradoxically, the term "witch trial," the *actual* remnant of that barbaric state, was effectively erased from the legal proceedings in the guise of American modernity.

News of the warrant for her arrest suddenly placed Anne in the center of attention of a media circus. The banter over her fate had already begun. The confusion over the indictment ensued: charges of being a common scold—or an "uncommon" scold, remarked a newspaper editor—set the stage for a courtroom audience that wasn't quite sure if it should be amused, or outraged, but certainly entertained.

Everyone understood the real charge: Anne Royall, as the exemplar of a disorderly woman, was walking to her trial for being a woman, one "with a serpent's tongue."

And more importantly, a woman of a certain age who engaged in the act of political satire.

The *New England Religious Weekly* described her as "the old hag." Even backhanded compliments captured a frozen image of an older Anne, as if she had never existed before the age of 57. She became the excoriating shrew. The "virago errant in enchanted armor," John Quincy Adams had famously called her. The "grandmother of the muckrakers," H. L. Mencken's snarky admirers at the *American Mercury* would declare even a century later.

The *Charleston Western Virginian* managed to expand the age issue into an element of slut-shaming, describing Royall as a woman with little "refinement and good breeding," whose writings served "the detestable purpose of a woman, whose brazen-faced effrontery is without parallel, and whose old age and the decay of personal beauty have unfitted her for employment, which at an earlier period in life, yielded her a comfortable, though infamous, support."

Placing the discriminatory ageism and sexism aside, Anne had her own version of the motives: "The good pious people of Capitol Hill were only the cat-paws of Dr. Ely and Pope Duffield, the agents of the General Assembly" of the powerful Presbyterians who couldn't handle the sharp edges of her sense of humor. "I had long thwarted the godly people," she boasted. "Now was their time to measure their strength, if ever. Many weighty state matters were at stake, the new Congress was soon to meet, I had influence there."

In the end, Anne also saw her extraordinary trial as bait for the incoming President Jackson, perhaps in an inflated sense of her own fame. "Put her in jeopardy," she posited. "This will show how far the administration is with us. It will prove whether the President is of the true evangelical faith or not."

In her mind, the politically savvy elders at the Christian congregation sought to brand Anne with a scarlet letter in the court of public opinion—to shame her lack of morality among the "respectable" class, silence her controversial voice in the public arena, and banish her and a growing number of other female writers to the backroom of what historian Rosemary Zagarri called for women a "new era of political invisibility." Besides, as an essay on "literary women" in *Sartain's Union Magazine of Literature and Art* pointed out in 1850, "the truth being conceded that no women but those who are ugly and unattractive, should or do write."

Royall made readers laugh about the machinations at play in politics and religion and forced them to feel uncomfortable doing so. She fanned the confusion with her own dark humor, lampooning a plot that implicated religious and political leaders in almost cartoon-ish terms:

> About this time a council was held to which all the good pious men of Capitol Hill repaired.
>
> Amongst these were some mighty good pious souls who were turned out of office, and others who expected to be turned out. This revived good holy pious feelings in their bosoms, and glorious were the out-pouring of the divine grace. "Oh that we had our holy religion established," said Mucklewrath, "we would bring this heretic to a speedy repentance." "Yes," said Hallelujah, holding forth, "the inquisition is the thing; it would open her eyes to the light of our holy and precious religion."
>
> Simon Sulphur, who had been closely engaged with the Lord, breathing pious ejaculations, begged leave to be heard. My friend Coldkail, who had been chosen moderator, said, "Speak on brother, for, Lord be thankit, I hae nae ill will against the leddy, gude though she hae call'd us names, and 'has set the world in a roar o' laughing at us.' "
>
> "I think, for my part," said Simon Sulphur, "this woman is beyond grace, and if we can fall on some plan to remove her, that we might serve the Lord in peace, it would be best and never mind her soul, a civil prosecution is our only hope."
>
> "I second the motion," said Holy Willy, "a little coercion is sometimes attended with salutary effects. Our holy meetings yields no refreshment to my soul so long as this heretic eats, drinks and sleeps, in peace." He spoke this with power and great boldness in the Lord—took a drink of water from a glass which stood before him, wiped his mouth and sat down.

Mucklewrath spoke next: not being a gifted man, he said but little. One of the Raws spoke next—"Gentlemen, if we let this woman alone, I mean if we suffer her, gentlemen, to write more Black Books, she will Black Book us all out of office, I can swear to that. I suppose you've heard of——being turned out to-day, and I'm of opinion she ought to be had up, that is I think, she ought not to be let alone for writing these Black Books. They say she is writing one now that's as bold as Beelzebub, and all them members of Congress bleevs every word that's in them books, quite probable and I'm sure there's not a word of truth in them to my sartin knowledge. I can swear that any day."

"Well, well," said Holy Willy, "we'll see about that very good idea, Mr. Raw."

Royall sent her characters on an adventure in search of a crime. They discovered an old book, blew off the dust, and began to read, only able to distinguish broken sentences, such as "Cart-tail—Ducking-stool—Sabbath School—Fine and imprisonment—Outpouring—Nuisance—Lord Mansfield—We'll tie her neck and heels—Glorious gospel—Virago—Only let us get a hold of her—Vital religion—I wish we could hang her—The Holy Bible—Drowning will do as well . . ."

Anne laughed: "All the statutes of England were read or searched down to George III. In true Christian spirit."

They had defined their criminal—"a troublesome and angry woman"—by unearthing an offense in the back of an ancient tome: "who broke the public peace by habitually arguing and quarreling with her neighbours."

Unfamiliar with the term "scold" but aware of Anne's reputation, the partisan newspapers went to work on the details of the trial with dueling depictions. Several would define Royall's legacy for the next two centuries. Either they took her too seriously, parlaying her vulgar sense of humor into criminal offenses against the religious and political mores of the times, or they didn't take her seriously enough, dismissing the author as an innocent old gadfly.

On one hand, the pro-Jackson newspapers recognized Anne as entertaining but nothing more than an eccentric old crank: the marshal "quaking in his boots," a friendly New York paper narrated, was less fearful of a "rhinoceros rather than come within the pale of Mrs. R's tongue," as if the older woman would fly to the courtroom on her broomstick. For *New York Enquirer* publisher Mordecai Noah, the trial was a blatant attack on Royall's reputation and right to free speech, and yet he couldn't resist dabbling in the vocabulary of disdain: "Anne Royall continues to reside on Capitol Hill," he joked, "receiving the daily homage of her friends, and dispensing terror and dismay among her enemies."

For the anti-Jackson newspapers, however, who feared the wrath of a woman's campaign against corruption in the government and religious usurpation of the executive branch, the terror of Royall was a real thing. They saw nothing humorous about her satire. One such portrait, reprinted across the country and in London, appeared as an editorial in the *Daily National Journal* and was most likely written by George Watterston, the novelist and former head of the Library of Congress who had been unceremoniously dismissed by Jackson and who would serve as a plaintiff in Royall's trial. "Many of the respectable citizens who reside on Capitol Hill appear to have been prodigiously annoyed by this gifted dame, whom Petruchio would have harder to tame than Kate the Curst: and such a universal terror of her, except among the boys, infects that whole region, that man and woman, priest and layman, would rather make a circuit of a mile than venture beneath her eastern window."

Such mixed and contradictory perceptions of Anne's legacy have been as illuminating as her impact in her own time. Depictions of her life and writings, given an outsized showcase during her "common scold" trial, tend to range from the apocryphal to the demonic to the hagiographic (albeit apologetic) praise by the Masonic Lodges.

The *Morning Courier* asked the nation: "Thus it is with great geniuses in all ages—Galileo, the starry Galileo, was imprisoned for his wisdom. Tarso was the tenant of a cell, and Columbus sighed in a dungeon. Why then should Anne Royall hope to escape the general doom of genius?—It is inherent in her destiny, and a concomitant of her greatness."

Anne hobbled up the stairs to the courtroom in the old City Hall, betraying the lingering pain from her attack in Vermont. Still, she strode with purposeful delay. Only months before, she had written about reaching a high point in her life, "blessed with friends, dreaded by foes, above want," a period of "bliss serene." She soaked up the attention of the crowd, which had overflowed the streets outside the courthouse. Anne had not yet even reached the door when a man pushed through the crowd and thrust a drawing into her hand. It revealed the "caricature of a ducking car" on a horse-pulled wagon, the sketched figure of Royall chained "hard and fast." Marshal Ringgold commanded the horse-driven wagon, his naked figure sporting "a tail like a monkey."

"This is the good people of Capitol Hill," Anne quipped, handing the picture to the marshal and immediately drawing guffaws from the crowd. Ringgold wasn't amused.

Days before the trial, a petition for the arrest of judgment of her case had already unleashed the first rounds of jokes in taverns and parlor rooms across Washington. Arguing that the court had to "adjudge any other punishment to a common scold than the ducking stool," Royall's appointed defense attorney, Richard Coxe, had motioned for the judge to dismiss the charge, as the required penalty of "ducking would only have the effect of hardening the offender." Coxe claimed the ducking stool was obsolete in England and had never been inflicted in the state of Maryland, "under whose common law the prosecution was commenced."

The judge deferred. After an in-depth review of the history of common scolds, District Court Judge William Cranch concluded with legal expert: "Sir William Blackstone, in using the word 'shall' in the passage cited, is not to be understood as having used it in its peremptory and obligatory sense, and as intimating that the court was bound to inflict the punishment of ducking upon a common scold," therefore, allowing the court to "punish any common-law misdemeanor by fine and imprisonment." On the other hand, the court "might sentence the offender to be ducked only; in which case, it would be part of the judgment that she should be placed in the stool; and the *residue*, in that case, would be, that she should be plunged in the water."

The city of Washington reveled in imagining the details. The punishment for Royall's crime almost overshadowed the charge itself—and before she even took the stand in her defense. "She is destined to immortalize the Tiber—alias Goose Creek," crowed one Boston newspaper.

Even the Navy Yard "prepared for this event," Anne noted, where shipyard hands constructed a machine "that I could not have survived." She described the model, which had been displayed at the City Hall. Its tall shaft rose "eleven to fifteen feet in length, and at the extremity of this, I was to be fastened," she explained. Powered by the push of a brigade, it would rotate like a windmill, "with such rapidity, that, from the circumference of the sweep, I could not have survived one sweep of the machine!" Anne understood the entertainment value—the extreme humiliation intended by fastening the female "criminals" to a large chair, swung over a piece of water. The "holy people" would shout and make a great noise, and her death "would have been inevitable."

At an earlier hearing, Anne had smiled "graciously" and miraculously refrained from responding when the prosecutor declared she "should enjoy the benefit of a cold bath with as much privacy as possible." It was all part of the spectacle.

Entering the courtroom, Anne silenced the sweat-soaked onlookers with her disheveled attire, her shuffle, and her grin. Her eyes memorized the details: society men and women dressed for the theater, a phalanx of journalists, Jacksonians and anti-Jacksonians, all "lovers of the ludicrous," declared the *Boston Patriot* correspondent. Francis Scott Key, composer of the "Star Spangled Banner," avidly found a seat, engaged as he was in his own trials as a rising district attorney and eager to take in the proceedings.

Journalists watched closely as Anne crept toward the front bench, taking her seat alongside her attorney Coxe. Their descriptions of her entry differed based on their political organs. Royall's friends at the *Morning Courier and New York Enquirer* took note of her demure presence, "the gentle captive smile upon her persecutors," and stated that she spoke quietly to the clerk. Still, the correspondent couldn't help but predict Royall would unleash a "forensic display unrivaled in this country" on behalf of "Life, Liberty and the use of the tongue." The anti-Jackson *Patriot* countered: she had laughed with contempt at her earlier grand jury hearing, and now "the appearance of the prisoner (loudly greeted by the boys around the door) and the reading of the indictment excited much mirth throughout the courtroom."

To Anne's right sat her young journalist friend James Gordon Bennett, who would in a few years go on to found the *New York Herald* and usher in the penny press of yellow journalism fame. Anne "scorned the public gaze," Bennett declared in his sympathetic portrait. He referred to the author as "her ladyship."

The accused, in fact, remained transfixed on the triumvirate of judges before her. Exactly the same age as Royall, Chief Judge Cranch had been appointed by President Thomas Jefferson to the bench. A cousin of John Quincy Adams, Cranch, from Massachusetts, played a leading role in Washington reform circles. Anne considered "the Yankee" as the brightest on the bench. To his right was Associate Justice James Sewall Morsel, appointed by President James Madison; the elder Buckner Thruston, who had served in the US Senate from Kentucky, rounded out the court.

Cranch possessed "a longer face, with a good deal of the pumpkin in it, though my friend said the pumpkin was in his head," Anne noted. On the other hand, "Judge Thruston is about the same age as Judge Cranch, and harder featured. He is laughing proof. He looks as though he had sat upon the rack all of his life, and lived upon crab-apples." Morsel, according to Royall, "his face round and wrinkled, resembles the road to Giandott, after the passage of a troop of hogs."

Shifting to her right, Anne scanned the jury box. "I would suppose twelve more ignorant men could not have been picked out of the District," she concluded. She gave them names: "George Upper Leather, Will Chissel, Overdone Carr, Jack Pill Box, John Stirrup Leather, Phil Yardstick, Tom Lapstone, Dick Tape, Bob Bouncer, Hall Saucepan, and others I did not know; but it would puzzle Hogarth to paint them."

Everyone understood that Royall, too, was having fun, even at her own expense. "Her debut" was like a "vernal morning, bright with sunny smiles," chronicled the *Bedford Gazette*.

"I shall make a proposition to my friends in Congress," she wrote, "to have the whole painted and put in the Rotunda with our national paintings, reserving a conspicuous place for myself."

Funny enough, Anne, like her defense attorney—even like Judge Cranch—assumed she was the first woman to be put on trial as a common scold, a legend that still persists among many accounts today. The sorry history of the gender-specific crime in the United States, however, had carried on a long tradition of humiliation.

Cranch disappeared into the chamber's dark archives and returned with dust-covered volumes of English legal scholar Giles Jacob's early eighteenth-century law dictionary and Sir William Blackstone's definitive *Commentaries on the Laws of England*, first published in 1765.

The *Niles' Weekly Register* explained to its amused readers: "Jacobs [*sic*], in his law dictionary, says 'scolds,' in a legal sense, are troublesome and angry women, who, by their brawling and wrangling amongst their neighbors, break the public peace, increase discord, and become a public nuisance to the neighborhood." Cranch continued the history lesson. He leaned heavily on Blackstone's English law book for answers: "A woman indicted for being a common scold shall be sentenced to be placed in a certain engine of correction called the *trebucket, tumbrel, tymborella, castigtatory or cucking-stool*, which, in Saxon, signifies the scold stool, because of the residue of the judgment is that when she is placed therein, she shall be plunged into the water for her punishment."

Written a little more than half a century after Anne's trial, Alice Morse Earle's *Curious Punishments of Bygone Days* provided some colorful examples of common scold trials and the ducking-stool, including a French writer's account of his visit to an English town in

1700: "They place the woman in this chair and so plunge her into the water as often as the sentence directs, in order to cool her immoderate heat."

Instances of this ancient punishment, of course, abounded over the centuries and across the British Isles. But its entrenchment within the American experience, dating back to the Jamestown settlement in Virginia in 1626, astonished a historian like Earle. "At the time of the colonization of America the ducking-stool was at the height of its English reign; and apparently the amiability of the lower classes was equally at ebb," she wrote. "The colonists brought their tempers to the new land, and they brought their ducking-stools."

Two centuries later, though, in Anne's time, the common scold offense and ducking stool had hardly become relics. In nearby Maryland, only ten years before Anne's trial, a "spinster" named Jenny Lanman had been convicted for being a common scold after a constable testified that she had been "flogged over and over again with a very good cow-hide" for her crime of being "noisy and troublesome," but "he could not quiet her tongue, for the more he had whipped, the louder she had screamed, so he absolutely despaired of a cure." The *American Register* detailed the punishment of ducking of Lanman till the "offender will hold her tongue." In that same period, the superior court of Baldwin County, Georgia, convicted a "Miss Palmer" in 1811 as a common scold and sentenced her to three duckings in the Oconee River. She had been recorded as being "rather glib on the tongue." In an attempt to save money, the sheriff, instead of building a ducking machine, apparently tied Palmer to the back of a cart and, accompanied by a hooting mob, ran the cart "down into the river." According to accounts, she exclaimed "glory to God," with each ducking.

Such drastic measures did not only take place in rural backwaters. Newspapers across the country recounted the trial of Catharine

Fields in New York City, who was convicted for being a common scold in 1821. "The trial was excessively amusing, from the variety of the testimony," according to a news report filed by the *New York Commercial Advertiser*, "and the diversified manner in which this Xantippe pursued her virulent propensities." Newspapers dwelled on the "merriment" of the trial.

That element of entertainment, at the emotional cost of the convicted, had actually prompted a little soul-searching among New York spectators at an earlier trial in 1813. Once again erroneously assuming that "no indictment had been found" for a common scold in a hundred years, the *Washington Daily National Intelligencer* ran an article from the *Commercial Advertiser* on the trial of Margaret Mullen, who, "when irritated, was a most outrageous and violent scold." Despite a number of witnesses, the jury found Mullen, a known alcoholic, not guilty.

Something else about Mullen's treatment bothered the New York jury and packed courtroom. While the trial generated "much amusement," the newspaper reported, it also caused some "anxiety to the female part of the audience; and some of them seemed to fear that this invasion of the rights of women might ultimately result in their being deprived of their principle weapon of offence as well as defence. And we congratulate them upon the defeat of this attempt to muzzle them."

Compared to the partisan news portrayals, the *Daily National Intelligencer* remained decidedly neutral on Royall's trial, though it clearly overlooked the fact that its front page had once aired concern over attempts to silence women in a similar common scold trial a decade earlier.

Writing in the Boston-based *North American Review* in 1828, eminent jurist Caleb Cushing advanced these concerns over the "barbarity" of the ducking-stool punishment for convicted common scolds. Cushing reminded readers that the Supreme Court in Pennsylvania had actually struck down the offense of common scold as indictable, ruling it an unconstitutional act. Reported across the nation, and even in newspapers in England, was the story of Nancy James, who had been convicted by a judge in Philadelphia for being a common scold and sentenced to three duckings in a nearby river.

The timing of James's trial in Philadelphia in 1824 should not have been lost on Anne, who had passed through Philadelphia in that period as part of the research for her first book, *Sketches*. She gushed about the city market, inspected the prisons and asylums, attended a Jewish synagogue as well as a Quaker meeting, took notes at Peale's museum, met all of the local editors, and interviewed people on the street. In light of William Penn's own persecution, she celebrated his statue on the "hospital square" in full Quaker dress: "Tolerance to all sects, equal rights and justice to all."

According to Cushing, Pennsylvania's Supreme Court in 1825 had "sufficient manliness to resist the attempt to revive the barbarous usage." The court's decision, in fact, obliterated the lower court's process and issued a stunning rebuke to Philadelphia. Despite the "ferment and excitement in the public mind," it ruled the decision was "cruel, unusual, unnatural and a ludicrous judgment."

In a lengthy ruling, the state's Supreme Court did not simply trace the history of the common scold crime and its ducking stool but expounded on the social ramifications of the convictions with an extraordinary sympathy toward women.

It destroys all personal respect—the women thus punished, would scold on for life, and the exhibition would be far from being beneficial to the spectators. What a spectacle would it exhibit? What a congregation of the idle and disorderly, of black and white spirits! And the day would produce more scolding, in this polite city, than would otherwise take place in a year. The city is rescued from this ignominious and odious show, and the state from the opprobrium of the continuance of so barbarous an institution; which would pluck from the brow of our legislators, that diadem of humanity, which the civilized world has award.

The Pennsylvania justices pointed out that the gender-specific crime also discriminated against women; though, an English judge once suggested that indictments for common scolds could be applied to men, given "our modern men of gallantry would not surely decline the honour of her company."

The Pennsylvania Supreme Court's final admonition somehow failed to travel the short distance to the nation's capital in Washington. Reminding the legal community that New York and Massachusetts had already declared "this strange and ludicrous punishment" as illegal, the court ruled that "we shall hereafter hear nothing of the ducking stool, or other remains of the customs of barbarous ages."

Cushing, a Congressman from Massachusetts who would soon serve abroad as a diplomat, added his own final blow in 1828 in the *North American Review*, a year before Anne's trial: "Our ungallant fathers of the common law provided a peculiar punishment for common scolds, but carefully confined the crime and the punishment to scolds of the female sex." The case in Philadelphia, he concluded, "furnished a safe precedent for all the other States in the Union."

A safe precedent for all—but the District of Columbia's courtroom. Royall may not have been the first American woman to be indicted, tried, and convicted as a common scold, but she was certainly the most famous. For Anne, of course, the trial had little to do with legal protocol. "We authors must always bleed for those fellows," she had recently written to her friends at the *New York Enquirer*. "My contemporaries Madame de Staël and Jemima Wilkinson did so. My rival, Lady Morgan, has been badly abused by the booksellers, and can Anne Royall expect to escape?" Placing herself in the company of such notable and revolutionary women authors, all of them the bête noire of their times—Staël as the banished French author under Napoleon, Wilkinson the Quaker visionary, and Morgan the controversial Irish author—Anne attempted to aggrandize her own sense of sacrifice on the altar of literary freedom.

Royall presented her literary credentials as evidence of the charge's misrepresentation: "One who writes as much as I do," she quipped, "has not much time to scold." A closer reader, however, would have reminded Anne that she had often used the word "scold" in her books. "The more I scold them, the better they like me," she mused about literary editors in Rhode Island, clarifying to her readers that the faux invective was more in jest than a serious attack. "The saucy rogues, they almost tore me to pieces, out of pure joy to see me." Unlike the pious religious stalwarts, who seemingly held out their chins awaiting every offense, Royall jabbed the literary crowd with a wink in her eye. "These literary people, whether cadets or not, are always doing one piece of mischief or another. But I shall *Black Book* them all."

Back in the courtroom, Anne faltered with the heat. While Judge Cranch continued the proceedings, the stifling humidity forced the court to open the windows, and a young teenager catered to Royall's needs, dallying by her side like a servant. (Richard Wallach, the 13-year-old who acted like an "affectionate son" to Anne, would go on to become the first Republican mayor of Washington, DC.) The plaintiffs sat to the left of the room, a block of ten men, solemnly dressed in "black coats," righteous in their stares; eight of them were current government clerks who feared the fate of Jackson's new administration changes.

Nonetheless, attempting to avoid freedom of speech and freedom of press issues, the plaintiffs aimed their wrath on Anne's personal interactions and abusive language and sought to distance themselves from her writing, even if it provided the narrative of their charges. The Plaintiffs' Complaint, which had laid the basis for the indictment, unfolded like an inventory from the devil's dictionary. She displayed "opprobrious and indecent language," they claimed, which accused them of "caterwauling and other false and offensive charges." She used "malicious and false sayings such as Thief, Villain, Hypocrite, etc. etc. to the Great annoyance of Females; and citizens of the Capitol Hill and to the disturbance of Said Good people in the discharge of their religious duties." She possessed the mark of the bête noire: "Some of the young ladies were actually afraid to pass" her window "without having themselves outraged by language, to which no delicate female could listen."

Before any plaintiffs took the stand, however, the court had to clarify two questions from the defense. Given that Anne was a "far famed and much maltreated personage," as the *Philadelphia Album and Ladies' Literary Gazette* would soon remind its readers, how did the definition of a "common" scold relate to the rather "uncommon" Royall? Second, definitions of "common scold" inferred that the transgressor was relentlessly "loud and obnoxious," when Madame Royall, as she preferred to be called, was well known as a soft-spoken figure. "More rational lawyers, however, seem to think that where the scolding is so loud and so frequent as to be a common nuisance," the *National Journal* reported, "it is sufficient to constitute a common scold."

"According to some of the witnesses, Mrs. Royall, although

frequent in her verbal exhilarations, was not always loud," the *Daily Commercial Gazette in Boston* countered, "but on the contrary has inflicted some of her linguadental severities in a very soft tone, and with a very smiling countenance, coming up, in fact, to the poet's description, and show that she can smile, and smile, and murder while she smiles."

The press bantered in rounds of jokes, awaiting some sort of judgment. Meanwhile, Anne praised the eloquence of her defender, his "style of feeling, energy and pathos, that would have touched the heart of the most untamable savage." Reaching back into the language of "barbaric" times, her attorney Coxe offered a combination of "Saxton, Roman and Norman" words to show the "illegibility of the law in toto."

While Anne smiled in confidence, the judges remained rigid in their stance on this "savage statute." The authoress returned to her pen portraits, "amused" by the look of the judge she preferred to call "my sweet Morsel." Royall wrote: "He kept his eyes shut, and looked as though he was peeping through rat holes. There was not much amusement in the looks of the other two. . . . Their faces grew as black as the hour they were appointed, and seemed to be taking different shapes. It was complete stage effect—nothing wanting but the rack, which was at that moment actually secreted in some part of the building."

The court admitted that the notably ambiguous charge of being a common scold referred to a general demeanor, not a specific action. As Reid Paul pointed out in his excellent study on the trial and concepts of "respectability" during the era, "In the Publick Streets," observers debated whether Anne's crime "was not her blasphemy or her politics, but her public displays of inappropriate behavior." Either way, her right to freedom of speech and freedom of the press somehow diminished in the haste to saddle her with a crime—and bring her satire to an end.

All jokes aside, Anne bristled at the language of the judge and prosecutors. As a wordsmith, she shook her head at their delight in taking her words out of context and dragging her reputation further across the line of irredeemable hope. Two years earlier, attending a trial in New York City, she criticized prosecutors who "coolly and deliberately turn the misfortunes and distress of suffering humanity into a subject of mirth and ridicule." She concluded: "Humanity weeps during the time any unfortunate fellow-man is on his trial. Those callous brutes, sneer, scoff and torture the feelings of the unfortunate, whom the one prosecutes, and the other pretends to defend."

Anne noted one poignant detail: only men testified against her. The reputable John Coyle Sr., whose Engine House congregation had brought the allegations to the district attorney, rose first and took the stand. He refused to look at Anne, though she didn't hesitate to capture his pose. "Hear, o Israel," she mocked. "He began to place his feet as though he had set in for a four-hour's sermon."

Coyle and his son, John Jr., were no strangers to the court. As clerks in the Treasury department, they belonged to the closed circles of civil servants that maintained a grip on civic leadership roles, including those that dictated the policies of the schools. Coyle also served with Judge Cranch as an official in the American Colonization Society, a movement that sought to ship enslaved and freed African Americans to Haiti or western African communities. As an elder in the Presbyterian Church, Coyle actively led local efforts in the Religious Tract Society, which disseminated Bibles and published materials, as well as the Washington Temperance Society.

Anne had written more colorfully about Coyle's activities on Capitol Hill. "Holy Willy," as she liked to call him, was the "commander in chief" of the Presbyterians that nightly assembled in front of her building. "They have a shy, gloomy look, with the countenance like the moon in an eclipse," she noted in one of her *Black Books*. "They are uniformly dressed in black, an emblem of their business. Their visage is long; their complexion a dirty wan." In one of her more outrageous stories, she had insinuated that "Holy Willy" had converted "an aged black sister" by resorting to "caustic specifics," including the "wounding of flesh." But any catcalls out of her window, Royall claimed, were precisely that—she often shouted colorful language at the feral cats that roamed the neighborhood, which the Presbyterians had clearly misunderstood.

"She called me a damned old bald headed son of a bitch," Coyle declared. "Not only once, but three times."

The courtroom erupted into laughter. Cranch demanded order. Anne shrugged. She would not deny it. The whole nation knew her, Anne declared, and no one else could make that accusation. "He is the only person in the world that ever heard me swear," she admitted, referring to Coyle. She offered some context in a later story. Running down the steps of her apartment building one evening in a great hurry, Anne had bumped into Coyle, who frequently lingered around her building. "I laughed, as usual, and said, 'we would have the pleasure of walking together.'" According to Royall, Coyle responded: "Ah, old woman, your time is short."

Coyle held court in his grave manner, giving testimony of "gross and abominable" affronts by the author. Coyle claimed, as recorded by a newspaper, that "none of the family had done aught to provoke the virago; yet she had not ceased to pour out on every one of them torrents of the most coarse, vulgar and obscene language, until they could not appear even at the windows of their own house. Other witnesses testified to the abuse of sisters and mothers (for had she confined her attacks to men alone, the prosecution would never have been undertaken), and that both in the public street and in their own houses."

The Engine House elder asserted his masculine duty to protect the endangered women on Capitol Hill. Anne's alleged attack on helpless women, as the *Boston Patriot* noted, was fundamental for the prosecution, whose case would have otherwise "never been undertaken."

"This old one C [referring to Coyle] is always around my house and annoying me with all sorts of noise," Royall countered. "So far did he go evening before last that he came to my own door and not in the street and threatened my life and I am about to have measures taken to bind him to his good behavior and therefore appeal to you what steps to take."

This self-proclaimed male role of protector outraged Anne with its hypocritical double standard, of course. "Is it not astonishing that those abominable defamers of mankind should be so countenanced as they are to the complete prostration of common sense, and that their slander does not raise the indignation of the people," the *Morning Courier* reported her saying. Long before the trial, she had written untold letters to newspapers across the nation and filled her books with episodes of her own persecution—often at the hands of women, who Anne claimed only functioned to do the bidding for their men and "priests." Alerting their readers to the undue attacks on their "authoress" friend, the evangelical renegades at the *Reformer* reprinted a Royall letter in 1828 that had appeared in New York and Baltimore newspapers: "It is also well known that these people made the first attack on me, and have never ceased to persecute me with the bitterest rancour."

Anne also reminded readers that she had been on the receiving end of her fair share of inappropriate behavior, including a scandalous letter written by one of these "godly women." Sent to her during an earlier visit in Carlisle, Pennsylvania, Anne had even displayed it for public outrage at the office of the mayor for ten days. "The most obscene pictures drawn on blank parts of the paper, and the most shocking . . ." She couldn't even bear to fill in the blank. "It was beyond shocking— beyond conception," adding that it was worse than the "vilest brothel."

Calling out the double standard of the trial, which only focused on her alleged misbehavior and not on that of Coyle and his Engine House minions, Anne maintained that the behavior of the "godly women" was even too contemptuous to notice. She, too, wanted to focus on the men, such as Coyle and the other religious zealots, who railed about their high morals and respectable society but couldn't even allow "an aged female" to pass through their city without being "beastly insulted by her own sex."

Anne laughed aloud. "A great beast like him," she had written. "How could so small a woman, as I, hurt him?"

Following Coyle, Lewis Machen advanced, though Royall stripped his testimony before he even took the stand. He "looked like Satan's walking staff," she quipped. Coyle's fellow clerk in the Senate and Presbyterian, Machen had a "long face, roached hair, and affected gaiety" that exhibited a "complete stage effect." Anne dismissed his stories as having no consequence. For the newspapers, however, the testimonies provided good entertainment—and quotes. The "sundry wicked sayings of their tormentor," wrote the *Daily Commercial Gazette*, "relaxed the features of the bench and bar," even if they would be found to be "insufficient to relax the stern countenance of justice."

Years later, the patrician John Quincy Adams attempted to explain to others that the author's words in the public street could not be separated from her writing: "Her deportment and her book," he wrote, were both feared and tolerated. She may have been "noxious,"

he remarked, but "lampooning" those who treated her with "incivil-
ity" provided the essence of her books—and identity.

One plaintiff understood this, though his testimony served up even
more bait for Royall's pen. W. J. McCormack, whom Anne had called
a "superannuated old man" whose useless service as a clerk was tan-
tamount to "cheating the government," actually invoked her writings. "He was a good natured simpleton," Anne wrote. "His very
countenance was the talisman to mirth. This was sport for the lawyers:
they saw at once he was their man, and set him down for the butt."

Referring to the description of a fellow clerk, McCormack said she
had slandered his friend. The prosecutor asked for clarification, aware
that Anne often used pet names for many of the characters in her books,
especially in terms of the Capitol Hill scene. How did McCormack
know that the unflattering description of "Tom Oystertongs" was, in
fact, his colleague? McCormack didn't hesitate. Anne's writing was
perfectly accurate. "I knew him by the description," he crowed, un-
wittingly causing the courtroom to laugh.

McCormack wasn't done. One day as he passed her building, he
testified, he noticed Royall sitting by her window, reading what
he presumed to be her awful *Black Book*. Anne narrated the rest of
the exchange: "The prosecutor asked if that was all. McCormack
replied that he could say more but that he didn't want to in the court."
Pressed by the prosecutor, McCormack went on (recorded by Anne):
" 'I was walking with some ladies, one day, and she asked me if I wasn't
ashamed to walk with them old maids.' Swann amused, commented,
'Well, maybe they were old maids.' McCormack drew back. 'No, they
wasn't for one of them was my sister.' "

The prosecutor snorted out such a laugh that he dismissed Mc-
Cormack and had to take a few minutes to compose himself; meanwhile, the courtroom rippled with laughter.

Quoting Thomas Bridges's *A Burlesque Translation of Homer's* Iliad, the "backwoods" Anne narrated: "Those who have the laugh upon their side, have the victory."

The testimonies continued in this fashion, though Anne mockingly declared that most of the men were "frightened to death" and "shook like aspins." She gave them more names, such as Harry Hedgehog, "his voice like the dieing notes of a saw under the hands of a butcher." Given the undertone of threat in Harry's testimony, Royall's friends advised her to take out a "writ de lunatico inquirendo" against him. "I had a notion of taking out one against the whole of them," she laughed.

Outside of Coyle's leadership, Anne cared most about witness George Watterston, who had recently been fired by President Andrew Jackson as the head of the Library of Congress. She still considered Watterston a friend and lauded his novels in her first book. His last novel, *The L. Family at Washington; or, A Winter in the Metropolis*, an epistolary satire on the travails of a Connecticut family navigating their way into the inner circles of Washington in the early 1820s, "abounds with humour, incident and sense," Royall wrote. "It is nothing more than a mirror, held up to reflect the follies of human life." In her first book, she portrayed Watterston as a gracious librarian of Congress and literary figure, "neither spare nor robust," with a "serenity over his countenance." Nonetheless, their relationship had grown testy, especially as she linked him to the growing influence of the "church and state" cause infiltrating government ranks.

Only weeks before Watterston's dismissal, Anne had visited the Library of Congress. Watterston acted "insolent" and "hostile in his language." She claimed he had called her a "squaw," owing to the fact that she had been "reared among the Indians." Anne brushed the comment aside. "No squaw had ever sold her king for a groat," she replied.

Charging that the novelist she once admired had "gone over to the black coats," Anne tore into the nation's librarian for allowing the Library of Congress to be blanketed by the very Sunday School Union pamphlets and religious tracts she had been fighting to keep out of government reach. Testifying in front of a congressional committee, Watterston had admitted to ordering some of the religious tracts and books and to working with Royall's dreaded nemesis Coyle. "I have delivered to Mr. Coyle the Sunday school books and as many Bibles and testaments as he wanted agreeably to the order of the Committee," he said.

Anyone who operated as a "traitor in the service of Doctor Ely," the dreaded Presbyterian leader, was an enemy of the state according to the author of the *Black Books*. Watterston's angelic figure had fallen. "He entertains shoals of these missionaries. Pass his house when you will, you will find it enveloped in a flock of black coats, like ravens round carrion."

She delivered her final verdict in her last book before the trial: "My friend Watterston ought to be hauled over the coals about his duties; being a man of sense and learning, he is more dangerous." Her suggestion: "He ought to be dismissed as soon as possible."

And he was. While the direct connection between Royall's writing and Watterston's fate could not fully be confirmed as the motivation to the political machinations at play, the muckraker's unrelenting attack on the religious subterfuge in the Library of Congress and among clerks heightened the growing tension in government offices. Jackson officials formally blamed Watterston's firing on his violation of posting a required bond as the Librarian of Congress. Nonetheless, everyone on Capitol Hill recognized that Watterston had supported Jackson's opponent in the 1828 election and, thus, remained at odds with the new administration. In the meantime, Andrew Coyle, the brother of John Coyle Sr., lost his job as chief clerk of the post office. "The poor wretch trembles like a leaf whenever he sees me," Anne scoffed.

Even Duff Green, the Kentucky-raised publisher of the *United States Telegraph* in Washington, DC, sided with Royall, writing his opinion of Watterston in a private letter to Jackson only months before the trial. Watterston belonged to that "little knot of corrupt aristocrats who have brought this city to the verge of bankruptcy."

Watterston took the stand and returned the favor to Royall. After offering a compliment to the authoress, he declared that she referred to "Presbyterians as cutthroats." Anne shrugged. "I suppose he learned his speech out of the Sunday School Union books."

She deflected his statements as nonsense—she was impervious to such comments now. Her writing spoke for itself. Anne didn't fire away indiscriminately at religious people; she loved Parson Obediah Brown, for example, a Baptist preacher and post office clerk in Washington, an "honest priest" who had none of that "long-faced hypocritical sanctification about him; he is a jolly, sensible man, and always gives me a smile, and a piece of bread, which I would have than a tract."

"Mrs. Royall, as it is well known in her writings and speech," the *Reformer* told its readers in an update on the trial, "has been very severe against the missionary schemes and missionary beggars, as well as tart and pointed in her remarks." The trial, according to the editor, was "to obtain revenge (as we have learned from disinterested individuals in Washington)" by Presbyterian leaders and a "certain man Mrs. Royall had called 'Holy Willy,' " who had set out a "plot for her downfall."

Born the same year as Anne, Judge Cranch probably felt the burden of his age on Washington's district court bench as he fended off the squabbles of the Engine House plaintiffs and dealt with one of the more formidable defendants of his career. The son of a justice for the Court of Common Pleas of Massachusetts, Cranch also witnessed the American Revolution as a child. His family shared a close acquaintance with the storied Adams family of Boston.

By the age of 24, the newly minted attorney had moved to Alexandria, Virginia, near Washington, DC, arriving in the muddy streets long before the judicial system had actually been established in the nation's capital. When Congress finally created the District of Columbia Circuit Court in 1801, President Adams appointed the 32-year-old Cranch an assistant judge. After a series of retirements and replacements, Cranch became the chief judge in 1806.

In the intervening decades, Cranch handled a number of defining cases and gained a reputation as a fair-minded but occasionally heavy-handed justice. According to a biography published by the Columbia Historical Society, "he never wore coif or wig; no gown of silk was needed to make imposing his judicial presence." As late as the mid-1830s, Cranch sentenced convicted criminals to the whipping post—and the branding iron, where officers burned a searing jail key into the hand of the offender as a punishment.

Only days before the Royall trial, Cranch had overseen the controversial proceedings for former Treasury auditor Tobias Watkins, who had been charged with embezzling $3,000. A close associate of former president John Quincy Adams, Watkins became a symbolic figure for the incoming Jackson administration, which claimed their intent to rid the government ranks of corruption—and the secretive operations of a bevy of entrenched civil servants who had dipped into the government coffers.

No one wanted to be the next Watkins—and the troublemaking Anne, forever roaming the halls of government, inspecting the ledgers, checking personal affiliations with religion, added an even more threatening element. While the election of Jackson in 1828 "cracked the old aristocracy wide open," wrote historian Arthur M. Schlesinger Jr., bringing the new president's Tennessean "rule of the people" to Washington, its actual ripple effect on government workings had yet to be seen.

As an assistant district attorney, a young Francis Scott Key also took part in the prosecution of Watkins—as did, ironically, Anne's appointed defense attorney Richard Coxe, who served as Watkins's defense. Key delivered a two-hour offensive on the auditor's fraudulent actions, drawing the attention of the bitterly divided newspapers. In the end, the court found Watkins guilty, and Cranch sent the Adams administrator to prison, the sentence reverberating throughout Washington. Who was going to be next?

This new era of government reform cast an additional shadow on the Royall trial. "Without any reference to the guilt or the innocence of the unhappy individual, who occupies at this time so large a space in the public eye," the *United States Gazette* warned, "there seems a deficiency in the public laws, or their administrators, when a man, if innocent, should be so harassed." In the wake of Watkins's trial, the *Gazette* insinuated that a less noble defendant like Anne had even been treated better. The anti-Jackson forces wanted a little revenge with Anne's case, as a signal to the Jackson rabble of its own poisonous and vulgar associates.

The press played with this flurry of political salvos—and close observers of the trial chose sides. The *United States Gazette* spelled it out in an editorial: "Our fair friend, the American Sappho, has actually been indicted, after all that has been said and done on the subject. The U.S. Gazette, however, is a coalition paper, and Mrs. Royall is a good Jackson man—therefore we are inclined to set this story down as a coalition slander."

The odd statement, of course—not to mention the funny gender designation—went beyond the banter over Anne's foibles, her stories of ridicule, the religious debates, and essentially came down to one main point: *Mrs. Royall is a good Jackson man and, therefore, fair game.*

On one hand, as the *Boston Patriot* noted, the aggrieved plaintiffs, such as Coyle, were "prominent and active promoter(s) of every object of a pious and benevolent character." On the other, Royall's editor friends at the *Morning Courier* and *New York Enquirer* invoked the unimpeachable cause of the American Revolution in her defense: "The widow of a revolutionary soldier," they responded, Anne had been "driven to hard expedients to obtain bread in her advanced age."

Cranch's biographer had little love for the "irate" Anne. He wrote, "Judge Cranch presided with dignity but Mrs. Royall was ever the foe of dignity, and although thoroughly frightened she maintained her side with sarcastic vigor."

To be sure, Anne had her defenders, especially in the sticky Washington courtroom that summer day. She claimed, however, that she had minimized outreach to witnesses, "knowing how it would end." Unlike the prosecution's case, the eight testimonies on her behalf also included women; likewise, government clerks and even a Cabinet secretary took the oath in defense. Only one witness refuted Royall's defense: an Irish ditch digger, according to a newspaper, who delivered his testimony "in the broadest accent of the turf," which "occasioned great merriment." He confessed, "Sure enough, I have heard her often shouting at people from her window—but I was too busy with my carts to give any great attention."

The rest of the witnesses touted Anne's reputable behavior, her adherence to a certain Capitol Hill social protocol, albeit an assertive one. The witnesses included Mrs. William Greer, the well-off wife of

Royall's new Washington printer, who had extended vast amounts of credit for her *Black Books*, and even gifted a bed to Anne for her shabby home. Mrs. Greer spoke on Royall's selflessness and her jolly, sensible ways. Sarah "Sally" Dorrett Stack testified next; she had befriended Anne as soon as the latter had arrived in Washington, and even provided her free lodging for six months in her house across from the Capitol. Stack attested to Anne's amiable relationship with other women, one of the key issues at hand. Stack, noticeably tall, thin, and wiry compared to the diminutive Anne, would become the author's closet collaborator for nearly two decades.

"Their testimony was clear and unequivocal, and directly opposed to the testimony of the prosecution," Anne noted. On the other hand, "Mr. Tims was true gold."

Senate doorkeeper H. Tims and his family lived nearby on Capitol Hill and were therefore familiar with the Engine House scene. Royall referred to them as "benevolent" Samaritans and found the Tims women "accomplished." Taking his seat in the witness stand, Tims faced the courtroom with a certain familiarity; his daily job at the Senate had put him in touch with many in the audience. The correspondent for the *New York Commercial Advertiser* described Tims for the rest of the readers: "His maniken shape, his red picked snuffy nose, and ludicrously pompous manners."

Delighting in the exchange, Tims struggled to answer the attorney's question over Royall being a common scold:

His eyes winked—or snapped, I believe the term is—his frame sea-sawed over the centre of gravity, and, with his right hand protruded, he answered the lawyer's question by another. "Pray, sir," said Tims, "what is the proper and legal definition of a common scold? When can a scold said to be common; for as being a scold you know all women are that." Now what gave point to this query, was the fact that it was the very question which Coxe himself had put to the court on a previous motion to quash the indictment.

The wary counsel gave it the go-by, and changing the shape of his question, said, "Well then, Mr. Tims, did you ever know of Mrs. Royall's slandering anybody?" Tims promptly answered, "Yes, sir—she has slandered me." This was a rather stumper—coming from her own witness. "You, Mr. Tims, how so?" "Why sir, she has said, aye and printed it too, in her book, that I am very clever—and to that I make no objections; in fact, I believe on the whole, it is true. Take me altogether I certainly am a very clever man; but she adds—and a very exemplary man. Now that is a slander!"

This was too much. The court roared; bench, bar and jury, all lost their balance, and while even the sedate Judge Cranch sunk his head between his hands and shook in his chair, Tims himself was the only person left unmoved. He looked round grave as an owl. Just opposite him stood Mr. ****** (Watterston) laughing immoderately. Tims catching sight of him, again opened his oracular jaws. "Yes sir, and I know her slandering one other person besides me." Indeed; who is that? "Why, there's Mr. ****** (Joseph Gales, local newspaper editor), she says in the same book, that he and ***** (Watterston) are two of the most handsomest men in Washington; now I leave it to the whole world if that is not a slander!"

The effect of this you may imagine. In vain, the constables roared out "silence." The Courtroom shook to its foundations, and it was some time before the trial could proceed.

Anne tried to stifle her own laughter, but even she succumbed to what she called such a "ludicrous farce" that had ever "played before a judicial tribunal." Nonetheless, she hoped the Senate would keep Tims on staff "as a reward for his honesty," or even better yet, that they would commission a "statue to perpetuate the fact that one honest man was found in government."

"Unfortunately for Mrs. Royall," the *Reformer* reported, "a court and jury were found willing to listen to the soft words and plausible tales of her enemies, and ready to lend their aid to gratify the vindictive feelings of an offended priesthood and their partisans."

President Andrew Jackson declined Anne Royall's request to testify on her behalf at the trial. Fatigued by a recent journey to Virginia and embroiled in a number of pressing White House matters, Jackson deferred to his secretary of war, John Eaton, in a move that carried extraordinary implications for the Washington gossip circles.

Judge Cranch concurred and invited Eaton to the stand to testify. Royall never failed to honor her "Tennessee heroes," Eaton being one of these. In her portraits, she had described Eaton as "noble and commanding," with a "great expression, his high majestic forehead and his whole deportment part of an elevated cast." Her first encounter with the secretary brought her back to her Alabama days, when she learned that Eaton, then a major serving under Jackson's command, had intended to write a book about their "brilliant victory in New Orleans." Following Jackson's lead, Eaton had served as the United States senator from Tennessee, occasionally crossing paths with Anne on Capitol Hill.

Nonetheless, the press wondered, could you blame the embattled Jackson, only a few months into his presidency, for not testifying? "It requires no ordinary share of animal, as well as moral courage, in any three and twenty men to make so daring an attack upon the rights of this belligerent authoress," the *United States Gazette* had commented earlier. Yet, the president harbored no fear of Royall—and, in fact, he considered her a friend, a fellow westerner, dating back to their first meeting at his plantation in Melton's Bluff, Alabama, in 1818. Not long after the trial, according to a letter by *Globe* newspaper editor Francis Blair, Jackson even invited Anne to dine at the White House after he had noticed a feathered partridge in her bag, which had been inadvertently revealed when she presented him with a new book. Realizing the tiny bird was the extent of her food, Jackson took pity on the author and made sure she was properly fed.

While the press considered her a "Jackson man," Anne's relationship with the president was far more complicated. She never denied her reverence for the military hero, though once he entered the White House she began to temper her comments, and over the years even criticized or broke openly with him over several policies. When Royall first met Jackson in 1818, she found the military hero's aura too powerful to resist. "General Jackson, General Jackson comes!" she wrote in her letters. Dressed in a blue frock coat, with epaulettes, a common hat, a black cockade, and a sword by his side, Jackson's tall and thin figure passed Anne with "a great deal of dignity." She called him "the hero of the south" and recounted being awakened at night years before in western Virginia with the news that he had defeated the British in New Orleans.

Less than two years older than Royall, the noticeably lackluster President Jackson had not recovered completely from the loss of his wife, Rachel, who had died a few weeks after his bitterly fought election of 1828. Rachel's mistreatment in the volatile campaign, in fact, stung both Jackson and Royall. Jackson had met Rachel in 1788 at her mother's boardinghouse, where she languished in an unhappy and apparently abusive marriage to Lewis Robards. In 1791, Rachel left

Robards, though the terms of their divorce remained uncertain, including Robards's own consent. Amid the confusion, assuming the divorce had been officially recorded, Rachel married Jackson, who brought Rachel with him to Mississippi. Whether he acted out of deception or not, Robards charged Rachel with adultery, using her actions for grounds for a divorce, which effectively meant that Rachel and Jackson had to marry again, though they did so from the awkward position of having cohabitated together outside the bounds of legal matrimony.

In the mudslinging pits of the 1828 election, a third of a century after the fact, Rachel and Jackson's marriage became fodder for the partisan campaigns and their allies in the press. Rachel's reputation took the worst beating.

Charles Hammond, an editor with the *Cincinnati Gazette*, obsessed over Rachel's reputation in numerous articles, charging that Jackson had forced his wife to dump her marriage: "Ought a convicted adulteress and her paramour husband be placed in the highest offices of this free and Christian land?"

The stress of the personal attacks angered Jackson; according to most accounts, they also affected the ailing Rachel, who died of a heart attack soon after the election. More than all of the outrageous accusations in the presidential campaign, including the charge by Hammond that Jackson's mother had been a prostitute, the treatment of Rachel wounded Jackson in a lasting manner. "In the presence of this dear saint, I can and do forgive all my enemies," he said at Rachel's funeral. "But those vile wretches who have slandered her must look to God for mercy." Months later, the widower Jackson arrived in Washington to assume the presidency, though he was clearly despondent.

It is unclear, and undocumented, whether the mistreatment of Rachel and the shredding of her reputation heightened Jackson's sympathies to Royall. Jackson clearly bristled at the references over the proper role of "respectable" women. In a rare glimpse into the lingering impact of Royall's trial, Jackson discretely hinted at it only months later in his "Second Annual Message" to Congress in 1830. Addressing the lack of uniformity in the laws of the District of Columbia, "particularly in those of a penal character," Jackson called out conflicts over differing legal codes in adjacent states. "And the peculiarities of many of the early laws of Maryland and Virginia remain in force, notwithstanding their repugnance, in some cases, to the improvements which have superseded them in those States."

Defending Anne's reputation on the stand, Secretary Eaton apprised the court of his limited time, given his governmental duties, and stated that he had never known Royall to make any of the alleged acts of "indecent language." According to Anne, Eaton had actually vouched on her behalf prior to the trial, when it was erroneously reported that she had attempted to flee prosecution and was imprisoned. Unaware that she was soundly home, Eaton sent a messenger to the marshal to release Royall. Anne wrote that "any man who would have not done so, must have had the heart of a beast."

The *Boston Patriot* stated that Eaton spoke "in short metre, with no appearance of delight." Eaton went on to testify that "Mrs. Royall had always conducted herself like a lady when she came to his office."

The courtroom murmured at the statement. The definition of "a lady" excited the crowd, and especially the press, given its association with Eaton's wife. Gossip over Margaret Eaton's disreputable ways already laced many of the conversations in Washington in those days, no less so when the issue of Royall's respectability came to trial.

In fact, a sordid web of scandalous gossip essentially entangled the disparate lives of Rachel Jackson, Margaret Eaton, and Royall in a strange way. "These men, as I expected," wrote Royall, "discovering Secretary E. was not a brute like themselves, immediately attacked

Mrs. E (whose worth they cannot imitate) with charges that were foul as they were false and malicious. The dastardly cowards, thus to make war on women!"

The relentless Hammond, who had hounded Rachel Jackson, chimed in on Eaton's own marriage: Jackson's new secretary of war "has made an honest woman of his mistress." His implication of Margaret Eaton's promiscuous past was hardly a secret. Hammond had also mocked Royall's writing in various newspapers under the title of "Gallantry."

The daughter of a popular tavern and boardinghouse owner in Washington, Margaret O'Neil grew up entertaining politically powerful guests. She played the piano, she sang, she interacted freely with men, she laughed without shame, according to accounts; one boarder described her "perfect proportions," and her "perfect nose, of almost Grecian proportions, and finely curved mouth, with a firm, round chin, completed a profile of faultless outlines." Even Margaret understood the sway and the sordid reactions to her beauty at a young age: "I was a lively girl and had many things about me to increase my vanity and help to spoil me. While I was still in pantalettes and rolling hoops with other girls, I had the attention of men, young and old, enough to turn a girl's head."

Margaret's first marriage to John Timberlake, who traveled often as a navy purser, didn't stop her extroverted nature. Her close association with Eaton, then a US senator and boarder at the home, drew particular attention, though more than one resident claimed to have conquered the tavern daughter in the bedroom. In 1828, after her husband died mysteriously at sea, apparently by suicide, those gossipy accusations reached a fever pitch when Margaret married Eaton in a ceremony four months later.

Jackson, who had known both Margaret and her family and his

Tennessee mate Eaton for years, encouraged the marriage despite the indelicate circumstances. "If you love the woman," he counseled Eaton, "and she will have you, marry her by all means."

A revealing letter by Washington doyenne Margaret Bayard Smith, the wife of the editor of the *Daily National Intelligencer*, written before she realized Rachel Jackson had died, tied together the rejection of both women, just as Jackson had often suspected:

> Tonight Gen'l. Eaton, the bosom friend and almost adopted son of Gen'l. Jackson, is to be married to a lady whose reputation, her previous connection with him both before and after her husband's death, has been totally destroyed. She is the daughter of O'Neal who kept a large tavern and boarding house whom Littleton knew. She has never been admitted into good society, is very handsome and of not an inspiring character and violent temper. She is, it is said, irresistible and carries whatever point she sets her mind on. The General's personal and political friends are very much disturbed about it; his enemies laugh and divert themselves with the idea of what a suitable lady in waiting Mrs. Eaton will make to Mrs. Jackson and repeat the old adage, "birds of a feather will flock together."

The attacks on Margaret Eaton came from two sides, both also at odds with Anne: the society circle of elite wives in Washington, whose husbands filled Jackson's cabinet and government office, and who had convinced Jackson's niece, Emily Donelson, his designated White House host, to be their ally; and the very Presbyterian religious ranks that pursued the "common scold" trial.

Less than three weeks after Jackson's March 4, 1829, inauguration, the president received a letter from Royall's arch nemesis in

Philadelphia, then-presiding Presbyterian clerk Reverend Ely. He laid out a long list of transgressions by Margaret Eaton, the "ill famed" woman who had engaged in "illicit intercourse." Aware of Jackson's grief, Ely suggested that "the name of your dear departed and truly pious wife is stained through Mrs. Eaton." Packing his letter full of sordid details, including statements by various men who claimed to have slept with Margaret, Ely noted that the "ladies of Washington" refused to meet or recognize her—even if it "should cost" their men their places. Ely placed his own vocation on the line: "As a minister of God, as a man, and a Christian, I would forgive Mr. and Mrs. E— and do them all the kindness in my power; but forgiveness does not imply that a woman of lewd character for years should on marriage be received, at once, into chaste society."

Such exile from the kingdom, of course, resonated with Royall, who had suffered a similar fate in western Virginia. In her writing, Anne mentioned numerous times when she had fraternized with the Eatons, including occasions when they had traveled together on steamboats. Returning from Philadelphia one evening, Anne saw the "elegant figure" of Mrs. Eaton, and "we all saluted and promised ourselves high times."

During the chaotic inauguration, at which an exhilarated crowd, set off by the firing of a cannon and roaring proclamations, literally rushed the White House grounds, Anne was "astonished to see—see I did not—but hear that this insidious traitor [Ely] was countenanced by" Jackson. The author, who remained on the margins of the great celebration, admitted her "jealousy" of "Doctor Ely," the avowed advocate of intertwining church and state, and "an enemy of course to Republicanism."

When Anne expressed to White House host Emily Donelson her regret at Ely's proximity to Jackson's seat of power, Jackson's niece responded that she considered Ely to be "a very fine man." Anne chalked it up to "proof of [Emily's] ignorance." She was a beautiful woman, "but a great bigot."

Jackson fended off the Ely letters with diplomacy; he refused any entreaties to send Eaton abroad to France as an ambassador or force him to resign. Throughout it all, he remained a defender of Margaret Eaton, if only out of loyalty to his wife's memory and his long-time friend John Eaton, whom he considered a son. The president also believed in Margaret's innocence: "I would resign the Presidency sooner than desert my friend Eaton," he declared, adding in a closed-door meeting with his cabinet members (except for Eaton) that Margaret was "as chaste as a virgin."

Ely had corresponded regularly with Jackson for several years. Earlier that January, he appealed to the incoming president to avoid traveling to Washington on the Sabbath, as part of his commitment to the growing evangelical movement that had set its designs on halting Sunday mail and virtually all Sunday traffic, ramping up evangelical outreach in the form of "missionaries" and publications, and implementing a level of Christian oversight on political decisions. Ely delivered a letter to Jackson from religious leader Lyman Beecher, "the most distinguished divine at present living in Massachusetts." Beecher expressed his "fear" that Jackson's travel on the Sabbath would "injure both us and him greatly." Ely quickly reminded the president that the religious leader was "not a bigot," but "no Christian ruler of a Christian people should do violence to his own professed, personal principles."

After the excitement of the inauguration, Jackson and his cabinet embarked on several administrative plans, though Ely and his shock troops, along with their women allies in Washington, refused to let the Eaton affair fade away.

On July 3, only days before Anne's trial began, Ely wrote a personal and manipulative note to Jackson. He first mentioned seeing Jackson's son at the Navy Yard, and then he turned to Jackson's grieving heart: "In the midst of your important national affairs," he wrote, he knew that the president's "immortal soul" continued to visit his departed wife. With great drama, Ely enclosed an old letter from Rachel Jackson—only on loan, because it was so dear he was unwilling to part with it—so Jackson could see the truly Christian spirit that dictated the hand. As a humble follower of Christ, Ely concluded, Jackson should be distinguished by Christian virtue, as much as the presidency.

According to John F. Marszalek, author of *The Petticoat Affair: Manners, Mutiny, and Sex in Andrew Jackson's White House*, the Eaton situation reached a breaking point for Jackson in July, during Royall's trial. While on a steamboat ride with various Washington society members along the Virginia coast, the pregnant Emily Donelson, Jackson's niece, fainted. First on the scene, Margaret Eaton had actually noticed Emily's fading look before she lost consciousness and quickly offered comfort, as well as a fan and a bottle of cologne. Her efforts were in vain: Emily refused any contact or assistance from Margaret and thus fainted. Outraged by the dismissal, Margaret openly reminded Jackson that he had promised to send his niece back to Tennessee for such behavior. Emboldened by her place in power, Margaret, like Anne, never surrendered to public disapproval—or the whims of a handful of covetous women. Jackson made good on the promise.

In that same week, Jackson wrote another Eaton detractor of his correspondence with Ely. The president vigorously defended Margaret, adding that he had replied to Ely "such as truth and justice required, and respect for the memory of my dear wife demanded, whose name had been so unjustly associated with a set of vile and secret slanderers."

According to historian Daniel Howe, the Eaton affair took up more of Jackson's time in the first year of his presidency than any other matter. The social conflict over Margaret Eaton's participation at dinners, dances, and even White House gatherings provided a handy wedge for political divisions still unresolved by the election. At one point, it appeared the Jackson administration might even collapse over the denial of a secretary's wife's invitation to a dinner party. Jackson retorted: "Do you suppose that I have been sent here by the people to consult the ladies of Washington as to the proper persons to compose my cabinet?"

With a deadlocked Washington, Secretary of State Martin Van Buren finally devised a scheme in the spring of 1831; everyone in Jackson's cabinet would resign, including Eaton, in order to allow for the government to recuperate its administration and attend to the pressing matters at hand. "The political history of the United States, for the past thirty years," wrote James Parton, the Jackson historian in 1860, "dated from the moment when the soft hand of Mr. Van Buren touched Mrs. Eaton's knocker."

Anne, like Margaret Eaton and Rachel Jackson, understood the power of supercilious gossip as much as any political decision in shaping Washington. So did Jackson: "I had rather have live vermin on my back than the tongue of one of these Washington women on my reputation."

The Eaton affair served as a reminder that Anne also had to negotiate her own exclusion from Washington society circles based on the perception of her errant ways, her ragged attire, and her "vulgar" expressions. To be sure, Royall didn't pull any punches with those she found to be sycophants for religious fronts, or even dilettantes who used their wealth and privilege as a shield against any efforts for education and engagement. Yet, for those who were independent, strong, even defiant, and especially caring—like Rachel Jackson and Margaret Eaton—Anne didn't hesitate to note their appeal. She was loyal, to a fault.

A century later, muckraker Samuel Hopkins Adams explored this relationship between Royall and the two women in his novel *The Gorgeous Hussy*, which was also made into a Hollywood film in the middle of the Depression that starred Joan Crawford. "Ladies of the Georgetown aristocracy who ridiculed Rachel Jackson's homespun manners," he wrote, were quickly answered by Margaret "Peggy" Eaton. Her feisty collaborator in the novel is Royall, who "did everything but sleep," writing nonstop "with a profound conviction of her own rightness." In Adams's fiction, Anne explains how she has managed to travel the country as a single woman, withdrawing a "six-shot pepperbox from under her capacious skirt." Eaton joins Royall as a "silent partner" in her journalism efforts, playing an insider on the discussions with government officials at her family's boarding-house. "Life is hard," Adams's older Royall concludes, "and sometimes hazardous. But it is never dull."

The *London and Paris Observer* watched the development of the trial of the "American Scold" closely, reprinting clips from domestic newspapers as well as making their own commentaries. While they had never enjoyed "visits of this ornament of her sex," the newspaper had been informed by friends in Philadelphia that Royall "never fails to shower the pearls of her eloquence," even if "she has proved more terrible elsewhere than here."

Poking fun at the possibility of Royall being convicted and sentenced to the ducking stool, the *Observer* admitted the obsolete use of the "stool of repugnance" in England, which had resulted in "awful consequences," including a sort of branding for life, "with impunity." Nevertheless, ducking Royall would be a "cheap consideration for this

inestimable privilege," it quoted the *Daily National Journal*. Even better, added one editor, the "ceremony of ducking" should be delayed
until the weather "becomes colder."

After nearly five hours of testimonies, all attention in the courtroom now turned toward Anne. The author praised the prosecutor for
his deliberate speech, with "great mildness, delicacy and tenderness."
She considered Swann to be a "gentleman," notwithstanding his collusion with the Engine House religious group. He drew a great laugh,
Royall noted, by announcing "he did not wish to press me too hard."

The *New York Telescope* provided the only transcript of her statement, albeit an interpretive one. "Advancing her wrinkled visage and
swaying their souls with the majesty of her outstretched hand," Royall took the stand and made her plea:

> May it please the court, and you gentlemen of the jury—I am
> glad it has come to this, although the proceedings against me
> are a blot on the country which ages will not wipe out. The
> motive is too evident to delude the understanding of the coun-
> try. There is a deep laid plot at the bottom, which ought to fill
> every citizen with solemn fear. It is not a question between A
> and B you are called on to decide; it is a question between Lib-
> erty and Slavery. This is clear from the quarter from whence it
> comes, and from the individuals who compose the witnesses. It
> is the mere echo of the Sunday mail men, whose scheme is
> clothed in wide disguise. These are the same men who have
> persecuted me with unceasing rancour since I began to expose
> their impositions on the people. In one instance they made an
> attempt upon my life—I mean the same sect—and with pens
> steeped in gall, have hunted me from one end of the Union to
> the other.

I am a stranger in your land, gentlemen of the jury, and one of those heathens whom these religious men pretend to counsel, yet they never attempted to counsel me, or give me a mouthful of bread; and though they have heaped every species of slander and falsehood upon me, down to this day, and have ransacked every corner of the city to hunt up my bitterest enemies, they have not been able to produce a single immoral act of my life. It is therefore clean as the sun at noonday, that I am persecuted for my religious opinions.

Not one who hears me this day but must be convinced that the prosecution against me, is one of fearful tendency, and should they succeed, no man will be safe. When they were defeated last winter, they wrote to their friends in Congress not to be discouraged. "We will gain a little now," said they, "and a little again." This is one of the littles. Let them once get the wedge in, and the Judge on the bench, and the President in his seat, may tremble for their liberty. I hope, therefore, gentlemen, that you will meet these encroachments upon our civil and religious liberty like freemen. Give this dangerous sect a precedent, and our liberty is gone. Permit me, therefore, to impress upon your minds that the moment has arrived when you are called on to say whether you will surrender your liberties to an aspiring priesthood, or nobly resolve to be free. The eyes of the world are upon you. Now is the time, in this temple of justice, to decide by your verdict the fate of posterity.

"Your fancy must add the graces of emphasis, gesture and expression of countenance, the collection of which made up the rich but unavailing eloquence of the persecuted Cassandra of our age," concluded the *Commercial Advertiser*, "alas, her appeal was unavailing."

Baptist pamphleteer Reverend Greatrake declared that Anne "may be rude, very rude—she may be deeply skeptical; but she has more intellectual energy and more moral courage than a thousand of her bitterest persecutors." The Baptist leader wrote that Royall had been "hunted at Washington, DC" by "mongering rabidness." He placed her in line with a heady list of other truth-tellers who "already came forward in multitudes of instances to sound the alarm—to warn the credulous and ignorant of the chains that are forged for and that now are being riveted upon their political, religious and social liberties."

Writing a century after the trial, legal historian H. S. Boutrell reflected on the dynamics of Royall's trial for the *Georgetown Law Journal*, calling her the "most remarkable woman of her time." Looking back at the trial, and Royall's lifelong trial in the court of public opinion, the *Philadelphia Album and Ladies Port Folio* judged her fate as a "consequence of an erratic career." The editors, though, were not without pity, or even admiration, for the "redoubtable author." They took umbrage at other malicious portraits of Royall: "Surely this lady deserves to be apotheosized." Teetering somewhere between judicious praise and the ridiculous, the journal considered Anne the "Mrs. Walter Scott of America," if not the "Mrs. Don Quixote of the same continent." Either way, Royall's original writing "placed before the public the proper nature of independence, and the portraits of many individuals who had never been heard of but for the medium of the *Black Book*, deserve to be duly appreciated by the admirers of modest women and literary geniuses."

In all of the media banter, no drawing or sketch of Anne at the trial ever survived or was recorded. In fact, no picture of the author exists, though two artists did apparently ask her to sit for a portrait. In Philadelphia, a teenage student of James Fisher captured her "flop-bordered cap so exactly," she said after looking at the drawing. Later in Lynchburg, Virginia, the state's celebrated miniature portrait painter Harvey Mitchell, who gained recognition for his series on the local gentry, managed to conjure her "likeness."

As Judge Cranch gave instructions to the jury, the news reporters exchanged notes and began to draw up their stories. The force of Royall's "eloquence" was in vain, the *Commercial Advertiser* surmised. It viewed this trial as comeuppance for the "trial of public forebearance" inflicted on Washington residents who had been subjected to her attacks. It charged that Anne had chosen the capital as her "city of refuge." Noting that she had been "driven from Alexandria by the threat of being carted and 'dumped down' beyond the city bounds, and from Richmond," as the first step of imprisonment in Washington, Royall brought her "august presence" into the metropolis, yielding her "dint of brass, begging and scribbling" to gain a great name.

For the anti-Jackson newspaper, the jury was neither "melted by suffering beauty" nor "fired by the remembrance of posterity in danger." Other journalists postulated that Anne's fate remained inexorably linked to Watkins's recent conviction; her case, tried by Swann, counterbalanced that prosecution.

Perhaps Royall's ducking, the *Charleston Gazette* suggested, could set a precedent for everyone in Washington, especially the politicians. "It would be advisable before the next session of Congress," the newspaper quipped, "to erect a permanent engine near the Capitol for the special reformation of all the over-talkers of the stern sex, for the lasting benefit of the country at large." The *Commercial Advertiser* allowed that "two to four hours will be thought long enough for her [Royall] to remain under water."

In fact, in less than half an hour, the jury returned with the verdict: guilty.

"This is a pretty country to live in," Anne responded. She dismissed the jury as "all Bladensburg men," a reference to the disgraceful defeat of American forces to the British in 1814, which allowed the Washington capital to be burned to the ground.

As applause competed with catcalls, and as members of the courtroom took to their feet, Judge Cranch demanded order.

Flabbergasted by the applause, the *Reformer* referred the "whole transaction" as a "stain on our country" and chastised the editors "who have fallen into the current against an unprotected female, and chimed in to the same tune of her enemies." The newspapers' role, ultimately, made the "stain more deep" and "more durable."

"This verdict was pumpkin pie to Judge Cranch," Anne wrote. "The sweet Morsel licked out his tongue. Judge Thruston looked as fiery as Mount Etna, so displeased was he with the result. The sound Presbyterians gave thanks, and I requested the marshal, the next time I was tried, to summon twelve tom-cats instead of Bladensburg men."

Then Cranch delivered the opinion of the court in a series of intricate descriptions and justifications, returning to the ancient texts on "common scolds." The jurors had found Anne Royall "an evil disposed person as aforesaid, and a common scold and disturber of the peace of her honest and quiet neighbors."

Standing before the court, Royall and her attorney Coxe now braced themselves for the sentence.

Cranch first reiterated Coxe's earlier plea for an arrest of judgment of the "common scold" charge, given that "the punishment of common scolds is quite obsolete in England, and never was in force in this country; that it is a barbarous and unusual punishment, and therefore is prohibited by the bill of rights annexed to the Constitution of Maryland." The judge noted the "playful expression" of one English Lord Chief Justice who admitted the severe penalty of ducking women was "intended, perhaps, only to excite surprise by their exaggeration; for surprise is sometimes an approximation to wit."

The threat of being charged a common scold and sentenced to a subsequent ducking played as much a role as an actual conviction. As literary historian Jennifer Steadman noted in her survey of women travel writers, the threatened punishment of the ducking stool was "a blatant symbol of the violent consequences ragged-edge women often faced for their constructive criticism of the nation."

This didn't mean that the patrician judge planned to let Anne off the hook. The earlier admonition of the author's friends at the *Morning Courier* now resonated: that she "may be dealt with in a lenient way, corresponding with her age and infirmities."

Contrary to the defense's position, "the offence" of "common scold" is not obsolete, and "cannot become obsolete so long as a common scold is a common nuisance," Cranch declared. "All the elementary writers upon criminal law admit, that being a common scold, to the common nuisance of the neighborhood, is an indictable offence at common law."

Mrs. Anne Royall was consequently a common scold *and* a common nuisance.

Cranch concluded: "The Court is therefore of opinion, that although punishment by ducking may have become obsolete, yet that the offence still remains a common nuisance, and, as such, is punishable by fine and imprisonment, like any other misdemeanor at common law."

In a chilling footnote, he reminded the courtroom that another woman in a similar case in England, who had abdicated her domestic duties and left a home in a "disorderly" fashion, was sentenced to a year in prison.

At this point, Swann stepped forward and read an affidavit from

John Coyle Sr., claiming that Anne had committed further outrages the night before the trial. Royall immediately issued a denial and offered a counteraffidavit that Coyle had endangered her life. "I have no peace in my life from the whole gang."

Again the courtroom murmured in laughter. Cranch dismissed both affidavits. He asked for quiet. Then Cranch announced the sentence: that Mrs. Anne Royall pay a fine to the United States of ten dollars and put up $250 to guarantee her "good behaviour" for one year. He required her to be jailed until her fine had been paid, which set off a chorus of hisses from the crowd.

Whether Coxe shook hands or hugged Anne is not documented, but the triumph in keeping the 60-year-old author out of prison called for a celebration. Royall's friends, including the journalist James Gordon Bennett, her young admirer Richard Wallach, and other Jackson supporters, surrounded the defendant and offered a mix of condolences, outrage, and relief. The ducking stool would be returned to the Navy Yard for other experiments.

Anne, of course, did not have to tarry long for her bail funds. While she assumed her friend Eaton or other government officials would cover her securities, Anne laughed at the mass exodus of politicos from the courtroom. To her surprise, fellow journalists stepped up to defend the "honor of the press," ultimately invoking Royall's journalistic bona fides apart from her Jacksonian politics. Sent by *Daily National Intelligencer* editor Joseph Gales, who Senate doorkeeper H. Tims had hilariously labeled as one of the aggrieved slandered because Royall had called him a handsome man, two young reporters paid the ten-dollar fine. Still in a daze over the conviction, Anne hardly noticed their initiative. Other newspapers did, commenting on the role of the press in preventing "the incarceration of an aged woman, the wife of a revolutionary officer and a mason, by entering as her bail on such an occasion."

Ironically, Gales had posed as one of Anne's first pen portraits of Washington leaders on her initial trip to the city. Describing him with a "keen black eye," she had praised Gales as a perfect model for politeness, "just, generous and humane." The *Daily National Intelligencer*, in fact, unlike virtually every other newspaper, took a rather unemotional view of the trial in its no-nonsense reporting.

"Though these gentlemen have done themselves and the noble fraternity to which they belong, immortal honor by this generous act," she wrote later, transposing a line from Shakespeare's *Titus Andronicus* and the persecution of the Moor, "all the water of the Potomac will never wash out the foul stain of this infamous prosecution."

The *New York Observer* relished the defeat of "the vituperative powers of this giantess of literature."

Anne Royall had officially been branded America's common scold; the term "communis rixatrix" resounded with a better sense of its archaic origins, but its translation simply amounted to modern-day "witch." She called the guilty verdict an "eternal blot" on the American character. Her only praise for the justice system fell on the marshal, who agreeably escorted her back to her Capitol Hill home in his carriage. The Engine House "blackcoats," as Anne described them, vanished back into their church.

"Still praying to convert me," she quipped.

The last American witch trial came to an end. Anne Royall, meanwhile, was already planning to cast her next spell.

# SIX

# The Huntress in the Den of Vipers

*There is many a journalist now languishing in poverty, while dozens to whose success*
*in life he gave the first impulse, roll by him in their carriages, and have forgotten*
*his very existence. There is no country, save ours, in the world, where journalists*
*are expected to do as much work for the special benefit of others without recompense.*

—THE HUNTRESS, APRIL 15, 1837

Disregarding the conviction's terms to adhere to "good be-
haviour" for a year, Anne immediately packed up her belongings and prepared to take a valedictorian's victory lap through the
South after her infamous trial. She also announced plans to publish
a three-volume series of *Black Book* travels on the Southern states.
With the national media attention from the trial, Royall's demand for
appearances soared, book sales flourished, and the author cleverly
sought to manipulate the notoriety for her own gain.

The trial had also upturned her role as an author: she became more
watched than read, her status shifting from that of a critical observer
into one critically observed as a cause célèbre. Her journeys now took
on a barnstorming element of performance, drawing a great deal of
newspaper attention and onlookers. The mirror focused on Anne for

the rest of her travel life, and suddenly every move or word became a news headline; she became her own pen portrait. Increasingly, the public cared less about what she wrote and more about what she said—or how she interacted in the commons. The temptation for more outrageous gaffes or declarations tugged at Anne's every move. In the process, she transformed from an esteemed author and social critic, in the minds of the public, to a peculiar roadside attraction.

One man who had mastered the art of self-promotion in his own singular way, Phineas Taylor "P. T." Barnum, reflected on Royall's unique role in this period. Before he became the great pioneering American showman, largely remembered in history for his freak shows and touring circus, Barnum had also enjoyed a storied career as a newspaperman and politician in Connecticut. In his first press battles, he confronted evangelical extremists, fighting against the sabbatarian movement and the Congregationalist attempt to fortify a state church.

Wielding the *Danbury Herald of Freedom* like a battle axe, the young Barnum went on the offensive against church leaders, eventually drawing three libel suits. Unlike Anne, who preferred to lampoon individual foibles and keep her invective largely focused on the hypocrisy of religious dogma, Barnum made personal charges against local leaders outside the bounds of their politics, claiming they had engaged in usury and fraudulent financial schemes. Sentenced to two months in jail, the impish Barnum seized the silver lining of his predicament like a vaudeville barker: "The excitement in this and the neighboring towns is very great," he wrote about his own trial in 1831, "and it will have a grand effect. Public opinion is greatly in my favor. . . . I chose to go to prison thinking that such a step would be the means of opening many eyes, as it no doubt will." Barnum turned his prison cell into an office; a line of visitors kept him busy throughout the sixty days. On the day of his release, Barnum threw a massive party, flipping his libel statements into a noble cause for freedom of speech.

"She strongly sympathized with me in my persecutions," Barnum wrote about Anne, saying that she always exhibited a boisterous joy at their meetings. He called her the most "garrulous old woman" he had ever met. "Her tongue ran like wildfire." He delighted in baiting the author into an exchange of friendly insults, especially in political matters: "Will you support such a monkey, such a scoundrel, such a villain, such a knave, such an enemy to his country?" Barnum recorded Royall shouting, "Barnum, you are a scoundrel, a traitor, a rascal, a hypocrite! You are a spy, an electioneering fool, and I hope the next vessel you put foot on will sink with you."

The showman loved her daily performance, the twinkle in her eye, her natural ways with the sardonic aspersion. In his autobiography, he admonished readers to not take Anne's "monomaniac" persona too seriously. She was a "good-hearted, generous woman," who loved to play with the "ebullition of her eccentricity."

Aghast at Royall's disinterest in her attire, Barnum couldn't help but notice that she took a seat once on the dirty floor when she tired, not even opting for a chair, as if more accustomed to living in the country. He couldn't resist: "My showman propensities were manifest," he wrote, "inasmuch as I tried to hire her to give a dozen or twenty public lectures upon government in the Atlantic cities, but she was not to be tempted by the pecuniary reward." Barnum scoffed. Working with her would have been a "profitable" venture.

Anne did not really need Barnum after her trial. Even the Washington press lamented her absence from the capital city: "SOMETHING MYSTERIOUS," ran the *United States Gazette* headline. "We have not a word, public or private, from Washington touching Royall and her case. We hope no injunction has been laid upon the press—we will vouch for the lady that she has not been silenced."

The "Southern Tours" had already been launched—after a quick trip to Baltimore, Philadelphia, and New York City, where Royall first needed to check in with her booksellers and salute her newspaper friends prior to returning to the southern "wilds, streams and forests, and lest some accident might befall me; for instance, an alligator might swallow me."

Within a short time, Anne boarded a steamboat and headed back to Richmond for the state constitutional convention, starting her tour in earnest. She visited James and Dolley Madison and chafed at the "mantua-makers and milliners" of society women who filled the galley seats with their "line of big bonnets." She greeted John Randolph, the former US senator from Virginia and states' rights advocate, who was distantly related to her husband. Randolph's own legendary sense of wit and sarcasm—he was a spellbinding orator—made him feared in the corridors of power, a trait Royall admired.

Anne may have carelessly set off in the tradition of Parson Weems's mobile book tour—her New York editor friend Mordecai Noah had once referred to her as a "traveling bookstore." But the author quickly realized that any attempt to draw on her "common scold" trial for publicity would face a brewing backlash stirred by the religious forces and the partisan press. Her own past in the South, as well, forced her to revisit some painful memories.

In a rare recognition of her slaveholding husband's past, Anne sought to visit with the enslaved families from her plantation at Peters Mountain, who had been moved outside of Richmond to the home of the attorney who had contested her husband's will. She wrote in a feigned sense of curiosity, but a clear undercurrent of betrayal and concern laced her words. While William Royall had granted manumission to a number of enslaved African Americans on his plantation, his vast family holdings had included many other lives. According to the records, Anne inherited a number of enslaved workers, all of whom she eventually lost as part of the court decision or to settle debts.

While Carter Woodson's groundbreaking *Journal of Negro History* in 1929 singled out Royall, along with radical pamphleteer David Walker, as "exceptions" to the pro-slavery Southern writers of their age, a closer look at Royall's work presented a more conflicting picture. Anne despised slavery's institution, but she paradoxically sided with states' rights over individual liberties, complimenting the treatment of some slaves by their owners while condemning as a crime the disregard for enslaved children abandoned by their white plantation owners. Throughout her books, she often denigrated free blacks and enslaved workers whenever they provided an obstacle to her journeys. In Washington, she feared the role of freed African Americans in overtaking the poorly paid positions of white laborers. In one of her most cringeworthy vignettes, she criticized enslaved men for their brutal treatment of street dogs, as if oblivious to their own state of servitude.

Years before in Alabama, however, when Anne gave a toast at a New Year's party, she invoked her "Irish ancestors" and defiantly called out, "Health to the sick, wealth to the brave, a husband to the widow, and freedom to the slave." Earlier in her *Letters from Alabama*, Royall had praised Andrew Jackson for his treatment of his enslaved workers on his cotton plantation, and yet she checked herself as black children played and followed her on a subsequent walk in the area. It forced Anne to reckon with the fate of her own "negro children," and "I discovered the traces of tears on some of their cheeks. The sight pierced me to the heart. Oh, slavery, slavery! Nothing can soften thee? Thou art slavery still!"

Perhaps Royall's most pointed statement on slavery took place in

Alexandria, Virginia. The huge ranks of slaves at the market over-whelmed her. In a rare denouncement of sexual assault, she also chal-lenged the inhumanity of predatory plantation owners who left their offspring in a state of slavery:

> Strange that a nation who extol so much, who praise themselves in such unqualified terms, as possessing in the highest degree, both moral and political virtue should afford no better proof of it than this before me. There is a measure even in crime. There is a point, beyond which the most daring will not venture. His-tory affords us many examples, amongst the most barbarous nations, in the most barbarous ages, where the most lawless ruf-fians become softened at the sight of human distress, to which they were impelled by no law, but that of common humanity. But for man in this free, and (as they say) enlightened country to doom his own children, to a state (to say the least of it) fraught with every species of human misery, we want no better evidence to prove, that such men must not only be void of vir-tue; but guilty of the most indignant crime.

Only days after her rendezvous with the Madisons in Richmond, Anne met head-on with the clash of her post-trial reality. She jour-neyed miles out of her way to visit Jefferson's famed Monticello residence, which she found in disrepair and the former first family's possessions scattered in a contemptible way. Mrs. Jefferson's beloved "spinnet," an early type of piano, sat in a corner in pieces; "slain" frag-ments of china ware and glasses littered the rooms. While "unspeak-ably gratified" to be able to visit the celebrated place, Anne also rued that the era of Jefferson reverence had come to end. New religious forces, she declared, ruled the region.

While in Charlottesville to visit with trustees from the University of Virginia the next morning, the now notorious author noticed a growing mob of students outside her tavern. A guard soon posted at the door. Within minutes, they rushed the building, chasing Royall and the landlord to her upstairs chambers. "The ruffians thundered at the door to break it open," Anne wrote. After one courageous student agreed to serve as an intermediary, the mob slid pieces of paper with "obscene sentences" written on them under her door and continued to "stamp and shout in the most insolent manner" for hours. The attack continued until the evening, when the mob dispersed. Royall placed the blame on the local Presbyterian minister, who had apparently incited the crowd in advance of her arrival.

With newspapers advertising her daily travels, the author was never without company or controversy. Touring with local dignitaries the Camden battlefield where her husband had served in the Revolution, Anne won the graces of the local newspaper, the *Camden Journal*, which gushed over her visit: "The annals of Camden will hereafter show 1830 as the year particularly glorified by the transit of Mrs. Anne Royall . . . our citizens look upon her as the Queen of Flowers." The *Camden Observer* retorted with their own version of the visit, pretending to write a letter to the citizens of Wilmington in advance of Royall's arrival there. The letter is a nugget of sarcasm, capturing both the lingering fallout from the witch trial, the anti-Jackson mockery retained for Royall's literary achievements, and even the process the author used to hawk her books:

> We have very gloom advices from Fayetteville. Mrs. Royall writes us that she is going to Charleston by way of Wilmington!—being under a promise to do so. Keep your promise, "Dear Mrs. Royall"—great as our grief is in seeing so

much felicity slip through our fingers, and we cried for two hours this morning by "Shrewsbury Clock," (without any assistance even from a Weathersfield Onion) when the mail first brought us the information that we were not to have the beautification of taking the Semiramis of Modern Literature by the hand—still we say, keep your promise, Mrs. Anne Royall, go to Wilmington or go to _____ if you please. We need not fill up the blank, for Mrs. R. knows that our constant prayer is that she goes to none other than a good place. If she does not consider Camden in that light, it is hoped that she will steer clear of it; much as we want to see her, and the wise know that this is inexpressible? She tells us however, that she intends to be here before long; this, if we may be permitted to use a sectarian, and to us a very sickening phrase, is very happifying to us. She has sent us she says, some twenty or thirty volumes of her books, which we intend to advertise in glaring capitals when they arrive. Mrs. Royall, or as we ought to say perhaps, Mrs. John Milton, Oliver Cromwell, Napoleon le Grande and Grant Thorburn, is without competition the great Lioness of the present day. There is an interest about her which is absolutely indescribable! Nay, what is more, she is comparatively young, for she tells us that she is 23 years younger than her husband, who was a gallant officer of the revolution and fought at the battle of Camden. This new information of our "dear friend's" juvenility will awaken troublesome sensations in many a bachelor bosom, we are afraid.

Such dueling editorials and articles dogged Anne's trip along the East Coast, across the Carolinas and Georgia, from New Orleans to Alabama, and finally up the Mississippi River to St. Louis, where she met the celebrated explorer and superintendent of the Indian Agency, William Clark. Traveling over six months, she soon found that an air of fatigue colored much of her writing. She observed a nation in decline. Corruption flourished everywhere. A pale of religiosity had infected the towns. The "once polished city" of Charleston seemed to belong to "another species," she lamented. "The only reputable people" were "Jews and a few Yankees." Despite a hero's welcome in Raleigh, North Carolina, her visit throwing the city "in commotion" according to the local newspaper, Royall seemed more infatuated with women who chewed tobacco. She found her Alabama an altered landscape, still recovering ten years after the collapse of its land rush from over-speculation and the Panic of 1819, when an economic crisis led to widespread bankruptcies. The sense of frontier intrepidness had faltered in Anne's view. "When I left the western country some years back, I left them a brave, virtuous, industrious, and independent people," Anne lamented. "What are they now since they began to spread the gospel."

In an attempt to mimic the sarcasm of her own detractors in the press, Royall circulated a letter to her friends at the *Morning Courier and New York Enquirer*, which would be reprinted across the country. Over the next century, several critics held up this letter as indicative of her lopsided sense of self-acclaim, or even suggested it proved an element of delusion, as if Royall's notoriety from the trial had begun the process of unhinging her from a firm sense of reality. Placed within the context of the nonstop exchange in the newspapers, however, where hyperbole and mockery had dislodged reporting in a tête-à-tête among partisan newspapers, the letter recognizes Anne's wit more than any unraveling mind; in fact, it demonstrates the writer's longing to return to the center stage of politics in Washington.

My Dear Friends: What is the reason that you make no mention of my triumphant march through the South? From the days of my predecessor, Queen Elizabeth, no woman has enjoyed such fame—such éclat as I have done. I say with all becoming modesty, for every one who knows me is aware of how sensitive I am on that point. There is no place in the Union worth living in during winter but the south. . . .

Before I left Washington I put Congress to rights, but they are such a set of sad fellows, that they cannot keep straight unless I am constantly with them. . . .

I was the other day in Charleston, and suffered much from the barbarians and blue skins. I have borne much degradation and contumely in South Carolina, and I am half inclined to put her down in my Black Book. The "Old Dominion" is a glorious state. She is the Sparta of the South—full of public virtue, public principle, firmness and integrity. I have not many Black Books there. . . .

There was I, Anne Royall, in Charleston, hunted into a grocery store by some of the mad caps, and not only that but cheated out of my passage to Camden. I have been told that South Carolina intends to put herself upon her sovereignty—she better put herself into an honest bib and tucker, and behave like an honest woman who was never yet married twice. I hate all those who married a second husband. It is a monstrous departure from the purity of our first love.

Arriving in St. Louis on the steamboat *Atlantic*, Anne's encounter with the celebrated Clark provided further evidence that the time had come for her to return to the nation's capital. Having already made her acquaintance with Clark at Jackson's inauguration, Anne assumed the superintendent of Indian Affairs would welcome her himself at the dock. Instead, Clark's soldiers greeted the steamboat stark naked and grinning, having just climbed out from their swim in the river. The government officials denied Royall's request for lodging; the "band of pirates in his name," she wrote, wanted to keep her investigative nose out of the city. Resolving to "storm the castle," Anne sought to witness how much "fingering of the annuities and fur" of the Native Americans took place under cover. Clark's assistant attempted to keep the author from the general's room, referring to her as a "crazy old woman." Royall pushed on. She finally found Clark alone in a room, "a superannuated old man, about as fit to do business as a child, and is kept on the pay by the government as a pauper."

Meanwhile, millions of dollars of fur trade passed through St. Louis, Royall noted, calling the city a veritable empire. "The lead trade, the Santa Fe trade, the pay of the Army, and the Army itself," she continued, were all unregulated by Washington. Unable to convince anyone to help her with lodging, Anne finally turned to a Spanish sailor, who took her across the river to Illinois.

Despite Royall's observations of his infirmity, Clark recorded his brief version of the event in his diary: "From Orleans, arrived the eccentric and no less strange Woman, Mrs. Ann Royal! Her turbulence, wanton vehemence, excites curiosity, while it keeps from her the real friendship of all."

Across the Midwest and then into Kentucky, the author moved deliberately back to Washington, where she felt the only recourse existed to seek the redress of government corruption and, ultimately, to halt the growing power of religious forces.

A final event in Pittsburgh brought Royall to a punishing end of the road on her tour. While visiting a bookstore, she had mocked the seller's effort to hawk her books, as well as his politics. According to a report of the incident in the *Pittsburgh Statesman*, the seller got a "cow skin, followed the complainant downstairs and inflicted the assault and battery." The whip tore into Royall's face, drawing blood. Anne claimed he took offense at her comments on the US Bank controversy, which had become a hot-button issue over currency stabilization and the recharting of the national bank. She only survived the incident, she wrote in her usual gallows humor, because she had purchased a "thick padded bonnet" the day before, which had blunted the force of the whip.

In comparison to her humiliating trial over a wrangle of words, the bookselling assailant's act of violence only brought a $20 fine, outraging Royall and all the newspapers. The *United States Telegraph* declared the man's name should be "gazetted in every press, and he should be punished by the frowns of every petticoat in the Union."

Anne had a different idea. Exhausted by traveling nonstop for the past decade, she reunited with her friend Sally Stack in Washington and bought an old Ramage press. Rounding up a handful of orphans as printer's devils, she readied to launch her new endeavor. It took her nearly a year to recover, but Anne had finally discovered her way to respond to her trial. The *communis rixatrix* would launch her own newspaper, *Paul Pry*—and regain her sense of humor with it. "To this end, let it be understood that we are of no party, we will neither oppose or advocate any man for Presidency. The welfare and happiness of our country are our politics," she wrote. "We shall patronize merit of whatsoever country, sect or politics. We shall advocate the liberty of the press, the liberty of speech, and the liberty of conscience."

Let all pious general, colonels and commandants of our army and navy who make war upon old women, beware—let all pious postmasters who deceive the government franking tracts, beware. Let all contractors who stop packages, beware. Let all pious postmasters who cannot read commence learning henceforth—never too late to learn. Let all pious booksellers who take bribes fear and tremble. Let all pious young ladies who hawk tracts into young gentlemen's rooms, beware. And let all Old Maids and Old Bachelors marry as soon as they can."

Few could have imagined that the "common scold" trial in 1829, one of the most bizarre judicial events in the nation's capital to test the bounds of freedom of speech, would end up spawning modern muckraking journalism. At the age of 62, Anne commenced a second act in "the first rough draft of history."

Far from defeated by the conviction, she overcame the ennui of her Southern tour and the fallout from the trial by reinventing herself yet again. To depict Anne as indefatigable hardly captures the sheer level of daunting challenges she faced in this period: failing health, debilitating injuries, a growing marginalization in the market that deprived her of daily bread, virtually no resources. Her future looked dismal; she quipped at one point on her previous Southern tour that the idea of retiring to a small plot of farmland in the countryside appealed to her. Not that she or anyone else could have seriously entertained such an idyllic retirement; Anne thrived on the rough edges of a tavern or amid the fray at the political stockades. Instead, joyously defiant of the odds, Royall came to the conclusion that publishing remained the only way for a woman in her persecuted state to be recognized on her own terms.

A frustrated Royall had actually sent out her warning shot to the inner circles of Washington before she took the stand at her witch trial. "There is no press in Washington to combat those traitors," she had lamented in her last book before the trial, foreshadowing her future literary endeavor and what she perceived as indifference by her squabbling news media friends to her own persecution by religious extremists. "They go on as they please."

No one paid much attention to Anne's challenge to her fellow journalists, assuming it was only another chapter in her series of *Black Books*. The patrician duo of Joseph Gales and William Winston Seaton, who founded the venerable *National Intelligencer* and took turns serving as Washington mayors, quietly tolerated Royall's outbursts, paid the fine at her trial, and even offered bills of charity, concerned about her level of poverty. Still, they refused to accept her payment for an advertisement for one of her *Black Books*. Gales defended her right to free speech and a free press—just not in his own publication.

The anti-Jackson *Daily National Journal*, with aggrieved author George Watterston now writing their editorials, had no patience for Royall. Nor did Duff Green, whose pro-Jackson *United States Telegraph* had been granted the lucrative printing operations for Congress. But Green did provide Anne with one consolation. He ordered his printers to round up all the discarded type at his operation and gift it to her and her band of orphans. Royall's Ramage press may have sported a few gaps, but it was hardly toothless.

"The time has arrived when we have to make our *congee* to the public," Anne wrote in the first column of *Paul Pry*, which she launched on December 3, 1831. From the same Capitol Hill apartment in proximity to the Engine House church, the writer converted her kitchen into a printing operation that would take her fervent belief in the freedom of the press to a new level. Dismissing the demands by potential subscribers and observers to formally align with Jackson, US senator Henry Clay's opposition, or Vice President John C. Calhoun and his Southern ranks, she announced the paper would transcend such "political humbug."

She remained irrepressibly independent, crowed her admirers at H. L. Mencken's *American Mercury* magazine a hundred years later. "An old lady of a perpetual liveliness, no property but a printery, no aspirations to bribe, no appetites to seduce, only a tongue and a cheek to put it in."

To be sure, Royall declared, the politically independent *Paul Pry* would show no mercy in the face of enemies of the state or those who waged war on the freedom of the press—or aged widows—including "those cannibals, the anti-Masons," whom the editor strangely compared to "the contemporaries of the negro insurgents" in a reference to Nat Turner's historic attempt at a slave rebellion, which had recently taken place in Virginia.

Contrary to much lore, Anne was not the first American female journalist. Among others, Elizabeth Timothy became the publisher of the *South Carolina Gazette* in 1739 after her husband died. In Royall's own native Baltimore, Mary Katherine Goddard took a leading role with her family to publish the *Maryland Journal and Baltimore Advertiser* before the American Revolution. She rebelliously printed a series of articles by radical Thomas Paine on the "American crisis" in 1779. As Jonathan Wells noted in his historical survey *Women Writers and Journalists in the 19th Century*, 65 women editors and printers took the reins prior to 1820, including 18 newspaperwomen in Southern states. Virtually all of them, like Sarah Hillhouse in Georgia, who took over the operations from her deceased husband, inherited them from ill, deceased, or incarcerated husbands.

Following up her decade of travel writing and *Black Books*, Royall carved out a singular niche in the history of journalism as the editor and publisher of the first female-owned and -operated newspaper based in the nation's bastion of political power. As provincial newspapers reprinted some of her pen portraits and editorials on the latest machinations in Congress, she effectively served as the first female correspondent in Washington.

"Our course will be a straight forward one," she wrote, reminding the readership—and her newspaper competitors—that she brought a literary legacy with her. One overlooked contribution by Royall to journalism was her pioneering use of the quoted interview, which she had employed as early as her first *Sketches* book, years before her friend James Gordon Bennett institutionalized the method in his *New York Herald* in the 1830s, and before Horace Greeley's *New York Tribune* took it to a professional level. "The same firmness which has ever distinguished our pen will be maintained."

As a journalist, Royall would demand the same feared deference that had come with her first *Black Book*. The early winter of 1828 had never left her mind. Still incapacitated by her shattered leg from the attack in Vermont, she once required the Capitol guards to carry her on a makeshift litter to the Senate floor so she could cover a contentious debate. Her appearance silenced the floor; senators offered their hands; women on the sidelines of the chamber raised their eyebrows. Everyone understood, begrudgingly or not: Anne Royall would not be silenced.

Ensconcing herself in the corridors of Congress, in the gallery of the courts, and at the front door of the White House, Anne launched *Paul Pry* with the same intent: "We shall expose all and every species of political evil, and religious fraud, without fear or affection." She left it up to her observers to interpret the impish beam in her searing blue eyes.

In her early days, Royall traipsed the halls of government in a flurry of inspections, dallying just long enough to churn out a pen portrait of an elected official or a story on a gallant or particularly deficient clerk. "She was the terror of the politicians," wrote John W. Forney, the clerk of the House of Representatives. "I can see her now tramping through the halls of the old Capitol, umbrella in hand, seizing upon every passer-by." As an official correspondent, Anne staked out her territory with even more presumption.

"How to disperse a mob," she laughed. "Present a subscription paper and they will all vanish in the twinkling of an eye."

A perceived level of terror, of course, was in the eye of the beholder; the hyperbole seeded by Forney took root in similar depictions of Royall. Despite her renewed appearance in public, a popular novel circulated widely in 1838 that served as a reminder of how the crafting of Royall's legacy as an eccentric panhandler had already begun. *Clement Falconer, or The Memoirs of a Young Whig*, written by Baltimore author William Price, depicted her as a "she-wolf" who arrives at the house of the narrator to hawk her books. "A squat old woman, with a green calash, plaid shawl, and a huge bag pending from her arm," Royall is described as toothless, with a lower jaw marked by a "voluble tongue." A guest mockingly pretends to be deaf, forcing Anne to scream her pitch; she begs for $50, an extraordinary sum, to pay for a new bonnet and cloak. Such portraits of Royall—as "profligate and treacherous, and as coarse as a Mississippi boatman"—gained favor among the elite in Washington, who still couldn't come to terms with her raggedly influence.

At the same time, she increasingly filled her newspaper with glimpses of kindness and friendship, especially about those same clerks in the government offices. Notes of gratitude appeared for the "watchman of Congress Hall" who escorted Anne up "the long stairs." The newspaper endorsed Major B. B. French as the clerk of the House of Representatives, regardless of the change in administration: "He is a friend that sticketh closer than a brother and is honest as the sun."

Mary Chase Barney stood out as one notable literary exception in

Royall's time. She launched the *National Magazine or Ladies' Emporium* in 1831 after her husband lost his appointment as a naval officer under Jackson. Chase Barney unleashed an invective that rivaled if not surpassed Royall's. She dismissed the president as "completely destitute of intellectual ability" and eventually called Jackson a "cancerous excrescence fastened upon the body politics."

Like Royall after her conviction, Chase Barney no longer feared the contempt of men, having already bottomed out in a period of despair. "The natural timidity of my sex vanishes before the necessity of my situation," she declared, "and a spirit, sir, as proud as yours, although in a female bosom, demands justice." The comparison to Anne, however, ends there.

Staking out her claim of independent journalism without any political party, religious sect, or family coat of arms, Chase Barney came from an elite family—her father was former Supreme Court justice Samuel Chase, who had been appointed by George Washington. Unlike Royall's, Chase Barney's publication in Baltimore collapsed within a year.

For nearly a quarter of a century, Anne would publish more than 1,200 issues of two newspapers—*Paul Pry* and *The Huntress*—becoming one of the longest-enduring independent publishers in Washington.

A widow herself, suddenly without means or a family, Stack became Royall's first companion and family in nearly two decades. Within a short period, they moved their orphan-powered operation to another house on Capitol Hill, which would fill up like a farm with a string of dogs, cats, and Anne's favorite hens. Everyone engaged daily in scrounging up enough food, wood, and printing materials, such as costly newspaper. Years later, an unnamed young printer would chronicle his chores in his own article: "I have to set type—learn Grammar—and spell words for Mrs. Royall—pump water (thank my stars the pump is at the door), and then I have to wash inky aprons. I saw wood and carry water and do heaps of things besides." Raised by Anne and Sally, the printer held fast to their promise that if he stuck to learning, he could be a great lawyer one day. "Mrs. R. learns me herself."

Within two years, the home-based printing operation moved again, this time to a house only a few feet from the vice president's residence. Royall enjoyed telling an anecdote about how future vice president Richard Johnson helped the aged editor round up guineas that had fled the coop.

The appearance of the two women together always amused observers; the tiny Anne, increasingly decrepit, rotund, always with a hat that hid her hair; and the tall, angular, thin Stack, whose bursts of energy made her look so much younger.

"Her fidelity, industry, and dispatch of business have never been surpassed," Royall wrote about her partner. "She is one of a thousand. Undaunted, yet modest and humble, fleet as a fawn, one moment you lose sight of her in Third Street, and the next she will reappear from Twelfth or Thirteenth. Again, she is off like a bird. She will face the fiercest storms whether of snow, wind or rain. Often have we been pained to see her come in with a cheerful laugh, though wet to the skin, and all this without fee or reward."

The sisterhood of publishing commenced: Royall in her sixties, Stack in her forties. The orphan children, whom Anne mentioned occasionally in her newspaper—regaling readers with anecdotes on their Latin, history, and math lessons, their work on the paper, or field trips to the theater—appeared to be quite young. "Should there be any shortcoming in the present number of our paper, we have a legal excuse, having just returned from Philadelphia, where we spent three and a half days," a typical note in the newspaper ran. "It was merely a visit of pleasure, and we took all of our printers along."

The folksy narrative suited Royall's purposes, staving off criticism over the quality of its content and providing a subterfuge for her idiosyncratic views. She never entertained any editorial pretentions; her newspaper, like an unedited modern-day blog, preferred to chronicle her views on what she considered to be the key issues of her time, rather than maintain a beat reporter on the breaking news of the day. In effect, *Paul Pry* and its subsequent incarnation extended a discussion with the rest of the nation she had already initiated with her first letters and books—at once personal, informative, provocative, and extremely vulnerable to bias. "We leave party questions in better hands, to our friends of the Union and Intelligencer," Royall wrote, "while we look after the great enemy of our country, Despotism."

*Paul Pry*'s name derived from a popular English theater comedy of the day, written by noted playwright John Poole. Armed with his umbrella, which he typically left behind and used as a ruse to spy on people, Paul Pry was a mischievous gossiper who couldn't resist eavesdropping on others. Poole credited an "old invalid lady who lived in a very narrow street" with the idea. Royall simply mentioned that one of her orphans, working as a delivery boy, had thrown out the name—and it stuck. "It's not the name that gives importance to the newspaper," she wrote years later after fending off friends who complained the name trivialized the seriousness of an independent newspaper. "It's the manner in which it [the newspaper] is conducted."

The ill-omened character plagued her for years, especially when other more scandalous sheets appeared in various parts of the country under the same name. Royall, in fact, had not been the first to use the "Paul Pry" title; an upstate New York publication ran under the

same name prior to her *Black Books* in 1828, along with a series of re-
formist publications in London.

Name aside, *Paul Pry* took its role as a muckraker seriously, though
not as a gossiper in the tradition of the British character; rather, the
paper published its issues with an unflinching mission to needle the
nation's power brokers with a witty, vulgar, and unceasing barb. *Paul
Pry*, like Royall, epitomized the concept of being inexorably dogged—
some critics would say obsessive, if anything—in the age of early
American journalism. Launched on the cusp of 1832, an election year
of upheaval, in a period when religion retained "a greater influence
on the souls of men" than it did in any other country, according to
traveling French writer Tocqueville, Anne's newspaper stuck to an
ambitious array of themes over the next 25 years.

In near comic repetition, she stated her refusal to profess an affiliation with a political party—denying allegiance to President Jackson. This pursuit of being nonpolitical did not suggest that Royall
lacked involvement in the political discourse of the day but reflected
instead her actual refusal to jettison her long-fought independence
from party dynamics. Within weeks of the paper's first issue, she
lambasted Jackson's rose-colored assessment of the country in his annual address, which championed an era of "happiness and prosper-
ity." *Paul Pry* countered: "We have just been through the U.S., and
with the exception of Louisiana and Georgia, we saw nothing but
fraud, violence and oppression—distress of all sorts, vice the most
abandoned." Anne added, playing on the name of her paper, "The
President, we fancy, does not pry into these things as we do, though
he need not go out of Washington to find ignorance, vice and distress."

The *Paul Pry* editor sought a loftier ground, forever mindful
that her ideals had been burnished in the American Revolution.
Her newspaper aimed to "defend the rights of people against

tyranny and corruption," and she remained dedicated to keeping the country "united." In the end, Royall announced, in an almost naïve voice of a dreamer from Peters Mountain, that "there ought to be no party—when all are in danger, all ought to unite."

For Anne, of course, one of the main dangers always lurked in the wicked schemes of the "church and state" party, whose imperial designs in her view still continued to threaten politics, infiltrate government, thwart efforts at enlightenment and education, foster anti-intellectualism, and turn schools into religious training grounds. In one of her main sections of the newspaper, "Church and State," she railed against the daily activities of the "money gospel," which had created a righteous alliance with misguided emancipationists and abolitionists, clergy-controlled women-reform movements, and a growing and more virulent anti-immigrant backlash in the country, all for the sake of "a money-getting scheme."

Reporting on a Temperance Society meeting near the Capitol, for example, Royall questioned the "large collection" of donations offered to the church for "dangerous purposes," while the moans and cries of a "poor sick man" turned out into the cold night went ignored.

Into this political cauldron she tossed the rise of the Anti-Masonic Party in the 1832 elections, the nation's first third party. Even still, it was "idle to argue with men so abandoned," the paper mused. Nonetheless, the party's ascent on a national level, even for a brief moment in the 1830s, provided the "perfidy of those money Christians, who have crept into our schools, and have corrupted the whole of our patriotic Union." Most of all, Royall despaired at what she considered the hoodwinking of the "masses of the poor and ignorant."

Unable to succeed in stopping the Sunday mail, the missionary groups "had gone another way to work," cheating "simpletons" out of "vast sums of money" to bankroll their efforts, wrote Royall. To underscore her point, she included a profile on a "little chimney sweep boy," who "resolved to save all the money which was given" him over six months to buy a Bible and religious tracts.

Such an attention to the improverished ranks and their exploitation by political and religious factions endured throughout Royall's writings. Only a few years earlier in her first *Black Book*, she had described Washington as unique in its numbers of the "oppressed" and that it contained "more indigence and human distress" and was "more cursed with dissipation" than any other American city. *Paul Pry* never hesitated to point out whether the collections for charity ended up in the hands of those in need or in the coffers of the religious institutions. When a cholera epidemic hit the capital city in 1832, Anne turned on her fellow newspaper editors for their silence, "lest the report might injure the bank-men, who own property in the city." With Washington "choked with filth," she chastised the national leaders inhabiting the capital for allowing an unfinished canal project to fill with "dead cats, dogs, puppies, and we grieve to add, infants."

In the process, she kept a running column of encounters with the desperate and the defamed, including a graphic depiction of a homeless pregnant woman who lost her child at birth in a dirt-floor cellar. "Such another instance of barbarity to suffering humanity," Royall wrote, blasting the "hypocrites" who were more concerned with raising money to convert the heathens.

As a nascent movement for guilds and trade unions took form, including a Workingman's Party and newspaper in later years, Anne raised her concerns over the plight of those at the bottom heap of the early industrial revolution. "These unions will form an era in the history of the world," *Paul Pry* declared, calling on them to "burst the chain of ignorance and set us free from the monster money craft." At the same time, Royall issued a political admonition that was remarkably shrewd and prophetic: "Oppression on one side will beget resistance on the other, and the strongest party, which is beyond doubt the working class, will become tyrants and usurpers in their turn. Therefore the present tyrannical acts to subdue the workingmen and reduce them to slavery, will have no other effect than to engender strife and discontent, which must end in the destruction of one party or the other."

With a decade of subscription-gathering experience, Anne immediately set out to enroll readers for her newspaper. Sally picked up a White House subscription; Anne took to Congress. Her bookseller contacts in other cities served as sales agents. Subscriptions ranged in the hundreds, though the paper circulated widely. Ads filled out the side columns and back pages. At $2.50 a year, the four-page sheet touted a phrase first attributed to Samuel Johnson (and then to Thomas Jefferson) under its banner: "Education, the main pillar which sustains the temple of liberty." Royall assumed an editorial "we," even to the extent of referring to "our husband, a Revolutionary soldier," and presenting views from the perspective of "the editors."

The initial response to *Pry*'s admittedly slapdash efforts brought the expected kudos—and the predictable dish from other newspapers, most of whom found Royall's tenacity endearing, or downright annoying. Even her detractors, though, begrudgingly took her tabloid seriously, given the Washington-based correspondent's insider view of the workings of government. No one doubted her access to President Jackson.

The most garrulous welcome *Paul Pry* received came from Thomas Dowling, the young journalist who had been sent to pay Royall's fine at the "common scold" trial and who now edited the *Greenburg Political Observer* in Indiana. Dowling remained awestruck of the notorious author's "fearlessness of spirit," which he said made her remarkable, and noted her flaying of the "Church and State party" and the anti-Mason crowds. While Dowling differed with Anne on her Jackson politics, he declared he would never dissolve their friendship.

The *New York Commercial Advertiser*, which had battled Royall on the anti-Mason front, found the name quaint but the Pry reference to eavesdropping to be a little alarming. While the *Commercial Advertiser* considered her newspaper a "hazardous" undertaking, it had to admit the author's "numerous works" demonstrated her "powers of observation and description." In an interesting gesture of a truce, it noted that Royall had been "severe" on some people in the past, but it was only because she sought to expose "their true colors." Writing for the *New England Religious Weekly*, Quaker poet John Greenleaf Whittier expressed his anti-Jackson views with little reservation. He charged Anne of sundry "blackguard" publications, suggesting she had "forgotten her late conviction" as a common scold, and accused her of applying herself to "her old vocation." Greenleaf Whittier let loose the hounds: "The old hag" was simply printing a strong Jackson rag that contained "all the scum, billingsgate and filth extant."

Anne's response to Whittier highlighted her incredible skill to flip the mockery of her work back into the face of her detractors: "Wonder in what part of the Bible he found that," she wrote, gleefully publishing his own comments in *Paul Pry*. In stinging and often witty rebukes, she made a habit of including any negative comments about her writing, if only to reaffirm her place in the thick of the controversies.

Biographer Sarah Harvey Porter tracked down an anonymous poem dedicated to Anne and *Paul Pry* that captured much of the romantic sentiment of the age, as well as the expectations of her writing:

> *Me to inspire ye sacred nine,*
> *Rifle your treasures—clothe each line,*
> *Send me choice flowers to gem her crown,*

*And give my favorite fair renown.*
*No heroine more brave than she,*
*Nor toil no danger doth she flee;*
*Ever prepared to take the field,*
*Restless power therein to yield.*
*O, may Paul Pry with Samson's jaw*
*Your Pandemonium smite with awe;*
*And the Black Books give rogues their due—*
*Lend each a glass his crimes to view.*

"Stay not your hand," a reader cheered. "Cut up the nullifers—give it to them, Mrs. Pry," another wrote. A "spry young widower" wrote a fan letter that included a fable, which he begged her to print as a member of "the Pry family." She did.

The most pressing challenge for the country rested with the Second Bank of the United States, according to *Paul Pry* in 1832, which took on an issue that many other newspapers had abdicated out of self-interest. In fact, Anne had essentially broken with her old friend Mordecai Noah when she discovered his struggling *New York Enquirer* newspaper had accepted a $50,000 loan from the central bank in Philadelphia. The New Yorkers were hardly alone; Royall's newspaper colleagues in Washington, such as Gales at the *Daily National Intelligencer* and Green at the *United States Telegraph*, had also turned to the banking institution for help. Founded in 1816, the Second Bank of the United States played an oversized role in financial concerns, serving as the depository for federal funds and as the principal lender to commercial interests in numerous cities. Operated by an independent board of directors and led by Philadelphia businessman Nicholas Biddle, a close associate of Presbyterian leader Ezra Ely, the bank represented "the strikes of Hydra" to Royall.

"I paid little attention to the US Bank until my last tour," she wrote in her final *Black Book*, right after her trial, even though it had long been a Jackson concern. Her swing through the western states had overwhelmed her with the bank's power. Referring to the bank and the missionaries as "two hideous monsters," Anne began to construct a narrative of the central institution's powerful speculation, wealth, and labor, even as "thousands of people are now in want of common necessaries of life." The brave, independent, honest, and industrious people she had left years ago had been "swallowed up by this voracious monster." Laying the blame on the foreign stockholders, she called for taking the bank out of the hands of individuals and placing a ban on foreign involvement. Two years before she launched her newspaper, she had already ramped up her rhetoric in her *Black Books*.

In his analysis of Royall's journalistic role as a "Jackson woman," historian Jeffrey Bourdon found *Paul Pry* printed "something negative about the Bank, its foreign influence on America, and its hidden opposition to the interests of the masses of the people" in almost every issue until a vote on the issue took place in the summer of 1832. In a daring move, Anne boasted about her influence over the president, according to Bourdon, vowing that Jackson would never sign the bill to recharter because he would then "strip himself of those honors acquired by years of devotion to his country." "They know little of General Jackson," Royall wrote, dismissing his critics.

Warning her journalist friends in New York that her brutal whipping in Pittsburgh had been the result of her writings on the bank controversy and not because of any defamation, she challenged them to consider the "foul deal" if the bank won its recharter. "Ye who value liberty," she admonished, "crush the monster before it be too late."

In a brash move to test Jackson's resolve, Biddle and his allies

THE TRIALS OF A SCOLD

worked with Congress in the spring of 1832 to introduce a bill that would issue a new charter for the bank, four years in anticipation of its deadline. With the support of Jackson's presidential opponent, US senator Henry Clay, the ploy was essentially a campaign tactic to place the controversial issue into the public arena, forcing Jackson to either make good on his promise to crack down on the powerful bank or accede to Biddle's forces. Either way, Clay saw it as an easy win for his election.

According to Jackson biographer Sean Wilentz, the president's war over the bank emerged as a way of defending his "reputation and honor." Royall, unlike most newspapers, stood by Jackson's side.

More importantly, Bourdon raised the question of whether Jackson's meeting with "the fiery, female editor" had an effect on the president's "characterizations of the Bank's Board of Directors." Along with her unrelenting reporting, she had posted a list of 12 reasons why Congress and the president should reject a renewed charter; a House representative ended up using some of the list in his own speech on the floor.

Over the previous decade, one of Anne's pet phrases for the hypocrisy of religious extremists in many of her books drew from Matthew 23:33, in which Jesus refers to the teachers of the law and the Pharisees as a "generation of vipers" (KJV). A "set of vipers" in a provincial town persecutes a woman in *The Tennessean*; in her last Southern tour, she complained that a "den of vipers" of Presbyterians took over Dickenson College in North Carolina; a theological seminary in Georgia hatches vipers; recovering from her attack in Vermont, Royall's *Black Book* attributes poor treatment at her guesthouse to the presence of the vipers.

In a dramatic meeting at the White House, according to handwritten notes by a pro-bank committee member that were transcribed years

later, Jackson unleashed a torrent of biblical images—and threats—
that closely echoed Royall's refrain. "Gentlemen! I too have been a
close observer of the doings of the Bank of the United States. I have
had men watching you for a long time, and am convinced that you
have used the funds of the bank to speculate in the breadstuffs of the
country," Jackson was recorded as stating. "You are a den of vipers
and thieves. I have determined to rout you out, and by the Eternal,
(bringing his fist down on the table) I will rout you out!"

The *Washington Congressional Record* noted Anne's prominent seat
at the front of the debate on the Senate floor. Despite his disdain for
her fervent anti-bank and pro-Jackson leanings, Clay insisted she sit
by his side, which he acknowledged in his opening speech, citing "a
lady of great literary eminence" in the chambers. Anne nodded her
approval. Clay's act of ingratiation spoke more of her power than his,
at least in her self-obsessed perspective. A bitter debate ensued. The
bill passed easily in both the House and Senate. The great confrontation
knocked on the White House door, the recharter of the bank in hand.

Jackson held his ground as Royall had predicted. He issued what
historian Daniel Howe called the most important presidential veto in
American history on July 10, 1832. The veto "frankly and fearlessly"
met the "corrupting monster," Jackson told his friends, who invoked
his plan to slay the "hydra."

In full view of a populist constituency, Jackson, in his Presidential Message, ultimately objected to the bank's recharter on political
and moral grounds, sharing much of Anne's concern: "The rich
and powerful too often bend the acts of government to their selfish
purposes," he wrote, adding that when laws "make the rich richer
and the potent more powerful, the humble members of society—the
farmers, mechanics, and laborers" have a "right to complain of the
injustice of their Government."

Though more commentary than actual reportage, Anne's investigative cajoling foretold the role of muckrakers in affecting policy. As historian Doris Kearns Goodwin noted in her book *The Bully Pulpit: Theodore Roosevelt, William Howard Taft and the Golden Age of Journalism*, muckraking journalists "ushered in a new mode of investigative reporting that provided the necessary conditions to make a genuine bully pulpit of the American presidency."

Less than three months from her paper's launch, Anne and her team triumphantly announced a time out. *Paul Pry* couldn't resist from crowing: "Having silenced the anties [Anti-Masons], and brought Josey [Gales] and the bank men to bay, and scattered the missionaries forces, we stop to breathe." Anne went on to "indulge" her "brothers of the quill" and answer some of their questions about her paper. "For though we have been busy, we have never lost sight of them."

Anne delighted in her new role as a guardian of liberty with a printing press. When challenged by other newspapers that her stunt with Clay on the floor suggested she had secretly gone over to the other side and supported bank interests, she replied: "The United States Bank never had enough money to buy us up."

Adapting her pen portraits into a regular column, Royall essentially ensured a published roll call of congressional members and movers and shakers on the Washington scene over the next two and half decades. Any new arrivals appeared in *Paul Pry* or *The Huntress* with the attention of a society column, though framed through her cultural lens:

Hon. Aaron V. Brown is a new member from Tennessee. . . . Mr. Brown is perhaps under middle age, as he has quite a young appearance. He is a tall, stout, well built figure. His face is round, very full, and of the middling shade. His eye is a dark grey, vivid and searching. His countenance is open and manly, and his manners are dignified, though affable and pleasing. These Tennesseans, as we have always affirmed, have an untaught dignity and self possession in their demeanor, that no other people have, and in size and manly beauty will lose nothing in a comparison with our finest looking men of Maine.

Mrs. Reynolds is the lady of Capt. Reynolds, of the Marine Corps in this city, to which station he has been ordered not very long since. Our readers will recollect the fine soldierly man mentioned in our paper last fall. Since then Mrs. Reynolds has arrived, and takes up her residence in the city. She is a New York lady, of rare accomplishments, and will add much to the society of Washington. She has a youthful appearance, though married some years. Her figure is tall and slender, and of the most interesting symmetry. Her face is oval and very fair, with beautiful, delicate features, a square, high forehead, and a soft brow, with eyes of deep black, and her coal black hair forms a contrast to her fair complexion. Her countenance is animated and happy, but it is the genuine warmth and suavity of her elegant manners that captivates the beholder. This is the handsomest and best matched couple we ever met with.

This type of adulation stood in such contrast to Royall's more typical critiques that some newspapers accused her of using the pen portraits as a fundraising scheme. "The fulsome flattery bespattered" by the "old lady," claimed the *Georgetown (KY) Herald*, "is perfectly disgusting." Anne denied any payment, reveling in how her writing infuriated "bigots" who sought to "exercise" the "tyranny over the mind." She invited the editor of the *Herald* to Washington for his own sitting. He declined. On the other hand, the *Montgomery (AL) Journal* reminded its readers, "Mrs. Royall has a rare knack of castigating the enemy. If they think she has no power to hurt them, they deceive themselves, for she cuts deep as any of the Washington editors."

Making good on a promise she made at her disastrous encounter at the Baltimore theater ten years earlier, when her theater queries were dismissed outright by the producers, in 1833 Royall cajoled an acting company into doing a production of one of her plays, *The Cabinet, Or, Large Parties in Washington*. Appearing at the Masonic Hall in Washington, the three-act comedy headlined as a farce, though it drew a modest crowd. Showings for charity took place at other venues. To her bona fides as a novelist, travel writer, publisher, and muckraker, Anne could now add playwright.

The publication of Frances Trollope's *Domestic Manners of the Americans* in 1832 brought another level of vindication for the Washington newspaperwoman—as well as more attacks. English author Trollope's searing critique of the United States was met with widespread criticism, as would be imagined. Most reviewers accused Trollope, who drew from her notes taken during a four-year sojourn, of attempting "to slander a whole nation." In the face of widespread disapproval, Anne gave her a starred review in *Paul Pry*, ran an excerpt from an embarrassing account in the book of a religious camp revival, and praised Trollope for a "most able exposition of clerical tyranny over our women."

Inspired by Fanny Wright's travelogue, as well as her utopian community for former slaves in Tennessee, a disillusioned and financially strapped Trollope found little to appreciate in the United States, the Americans most of all. "I do not like them," she wrote, rather conclusively; "I do not like their principles; I do not like their manners, I do not like their opinions." When a merchant scheme she launched in Cincinnati failed, Trollope cut her losses and roamed across the Ohio River Valley and along the East Coast, where she met largely uncouth, disrespectful, and lawless inhabitants—and their "frightful manner of cleaning the teeth afterward with a pocket knife." Royall laughed at Trollope's uncomfortable experiences, especially among tobacco-chewing women in the South. She found her insight into the role of women, however, especially within the confines of the religious orthodoxy of the Presbyterians and at Protestant revivals, to be particularly damning.

Trollope ranked the influence of the Protestant clergy nearly at the same level as that of Inquisition-era Spanish Catholic priests, noting that the strict oversight of both institutions ensured that women rarely appeared in public—or at best, only when they were en route to a religious meeting. "Were it not for the churches, indeed, I think there might be a general bonfire of best bonnets," Trollope joked. The separation of the sexes stunned her. "All the enjoyments of men are found in the absence of women." Women never attended the theater or took part in public celebrations. Conversely, the cloistered nature of their relationship to the church and priest, Trollope wrote, provided American women with a degree of importance that they defiantly sought to preserve. "I never saw, or read, of any country where religion had so strong a hold upon the women."

Like the legendary Wright, who had notoriously said Christ's fishers of men had become "fishers of women," Trollope echoed the sexual predatory nature among religious leaders that Royall had noted in her own travels: "Many of these wretched creatures were beautiful young females. The preachers moved about among them, at once exciting and soothing their agonies. I heard the muttered 'Sister! Dear sister!' I saw the insidious lips approach the cheeks of the unhappy girls; I heard the murmured confessions of the poor victims, and I watched their tormentors, breathing into their ears consolations that tinged the pale cheek with red."

Trollope did find one point of light in the United States for women, which actually touched on Royall's new profession. Unlike the English, American women had the right to observe Congress from designated galleries.

While the writing and life experiences of Wright, Trollope, and Royall are inexorably connected, especially in their roles as the main female social critics of the "church and state" apparatus, Anne wrote how she differed from the "free inquirers." They shared her objective to "expose the hypocrisy and impositions of the clergy in general," she noted, but she hesitated to include herself on their "lists of able writers" full of "talent and learning." The self-conscious "backwoods" editor did not simply defer for a lack of education; she also objected to the snobbery and intolerance in the women who refused to consider the opinions of others who believed differently. Royall loved to engage, spar, and debate ideas, freely and often relentlessly, rather than liquidate her opponents without a matching word. "Opinion injures no one," Royall wrote, "actions alone injure mankind." Somehow attempting to compliment but distance herself from Wright and Trollope, Anne clearly felt a need to stake out her belief that freedom of speech mattered above all else. "As for our hating Priests," Royall attempted to explain, most likely convincing few, "we hate nothing but deception and hypocrisy." While she never held back an inch on her own vituperative and belittling attacks on the clergy—and anyone who disagreed with her, for that matter—she took greater pleasure in the clash of ideas in the public arena than a snide barb from afar. To her credit, she published articles from religious newspapers, prompting her subscribers to decide for themselves. Letters from readers abounded, including those who asked her to intervene on obscure church matters, indicating a religious readership who somehow abided Royall's unceasing castigations.

The columns of her newspapers, Anne wrote, "will be open to any and every party or sect, who may consider themselves aggrieved, provided their appeals are decorous and respectful." In a rather remarkable departure from other newspapers, which still toed the party line or the interests of its financial backers, she sought to distinguish hers as a "public press" where the pages served as forums for ideas, as the "bona fide property of every citizen." In the larger context, her station in Washington allowed her to serve as a safeguard for the nation, a watchdog over the Constitution itself, in a city of "pollution and infamy" on every street.

In contrast to Wright, who as a towering lecturer addressed the minions below her in the great halls of the cities, and Trollope, who wielded her literary prowess from a long distance, Royall thrived in the center ring of public debate and raucous controversy, using her words like an aging and puckish street brawler—albeit a "decorous" one. "Our paper is small, the weather is cold, the times are hard, our fire is low, our candle is dull," Anne wrote cheerfully in an editorial. "But we will send over to our neighbor for a little more cayenne."

Beyond their writings, Wright and Trollope asserted a brash counterpoint to the rules of domesticity that also defined Royall's own experience and galvanized her role as an independent editor and publisher. That both women traveled with unmarried companions drew wide scorn as "singularly unladylike." On her previous Southern tour, Anne had encountered a similar moment of disparagement as a solitary woman traveler, which reinforced her determination to not only challenge the boundaries of so-called true womanhood but to shatter them. "Have you no man with you?" asked the wife of the president at the University of North Carolina in Chapel Hill. What did she mean by asking the question at all? Anne asked. "I always have a bad opinion of women, when I find them suspicious of their own sex."

She drew out the distinction: "What did I want with men? I was no missionary; they have men."

Like Trollope, Royall largely placed the blame of the entrenched religious hierarchy on female obeisance, and often took her most brutal censure for such stands. "A friend, now present member of Congress, says, 'Mrs. R, the people say they don't care how much you lash the males, if you would let the FEMALES alone,'" she wrote, dismissing the overture as the whine of a henpecked husband "led by the nose" by his wife. "You ought to let your own sex alone," another demanded. Anne fired back: "My own sex have brought my country to the brink of ruin, by supporting a legion of blue-skin priests. I disown my sex. I will attack the enemies of my country, come in what shape they may— whether in the shape of angels or serpents." She held out a chance of recourse: "When women cease to gad after priests, I will let them alone, and not before. It is understood I do not mean respectable women."

To be sure, Anne called out this double standard: "Were I a man, this fallacious argument ought to have no weight." She challenged those who preferred to "sacrifice truth to falsehood, virtue to vice," and reminded her readers that her role was to root out corruption. "Nor is any history valuable but in proportion to the integrity with which it is written." Royall viewed her criticism of women as a way of not only "rescuing them from the obscurity of history" but also prompting them to challenge their assigned places.

She did not want to be misunderstood, though. "Is it not to woman we owe our civilization?" she asked. "What would the world be without women—a mere herd of savages." Yet for Royall, while women had always served in advancing civilization, their recent downfall had come at the hands of the Christian "missionaries" who had deprived them of education and stripped their influence from "men of sense and taste." Declaring that all women—not just the "distinguished females,

queens, empresses"—are "like men, born free, and have equal
rights," Anne asserted a higher standard of actions "of females in all
ages" as the basis for understanding history.

In *Paul Pry*, Royall did not relent from her reproach of women from
this clergy-bound angle. She chastised the charity collections of a once
"amiable" Lutheran women's group, suggesting that they were latest
"victims of priestcraft." She saw it as a sign of darker times. "If ever
the liberty of America is overturned," she told her readers, "it will
be the work of women and priests." The courageous men of 1776, she
concluded, had shriveled up into "poor henpecked creatures," powerless in the face of such money schemes.

Years later, Anne praised the women in Washington who frequented the theater and insisted on attending the debates in Congress
despite a newspaper's call for females to "stay at home, wash, cook
and mend their husband's clothes." Such a slight was an affront to the
rights of women, she noted. She quipped that women had a "hard time
of it in this world," at the same time telling her male readers such concern was "no business" of theirs. "This is a free country."

The question over slavery, however, divided the three women.
Wright rose to prominence as an abolitionist; Trollope excoriated
American hypocrisy over the issue. "We do not oppose abolition,"
Royall wrote repeatedly in her newspapers; "we oppose the use that
is made of it—being on a repetition of the Sunday mail plan." The
overriding obsession with the "Church and State" conspiracy punc-
tuated every single article in *Paul Pry* and its eventual refounding as
*The Huntress*, not once fading in Anne's nearly 25 years in newspapers. She envisioned herself as the lonely bulwark against the "plot
of the Church and State party" in the guise of abolition, "insidiously
brought about by their untiring, unceasing endeavoring to shut out
knowledge from the present generation." While Royall openly

published excerpts and advertisements from antislavery newspapers, including a series of articles by the *National Era* and the more rebellious *Appeal*, she increased the pitch of her alarm as the cause of abolition grew. Under the headline "Fanaticism—Abolition—Church and State," she called on her readers to confront the "deadly blow aimed" at liberty and defend the civil and religious rights of all. Over the years, she singled out abolitionist leaders like William Lloyd Garrison and Wendell Phillips as incendiary religious agitators seeking to spark a violent uprising; she criticized the hypocrisy of British abolitionists who spoke about slavery on American soil while their own country had overrun the rights of the people of India with a "vengeance."

"The poor abolitionists are not the prime movers of these appalling principles," she wrote in an editorial, addressing the issue of prohibiting slavery in western territories. "There are most of them morally honest, even scrupulously so. They are kind neighbors and charitable on many occasions. But they have been erroneously educated." The problem with the abolitionist movement driven by the Christian church, she concluded, resided with their belief that "their religion is the only true religion on earth."

Anne's most pointed condemnation fell on religious reformers—especially women—whom she deemed as insincere "notoriety seekers," including the growing ranks of "convention spouters" and "fiction writers." She lambasted the hypocrisy of Harriet Beecher Stowe, the daughter of Lyman Beecher, the Presbyterian who had battled Royall on Sunday mail delivery and the sabbatarian movement years earlier. Stowe's best-selling novel *Uncle Tom's Cabin* had swept the nation. Reprinting the coroner's report of an African American woman who had recently died in Washington from starvation, Anne juxtaposed it with Beecher's novel: "How little do 'Uncle Tom's' sympathizers know or care about the suffering that exists among their own colored dupes in all of our principal cities."

In this respect, Anne's decades of writing left behind a trail of tirades, especially on the "Church and State" issue that many interpreted as fanatical, if not downright delusional. At the same time, no other writer of her time held so dearly to the Constitution as her religious foes did to their Bible; as the defender of eighteenth-century Enlightenment in the age of the Second Great Awakening of the nineteenth century, Royall's dissenting voice, if anything, kept the light of skeptics flickering during the darkness of the contemporaneous religious sweep.

To be sure, Anne excelled in the art of the rant, often writing in an effusive style that teetered between biting sarcasm and a sort of unhinged fury. When officials failed to provide fireworks for the Fourth of July celebrations in Washington one year, *Paul Pry* hailed it as a "plot to make this place the seat of MONARCHY." At the end of one of her frequent diatribes on the "missionaries," pushing the bounds of coherence, she regained herself and simply concluded with a wink to her own past: they are a public nuisance.

In an era of the partisan press, however, Royall's outrageousness often paled compared to the open threats of violence issued by many of her fellow newspaper colleagues. *Paul Pry* constantly reprinted articles from other journals, detailing the latest "abominable plot" of the "Church and State," perhaps as a way of disputing any aspersions and showing the widespread agreement of such a sentiment, at least from her side of the political aisle. For example, Anne reprinted an article from the *Niles' Weekly Register*, a leading news weekly in Baltimore that was considered a voice of moderation, that showcased the editorial of another newspaper, the *Microscope* (Albany, NY). Examining the "Church and State" forces aligning with the Anti-Masonic Party in the upcoming 1832 election, the *Microscope* called on readers to resist the movement at all costs. "The people in these United States," the paper admonished, "cannot be blinded by these rotten-hearted pretenders, until the noose is fairly placed upon their necks. . . ."

On the heels of the 1836 election, Royall announced the transformation of *Paul Pry* into a newspaper called *The Huntress*. With the increasing difficulty of maintaining subscribers, especially those reliant on the contentious postal service, she hoped a facelift would provide a better chance at survival. *Paul Pry* didn't go down in vain, she told her readers. In the "van of the editorial corps, attacking the enemies of the country in their strongholds," her newspaper had been the first to root out "traitors in the camp" and corruption at the post office, challenge fraudulent Indian land schemes in the West, and expose the "perfidy of the southern Jackson men in selling the country to Mr. Van Buren and his political intriguers to conceal those frauds." *Paul Pry* had put an end to "pious rogues" who had manipulated corporate debts from Congress. "The editress has only to say that if the people will do their duty to themselves as faithfully as has been done by them, all will yet be well. But let no man sleep at his post. Remember, the office holders are desperate, wakeful and urgent."

In an era dominated by the Jackson presidency and persona, Royall remained a persistent gadfly on government spending, patronage, and any hint of corruption. The post office became one of her main targets. One criticized postal worker showed up with a pistol at the newspaper, outraged by one of her critiques over the department's poor services; another government employee, angered by her investigations into spending improprieties, was indicted for "taking summary satisfaction on the fair lady" in a drunken fury at her home. She commended Congress for passing a bill that relieved debtors from prison. In the face of the devastating consequences of Jackson's

Indian Removal Act, Royall would paradoxically side with Jackson in the removal of the Cherokee from Georgia, in support of westward expansion, while filing numerous stories over the years on land fraud schemes and exploitation of Native Americans. "We understand the removal of the emigrant Creeks has been let to the lowest bidder," she wrote. The death rate among Creeks, "urged forward by white savages," was unacceptable. "What is our country coming to?"

An editorial in 1837, which lamented the "inhuman actions of our people" toward Cherokee leader John Ross and his nation, echoed her first letters from Alabama in 1818, when she described riding through an abandoned Cherokee village on horseback. Anne noted, "There could not exist a greater evidence of unbounded avarice and ambition which distinguished the Christian world." Two decades later, she accused the government of "shameful" treatment of the Cherokee, calling it a "barbarous, astounding and unjust" case of cruelty.

Her support of Jackson's showdown with Vice President John Calhoun and his nullification advocates in South Carolina in 1832, which erupted from disputes over federal tariff issues and state sovereignty in a chilling forewarning of the Civil War, stemmed more from Royall's prevailing commitment to the "union" over any states' rights policies she had previously supported. "While we advocate equal rights," *Paul Pry* noted, holding both South Carolina and merchants accountable, "we shrink from the idea of treason and the civil war of the nullifier, as much as we do from the manufacturing monopolist who from a selfish desire of individual wealth would see the United States sunk ten thousand fathoms under water, provided he could heap up money."

Years later, committed to the forging of a national identity as a process of uniting the country, Royall openly advocated for the annexation of Texas and hailed the expansion to the western territories with the same fervent belief in the "glorious cause" of liberty brought by her husband's Revolution. In a stunning juxtaposition of history, she praised the American war in Mexico in 1846 as liberating the "peaceable natives" there from the monarchy of Spain. With no hint of irony at her country's own tragic experience with natives, Royall framed the American invasion as "vengeance" for the slaughtering of millions of "innocent, unresisting natives in cold blood."

Sensitive over the criticism she took for naming her newspaper *Paul Pry*, Anne went on the offensive with *The Huntress*, a moniker that had been associated with the legendary Anne Bailey, her first pen portrait in the Appalachian Mountains. "The name is not inappropriate, as we have often followed the chase in our young days," she noted. "But the novelty and smoothness of the name, and its associations with our dear western rivers, woods and scenery, will no doubt find for the *Huntress* a hospitable reception."

In an odd aside, Royall casually announced she planned to move the newspaper to the Mississippi Valley. Whether she had reached a level of capital fatigue or financial struggle, especially during the economic crisis and recession of the Panic of 1837, she never alluded to her motives; nor did she ever mention the move away from Washington again. Nonetheless, as she noted in *The Huntress*, the people of Michigan passed a notable constitution that didn't require a religious test: "The (Mississippi) Valley is now the only asylum for freedom in the true sense of the word."

*The Huntress* prowled Washington, DC, until 1854. Every now and then it ran requests for "provisions and wood." The paper engaged in every election, almost vehemently, while denying party affiliation. Anne couldn't resist taking one last swipe at Jackson when Van Buren took the presidency: "One was always pained by the great numbers of 'I's' in Gen. Jackson's written speeches."

*The Huntress*, Anne declared, had never veered from its original stand: "On the side of the people." While the new version of the paper included a front-page fiction story, typically a reprint of an adventure or romance, *The Huntress* continued its weekly exposés on "corruption, hypocrisy and usurpation" without rest.

"Mrs. Royall owes an apology to her friends for the very limited editorial matter," ran a classic note in the newspaper. "Having important business to attend to in Congress (at least to her it is so), Mrs. R will have to curtail her editorial duties during the rest of the residue of the (Congressional) session, to look after those saucy *wights* [an archaic word for "creature"], the members."

Royall returned to the national debate when she launched a series of attacks on the anti-immigrant and "Native American" societies among the East Coast cities and elsewhere, charging that they acted as fronts for Protestant groups seeking to whip up hysteria for their own political gain. "Our country is an asylum for foreigners, and long may it be so!" she wrote. Her papers filled with letters from both sides, including a statement from a hundred signers at the Native American Society in New York who took Royall to task for associating their group with the "church and state party." Deconstructing every paragraph of the letter, Royall reaffirmed her point on their bias, noting the role of the Presbyterian Church; mocked their fear-mongering reference to immigrants as the "refuse of Europe"; and concluded that the main signer was a "dupe or a tool." Newspapers in Louisiana ran open debates over her accusations that the Native American Association was essentially conducting a witch hunt against Catholics "under the sham name of foreigners." A New Orleans Native American newspaper responded that Royall's assumptions emanated from a "disordered imagination, of an intellect weakened by the increasing years of a poor old woman," and chastised the *Louisiana Advertiser* for reprinting her column. "Well, what of it?" Anne quipped in

THE TRIALS OF A SCOLD

reply. If anyone ever had doubts on the religious attacks on freedom of press, she continued, the association's letter served as proof. Only "knaves and tyrants, and would-be tyrants" feared the press.

The deadly "church and state" riots in Philadelphia in 1844 underscored Royall's worries. In one of the bloodiest demonstrations of the antebellum period, anti-immigrant forces attacked and torched Catholic churches in an Irish neighborhood. Anne couldn't resist the temptation to place the blame on her old nemesis Ely. Whether or not he had "any agency in the lawless destruction," her paper wrote, "he did not prevent it."

In an increasingly alarmed voice, Royall obsessed over a brewing civil war in the country. The disunion of her beloved nation always tried the elder patriot's patience. The anti-immigrant riots, "under the pretence of fighting battles of the lord," mirrored the sectional divide between the industrial North and the nullifiers in the South. While an expansionist at heart, Anne wondered aloud if the nation had become too big geographically to contain all its aspirations under one flag. Beyond regional conflicts, she also raised the question over the unacceptable disparity between the rich and poor, especially during the depression of the late 1830s. "If it be happiness for one portion of the people—and no inconsiderable portion—to do all the labor and yet suffer for the necessaries of life, and in many cases, after laboring hard a lifetime, perish of want in our streets or in the poorhouse (the same thing), while another portion lives idle, dresses gay, visits, has splendid houses and furniture, fine carriages and every luxury for the table that money can buy," Royall warned, then the prospect for America's future looked dim.

"There is nothing more unpleasant to us than political controversy—the very sight of a political dispute gives us a fever," Royall wrote in a Saturday edition of her newspaper in the 1840s.

Nevertheless, at her age, "never while we wield a pen will we suffer the rights of the people or the liberty of the press to be trampled."

In 1845, *The Huntress* announced that Anne had collapsed from typhus, and her fate looked dire. Forever cordial, Joseph Gales at the *Daily National Intelligencer* expressed concern for his fellow publisher and printed a "touching appeal" for her support: "Those who feel an interest in the lonely and suffering condition of the widow, who for many years has held weekly intercourse with citizens of Washington of the first standing and respectability," the time had come to provide their "Christian ministering" for her comfort.

Royall recovered in full force, returning to the halls of Congress on a weekly basis. Three years later, a congressional bill made revisions to the statute of limitations on pension requests, ending a 24-year campaign by the Revolutionary War veteran's wife; nearly 80 years old, Anne was finally granted a lifetime annuity for her husband's service in the American Revolution. The Roane family, which had stripped Anne's inheritance, successfully won part of the claim. After paying off her debts and upgrading the paper's type, she purchased dresses for herself and Sally Stack with the remaining few dollars.

Despite her diminishing newspaper, Royall's presence still commanded an aura of deference from other journalists. By 1851, she had outlasted many of the correspondents who had covered her trial. "Among the notices of the press," announced an upstart publication in Boston, *Carpet-Bag*, it was "most honored" by being recognized by the "amiable editor" Royall in Washington. Traveling in Mexico in the late 1840s, author Corydon Donnavan founded the *El Republicano* newspaper in that nation's capital to be modeled on *The Huntress*.

Unable to keep a grudge, she had noted her delight in meeting a frail Judge Cranch at a groundbreaking ceremony for the Smithsonian Institution.

Still seeking to shine a light on the treatment of the poor, Anne published a series of articles in 1852, "The Responsibilities of Christians in the United States in Regard to the Suffering Classes," that drew attention to part of the country where "poorhouses are fast growing more populous."

In the spring of 1854, New York suffrage leader Susan B. Anthony paid a surprise visit to Anne at her home. She found the 85-year-old editor tutoring two little boys in Greek and Latin, as well as geometry. As Royall wrote her editorial for the week in the dim light of a lamp, Anthony looked around in a combination of awe and disgust, overwhelmed by the dilapidated confines. The house reminded her of a country barn, as the editor and her wards surrounded themselves with a huge black Newfoundland dog and a litter of kittens.

"What a wonderful woman you are," Anthony told Royall, who acknowledged the praise. She presented the suffrage leader with a gift of some of her older books.

Nine years old at the time of Anne's witch trial, in which the "voice of woman" had been held up as a dangerous and scandalous weapon, Anthony returned to her guesthouse that night and wrote about her visit with the famous author. She referred to Anne as "the living curiosity of Washington." But the Quaker-educated Anthony, on the verge of her own national prominence, could not shake the requirements of domesticity from her views. The pioneering muckraker Royall, in her mind, was the "most filthy specimen of humanity I ever beheld; her fingers looked like bird claws, in color and attennuity, they shone as if glazed." Still 15 years from launching her own weekly newspaper, Anthony apparently did not realize that an ailing Royall had worked the printing press that day.

Four months later, nearly 25 years to the day that Anne faced her conviction as a common scold in Washington's circuit court, a diminutive last issue of *The Huntress* rolled from the printing press. With fresh type, the paper was more readable than it had been in years. A page and a half of ads filled the back, including a long tribute to "Dr. Morse's Invigorating Elixir or Cordial." The text recommended the elixir as a cure for "the diseased, debilitated and shattered nervous system" and hailed it "the medicinal wonder of the nineteenth century."

In a small article, Royall also thanked a "ministering angel" for helping her get a drink at the Capitol fountain during a fainting spell. The front page featured a speech on the House floor over the controversy of the day—slavery in the territories of Nebraska and Kansas. Royall joked that Congress kept at it, "ding, dong—to provoke a civil war." Feisty as ever, she included a few pen portraits of new members of Congress, including the Honorable N. G. Taylor from Tennessee. "We cannot say whether Mr. T. is tall or short, for he would not get up."

In a final message addressed to Congress, Anne declared her "trust in heaven for three things." First, despite the fact that she and Sally possessed 31 cents and failed to pay their rent for the first time since she had arrived in the city three decades earlier, Royall appreciated having the means to publish the newspaper. Second, she expressed hope that Washington would escape its latest scourge of cholera. And finally, "our third prayer is that the Union of these States may be eternal."

"Perhaps we may never publish another paper," Anne wrote. "Life is uncertain, though we are at present writing in perfect health."

Less than three months later, Anne Royall died at her home. With the same fate of the destitute and forgotten souls she had chronicled in her writing, Anne Royall was buried by charity workers in an unmarked grave at the congressional cemetery.

# EPILOGUE

## The Trial of Public Opinion

*I shall be told that historians confine themselves to great females—distinguished females, queens, empresses, dutchesses; ladies, and princesses, and sometimes they condescend to mention the wife of an officer, and now and then an actress, but to descend so low as to notice Common women, it was out of the question. I am not so; I contend that all women are like men, born free, and have equal rights, and "we are the most enlightened nation on earth."*

—ANNE ROYALL, *MRS. ROYALL'S PENNSYLVANIA*

In the fall of 1951, a bewildered Shirley Graham Du Bois, the wife of renowned African American author and social critic W. E. B. Du Bois, wrote a letter to her friend Joseph Goldstein at the *Yale Law Journal*. In the wake of the United States' criminal case against her husband, who was indicted for failing to register his Peace Information Center as a foreign agent, Graham Du Bois felt like her latest literary work had been a casualty of the anticommunist McCarthy forces. "A trial of public opinion" was afoot, Graham Du Bois warned, led by the insidious American Business Consultants behind the *Red Channels*, the "bible of the black list" of radical authors, artists, and entertainers whose so-called communist affiliations and sympathies were deemed unfit for national broadcast or publication.

"Anne Royall made her way from frontier obscurity to places unheard of for a 'female' in her day, yet now has no place at all in American literary history," stated Graham Du Bois, who claimed that appearing on the *Red Channels* blacklist had resulted in the removal of her books from libraries, plummeting sales, and now the strange rejection by all publishers of her latest novel on Anne Royall. "Six months ago I completed my first novel," she wrote, noting the enthusiasm of her literary agents and the fact that no publisher had actually criticized the writing in the manuscript. But no one would touch the Anne Royall novel now.

Graham Du Bois had learned about Royall from literary critic Van Wyck Brooks, who had included her in his works on the history of American writing. "The dynamic personality of this early nineteenth century woman stirs the imagination," Graham Du Bois wrote in her successful application for a prestigious Guggenheim fellowship. As one of only two African Americans to be recognized by the foundation in 1948, Graham Du Bois planned to write about Royall's "contribution to the American mind."

She had already incorporated a slice of Anne's life into her last book, *There Once Was a Slave*, a young adult biography of abolitionist Frederick Douglass. As the subversive editor of a newspaper in Washington, DC, the fictionalized Royall trains a young woman who serves the abolitionist cause.

"Does she know I'm a criminal—a convicted criminal?" the mysterious and impish Royall character asks another abolitionist.

"You tell her, Mrs. Royall!" the man responds.

" 'Tis very sad.' There was mockery in her voice. 'A "common scold"—that was the finding of the jury. In England they would have ducked me in a pond; but here there was only the Potomac, and the honored judge deemed that might not be right—the waters would be contaminated. So they let me go.' They were in the house now and she was setting out china cups. 'You know,' she frowned slightly, 'the thing I really objected to was the word "common." This I did not like.'"

In Graham Du Bois's rejected manuscript on Royall, *The Woman in the Case*, which the author had also used as part of her PhD requirements at New York University, Anne takes part in another major trial, though not her "common scold" tribunal. Graham Du Bois's highly fictionalized account turned Royall into a passionate backwoods dreamer who meets the treasonous Aaron Burr in 1806, when he is brought to William Royall's Peters Mountain plantation after a horse accident. As he traveled toward the boundary of the Louisiana Purchase, beyond which he planned to organize and lead an insurrection against the Spanish Crown in Mexico, Burr falls in love with the young Anne, a curious beauty who still speaks in a mountain dialect. Perhaps to cushion the dynamics of the affair, William Royall is depicted as a feeble old eccentric from the Revolution, nearly 40 years older than the young Anne.

When associates finally reveal Burr's conspiracy, taking him back to Richmond for his historic trial for treason, a love-struck Anne saddles up a horse and secretly joins Burr at a remote farm, where he is being held. Their dangerous love affair mirrors Burr's high-stakes trial. The audacious former vice president, whose fatal duel with Alexander Hamilton ensured his place in history, discusses his thinly veiled plans to launch a war with Spain and establish an independent western country, with New Orleans as its capital.

In a strange twist of history, General William Eaton, who testified at Royall's trial in real life, served as the first witness in Burr's fictitious trial. In Graham Du Bois's novel, Anne huddles on the sidelines of the courtroom, dressed in men's clothing, her hair cut to a short bob. Despite the intense scrutiny of the press, including Washington

Irving's roving eyes, Burr and Anne steal away in the evenings, dodging guards, as a last resort for love.

Anne knew that she was overstaying her time. But each day overflowed into the next until she scarcely marked their passage. The rose-entwined cottage in its garden was sent down from heaven just for her and Aaron. They never approached each other in town. Outside the garden these two remained utter strangers—except for an occasional glance neither could control. Burr left her at dawn every morning and never returned until after dark. The nights were all their own. They walked beside the river and swam in its warm waters. They sat on the porch watching the stars reflected in the water. They stretched out on the grass and melted into the sweet, throbbing earth. Their passion flowed into ever deepening and widening channels. As prospects grew for a speedy ending of the trial they dared to look into the future.

Despite President Thomas Jefferson's insistence for a conviction, the jury found Burr not guilty. Anne's own future trial, as Graham Du Bois shows, has just begun. While Burr would eventually sail off to England, albeit in disgrace, Anne returns to a dying husband she has betrayed and then deals with a protracted legal battle of her own that will burden the rest of her life. The cost of pursuing one's love and passions, ultimately, is not only steep; it also forces one to abandon one life for another.

Matt [Anne's attorney] recognized the name of the family law firm. His eye quickly picked up certain legal phrases as he scanned the pages. ". . . certain evidence before us of a grave nature that the honored name of William Royall has been sullied." Matt's jaw stiffened. "It becomes imperative the Major William Royall protect the honored name of his family . . . the woman who now clothes herself in that name lacking both in moral rectitude and loyalty to her country."

As a radical woman writer of color in this troubling period of persecution in the 1950s, Graham Du Bois creates a somewhat daring and romantic portrait of Royall as a renegade, whose betrayal of her husband is considered a betrayal of her nation in the eyes of the moralists. In 1951, the period in which she struggled with Anne Royall's narrative, the 54-year-old author actually married the 83-year-old W. E. B. Du Bois; within a decade, they would seek citizenship in Ghana. She went through a half dozen drafts of the Anne Royall novel, unable to let it wither from rejection.

While caught up in the machinery of her times, Graham Du Bois's Royall does not appear as an unwitting victim to older men or a moralistic society, but as a bold, passionate, and defiant young woman, prepared to disobey societal mores to pursue some higher purpose. As a cross-dresser, Anne leaves the "cult of womanhood" in tatters. Just as Royall never denied her premarital cohabitation with William in her actual trial over his will, Graham Du Bois places the young Anne among early nineteenth-century feminists who saw "free love" as a more nuanced act of "spiritual affinity": as a right to freely choose a partner based on love and commitment, beyond social or economic obligations, and not have it seen as an act of promiscuity.

Anne emerges as a singular icon in Graham Du Bois's novel—at once restless, rebellious and with an insatiable desire to thrive, unrestrained, naïve and yet aware of the consequences, and ultimately undefeatable. While Royall's historical use of the word "redneck" referred to the bloody legacy of the Presbyterians—and introduced the term in American letters—it was Du Bois who ironically first explored the cultural dynamics of Royall's Appalachian background in her character; more a de facto feminist from the backwoods than a pioneering "redneck" feminist, her Royall character is a young woman who would scoff at the very terms of feminist independence that she embodies.

For the first time since she wrote of the fictional Anne's flashbacks to her youth, Graham Du Bois provides Royall with a persona outside of the "old hag" that dominated her character in the media, humanizing her in the process.

When another politician reveals her affair, Anne runs away and leaves Burr to his destiny, while returning to a life she has irretrievably altered.

"Ah, madam," Burr tells Royall in the novel, "you'll write your story yet."

Anne Royall wrote her story, indeed, though her "voice of woman" somehow got drowned out in the din of the controversy it inspired.

Despite Anne's prodigious output—she had few contemporary rivals among women writers—her story remains paradoxically one of the most unfamiliar in the nation. Ironically, her place in history has not been crafted by her own prolific pen but by the largely scolding interpretations of others. The primary focus on Royall's travails as a "beggar, blackmailer and common scold," as the *New York Times* noted in 1909, in the first century after her death, overshadowed any consideration of how her trailblazing literary path through the ruts and back warrens of the early nineteenth century might have opened a thoroughfare for subsequent generations of writers, both male and female.

In the trial of public opinion, as Graham Du Bois noted, some of the most important historical lessons tend to get lost in the cycles of controversy. The value of pioneering endeavors, however factual and innovative and bold, often wanes in the light of ensuing and more compelling work, until it no longer exists. While Royall defied convention as a groundbreaking traveler, writer, muckraker, and agitator, the subsequent marginalization of her erratic but compelling story has made it unthinkable that critics would consider her impact on other writers and agitators who broke through the barriers of their own periods; that the frontier masterpieces of humor and hypocrisy-stripping social commentary by Mark Twain were preceded a generation earlier by Royall's satirical travel books along the same waterways; that a host of remarkable women editors at the vanguard of journalism in the mid-nineteenth century, like Margaret Fuller at the *Dial* and Mary Ann Shadd of the African American *Provincial Freeman*, came a decade after Royall's autodidactic *Paul Pry* and *The Huntress* needled the political elite in Washington; that the investigative reporting of *New York World* journalist Nellie Bly on her sojourn in the insane asylums took place half a century after Royall's relentless examinations of the prisons, hospitals, and mental wards across the country; that the very birth of reform-minded muckraking journalism in Ida Tarbell's brilliant *McClure's Magazine* stories, which exposed the brutal tactics and monopolization of the industry by John D. Rockefeller and Standard Oil, appeared 75 years after Royall's splenetic newspaper crusade against the unfair financing policies of the United States Bank.

The main obituary for Anne Royall propagated more urban legends and falsehoods than the worst yellow journalism rag. "This eccentric woman whose death we noticed yesterday was aged ninety-two years," began the *Washington Evening Star* on October 3, 1854, getting her age and most of her life story incorrect.

Somehow in the process of her fading, Royall also lost her voice. She became a sour old unsmiling shrew. A witch.

The recognition of her wit as much as her wrath—the latter making Washington "bow down in fear," as the *Washington Post* wrote after her death—remains the most telling oversight of her story. The prominent political and religious leaders of the time, enmeshed in their intrigues, didn't simply object to Anne's writing; they couldn't handle her hilarious derision at their expense, as if she had cast a spell on them. The modern-day equivalent of "ducking," Royall was simply to reduce her witty legacy to the tediousness of a humorless, eccentric "old hag."

The disparaging of Royall's age, as well, beyond the abuse of her gender, often stood out as the main aversion to her prolific work and cemented her witch-like persona. In a sarcastic column in *The Huntress*, she mocked the belittling stigma of the "old wives' tale" epithet as she traipsed the halls of Congress. She referred to it as the "old wives' trot," a storytelling effort begot from labor and persistence, not superstition.

When the *New Yorker* mocked the demise of *Paul Pry* in 1836, calling Anne a "wandering piper," it captured the severance of an aged author from the accepted confines of womanhood with a single line: "We can hardly afford to coin a feminine appellative for the dame."

Royall, of course, has not been alone in her displacement in history—or the denial of her "wicked" sense of humor. "Obituaries that mostly stressed her satirical gifts missed the main point," *New York Times* columnist Paul Krugman wrote about the death of bestselling journalist Molly Ivins in 2007, in a tribute that could have easily been applied to Royall. "Her satire was only the means to an end: holding the powerful accountable."

For Ivins, whose nationally syndicated columns and popular books skewered the shortcomings of policymakers and the collusion of corporate money and interests in politics, there were two kinds of humor: "One kind that makes us chuckle about our foibles and our shared humanity—like what Garrison Keillor does. The other kind holds people up to public contempt and ridicule—that's what I do. Satire is traditionally the weapon of the powerless against the powerful. I only aim at the powerful. When satire is aimed at the powerless, it is not only cruel—it's vulgar."

While Anne excelled in such humor against the powerful, her tenuous platform and ultimate powerlessness made her a casualty of cruelty by subsequent writers and historians.

Only a few years after Royall's death in 1854, a catalogue advertising her books could have served as testimony for the Engine House plaintiffs in her "common scold" trial: "This Amazon would have been more appropriately employed as a fishmonger in Billingsgate Market, or a Meg Merrilies heading a gang of Gypsy Smugglers, than the author of books or editing a newspaper. She was the terror of every member of Congress while she resided at Washington."

As the nation shifted toward the impending disunion that Royall had cautioned against for years, the disappearance—or even disappearing—of Royall began soon after her death. Her fellow pioneering "editress" Sarah Josepha Hale, whose "respectable" magazine *Godey's Lady's Book* ran concurrent with Royall's publications for nearly two decades, didn't even bother to mention the muckraker among so many less-known women in her 918-page opus, *Woman's Record, Or, Sketches of All Distinguished Women: From the Creation to A.D. 1868.* The raggedy Royall stood too far outside the bounds of domesticity and the "housewifery arts" that were featured like benchmarks in the "ladies" magazines of the day.

Royall's dismissal of women-driven reform movements— including suffrage, abolitionism, and temperance—as disingenu- ous attempts by the evangelical church to gain members and money also alienated the reform editors and authors who determined the entries into the early canons on women. "Female irreligion," as his- torian Barbara Welter noted in her landmark study *The Cult of True Womanhood: 1820–1860*, had been the "most revolting feature in human character" for Royall's detractors. At the same time, as Karen Ramsey Johnson and Joseph Keller noted in their study of Royall's "Apocalyptic Rhetoric," the notorious author actually formed an early narrative of the nineteenth-century "parasitical" relationship between women and the clergy more often associated with a subse- quent and better-known generation of writers like Margaret Fuller, Catharine E. Beecher, and Elizabeth Cady Stanton, who cast "evange- lists and other clergy in the role of seducers, exploiters and oppressors of women." For Johnson and Keller, Royall's "ethos of a politicized American womanhood," based on a "secular and intensely personal" rhetoric outside the realm of the religious fervor of the times, some- how fell through the cracks of historical consideration.

In their monumental *History of Woman Suffrage*, authors Stanton, Susan B. Anthony, and Matilda Joslyn Gage recognized Anne's life work with a single sentence—that she published *The Huntress* for a quarter century, misspelling her name in the process—while focus- ing extensively on other writers and editors of the period, including Fannie Wright and Fuller, whom they deemed "the precursor of the Women's Rights agitation."

In the late nineteenth century, John Seely Hart, in his well-known textbook *A Manual of American Literature*, saddled a legacy on Roy- all that remained for decades. She was the "special pest of Washing- ton city," students learned. Hart continued: "As an example of the literary virago, she was probably without a parallel," repeating what had become the caricature of her life. "She was the terror of politicians and especially of Congressmen."

The initial rescue of Royall took place in 1908, when educator and writer Sarah Harvey Porter put together the first biography on the "vilified woman" whose "personal history is more closely intertwined with, and more analogous to, the growth of the Republic than that of any other woman of whom record is preserved." Porter's admittedly romantic portrait of Anne didn't exaggerate her importance in national affairs, but it drew attention to a unique "voice, a strident voice, crying out for national righteousness" when nearly all other women writers "were uttering themselves in sentimental verse or milk-and-water prose."

Porter's effort drew the attention not of women's groups or reformers but of the secretive all-male Masonic Lodges, who raised the money to provide a proper tombstone for Royall, which they dedicated in a special ceremony in 1911. The warm tributes to Royall "brought tears to the eyes of some of the listeners," according to the Masonic newspapers. They came not to salute a saint, but to pay tribute to "an old woman" to whom the "vituperative epithets 'crazy Anne Royall,' 'old hag,' 'common scold,' were mercilessly applied by hateful tongues, who was despised and rejected of men, upon whom neglect, poverty, injustice, contempt, vilification, were piled heap on heap, but in whose character we now discern in some measure the heroism of the soldier patriot, the loyalty of the honest publicist, the foresight of the prophet."

Royall's reputation, therefore, was not rehabilitated in light of her contributions as a writer or innovator or feminist; instead, she gained recognition as the wife of a Mason, as an eccentric victim of censorship, and as a casualty in the denial of the freedom of the press. During World War II, the *Cavalcade of America* radio program seized on this patriotic notion, churning out two radio stories on Anne in the early 1940s, with war and Nazi book burnings in the background. "People laughed at Anne Royall," intoned the radio narrator. "Some pretended not to hear. But everyone did hear all the same, it was even heard in the President's mansion." As Secretary Eaton tells President Jackson about his wife's admiration for Royall, "a real power in Washington," the folksy writer enters the White House as "tired as a Mississippi mule tramping around these streets." The radio listeners learn that she has the "power of the pen to stop US Bankers."

While other books and scholarly articles on Royall began to appear, it wasn't until 1974 that she finally made her debut in Gloria Steinem's *Ms. Magazine* as America's "pioneer woman journalist." A generation later, by the time National Public Radio journalist and long-time Washington correspondent Cokie Roberts included Royall's apocryphal tale of her dalliance with John Quincy Adams on the Potomac River in her collection of essays *We Are Our Mothers' Daughters*, any ambivalence over Royall's legacy had long been supplanted by a kinder, gentler attitude over her infamous trial.

Anne's most enduring fame today rests on this urban legend with Adams, which can still be found in most histories of Washington, DC—even in White House lore. In 1988, President Ronald Reagan entertained members of the Center for the Presidency with the tale, drawing details from a favorite story of President Harry S. Truman, who had once regaled author John Hersey, on assignment from the *New Yorker*, with the tale. The story goes that Anne had sat on President John Quincy Adams's clothes as he took his morning bath in the Potomac River in order to secure an interview. In truth, Royall and Adams were close friends—the former president donated money to the desperate widow's book efforts during her first days in

Washington. Adams's wife gave Anne a shawl. Adams petitioned for her right to a Revolutionary War soldier widow's pension for years; the traveling author visited him at his home in Boston.

This legend, though, most likely took root in Royall's own lifetime. Only months after her "common scold" trial in 1829, the *New England Weekly Review* published an article about Anne's supposed first meeting with Adams, a chance encounter while she was in the company of editor Alexander Everett. When Royall requested to be introduced to the president, Everett responded: "Would you wish to see him now, ma'am," and gestured toward Adams in the river "enjoying the comforts of a cold bath."

The story became its own landmark. In 1913, groundskeepers made national news, including the *New York Times*, for removing "Anne Royall's stone" at Potomac Park, across from the White House.

President Truman's daughter Margaret interpreted the famous legend for its meaning: in an age when women were "practically nonexistent" in political journalism, especially at the White House, Anne served as a feisty example of perseverance.

An air of scandal from Royall's witch trial tainted any meaningful consideration of her life's work; in one case, she was reduced to "America's first nationally recognized gossip columnist." That she had likely covered more American territory as an itinerant chronicler—on horseback and broken stagecoaches, on boat and barge, and often on foot—than any of her contemporaries never seemed to matter. The soul-searching in her books as she grasped for a sense of national identity—especially in the year of the country's jubilee, the fiftieth anniversary of the historic call for America's independence—and the observations and recordings of languages and dialects were set aside. Royall's descriptions of nature, technical and intricate coming from someone who was raised in the woods, understood medicinal herbs, and spent the first half century of her life in the southern Appalachians, were rarely mentioned.

To this day, the burden still falls on Royall's biographers to defend the writer's character and her right to freedom of speech and freedom of the press. Anne's lament over the double standard of the witch trial remains unresolved, where the abusive actions of men and the duplicitous case of the prosecution did not "raise the indignation of the people" or ever enter into the conversation.

In the same way that the extraordinary person whose life and stories instigated such a bizarre witch trial has remained a footnote of the mercurial Jackson era, few observers have recognized the unyielding power of the extreme religious and political forces that could justify such an appalling federal trial. Social critics have shrugged at this episode of American history, or have forgotten it completely. In the meantime, Anne's concern that the inculcation of unchecked political power and the insidious efforts of evangelical "church and state" advocates would one day obscure constitutional violations continues to resonate today.

"I feel that if this were a crime today," Roberts concluded, "some of us would be in deep trouble."

In an age when the federal government can make an argument over the "balance" of national security and freedom of the press, as whistleblowers risk their own arrests and prosecution for the sake of investigative journalism, Roberts's aside seems chillingly real.

It certainly asks the question: What is the role of crusading muckraking journalism today, in illuminating corruption, exposing inequality and disparity, ensuring freedom of speech, and serving as a watchdog of systematic collusion between Wall Street corporate interests and Washington or statehouse policies, or the undue influence of religious forces in politics? Is there room for independent voices like Royall, who can issue their own views—however inconsistent and quarrelsome—without facing marginalization, scorn, or prosecution?

In a social media age of unruly satire and outrage, would Anne still be tried in the court of public opinion as an "evil example" and a "common scold"?

The memory of Anne Royall and her unique story—or stories, rather—serves as a safeguard to an important moment in history when "common vengeance writes the law," as Arthur Miller wrote in *The Crucible*, and the trial of public opinion becomes a form of entertainment. The stain of America's last witch trial, as Royall's friend Theophilus Gates at the *Reformer* noted, remained as long as the news media allowed it to stay unchallenged. In Anne's case, it has never really been erased.

In the end, her relentless stands for the Constitution, upholding the separation of church and state, and forever serving as a bulwark against the entry of religious extremists into the corridors of power and education, remain timely and timeless lessons today, especially among the harrowing excesses of judicial execution in the hands of fanatics who believe in the rule of their exclusive God.

"Be kind to the old," *The Huntress* admonished in a good-hearted column, appealing for a bit of charity herself. "For doubtless many and severe have been the crosses and trials of earlier years."

In her eulogy of John Quincy Adams in 1848, Anne faced the question of mortality, casually overlooking all of his accomplishments as a statesman and a sage for a more personal touch. Anne memorialized their first encounter, long before the supposed meeting of Potomac lore, when she walked the streets of Washington, a "stranger, the indignant and the distressed," and Adams promptly gave her money for her book subscriptions.

"The world is my country, and to do good is my religion," Royall wrote, proclaiming it as Adams's legacy, as she borrowed the words from freethinker Thomas Paine. They became her legacy as well.

One of her first pen portraits in *Sketches*, in fact, of Anne Bailey, the "celebrated heroine," provided a prophetic rendezvous with Royall's own future. Hailed as "Mad Anne, the Huntress," the fearless scout and frontier fighter in the wartime aftermath of the American Revolution, Anne Bailey's legend had dimmed somewhat until it was rescued by Royall. At the time of their interview, Bailey was in her eighties, and apparently as forthright and vulgar as ever. Royall noted her Welsh origins and speech, though Bailey had actually been born in Liverpool.

In 1791, with one of the western Virginia forts under siege, Bailey had volunteered to ride through enemy territory to retrieve a shipment of gun powder for the faltering forces. No other man had been brave enough to answer the call. The death-defying assignment, while crucial to the fate of the fort, called on a certain level of faith and madness, daring and shrewdness, and a whole lot of luck. Royall clearly viewed Bailey's heroic act as emblematic of another kind of respectable womanhood, shouldering a rifle, leading a horse laden with ammunition.

"And what would the General say to you, when you used to get safe to camp with your ammunition?" Royall asked. "Why, he'd say, you're a brave soldier, Anne, and tell some of the men to give me a dram." Royall offered her a dram.

Bailey's miserable condition affected Anne. "She richly deserves more of her country, than a name in history."

A similar tribute could be made for Anne Royall.

# Notes

## INTRODUCTION

1 *Abby Kelley Foster quotation:* Dorothy Sterling, *Ahead of Her Time: Abby Kelley and the Politics of Antislavery* (W. W. Norton, 1994), 268.

1 *Grace Sherwood:* "Grace Sherwood, The One Virginia Witch," *Harper's Magazine* 69 (1884): 99.

1 *sport for the mob in ducking women:* Reports of Cases, 1754–1845, vols. 27–28, Supreme Court of Pennsylvania, Vol. 12 (Kay and Brother, 1874), 230.

2 *vituperative powers of this giantess of literature:* "Domestic News," *New York Observer*, July 11, 1829.

2 *She was a Holy Terror: Washington Post*, February 22, 1891.

2 *the men with the muck rakes:* Theodore Roosevelt, address at U.S. House of Representatives, Washington, DC, April 14, 1906.

2 *She could always say something:* quoted in Sarah Harvey Porter, *The Life and Times of Anne Royall* (Torch Press, 1909), 122.

2 *bow down in fear:* "She Was a Holy Terror: Her Pen Was as Venomous as a Rattlesnake's Fangs; Former Washington Editress: How Ann Royall Made Life a Burden to the Public Men of Her Day," *Washington Post*, February 22, 1891.

3 *serpent-tongued:* Benjamin Buford Williams, *A Literary History of Alabama: The Nineteenth Century* (Associated University Press, 1979), 14.

3 *redneck:* Anne Royall, *Mrs. Royall's Southern Tour, or, Second Series of the Black Book*, (Washington, 1830), Vol. 1, 148.

3 *virago errant in enchanted armor:* John Adams, diary entry, August 9, 1827, in Charles Francis Adams, ed., *Memoirs of John Quincy Adams, Comprising Portions of His Diary from 1795 to 1848*, 12 vols. (Philadelphia, 1874–77), Vol. 7, 321.

4   *The missionaries have thrown off the mask:* Anne Royall, *Black Book I* (Washington, 1828), 163.

4   *her travels around the new nation as its storyteller:* Patricia Bradley, *Women and the Press: The Struggle for Equality* (Northwestern University Press, 2005), 62

5   *bitter end:* Anne Royall, *The Tennessean: A Novel* (New Haven, 1827), 60.

5   *cult of true womanhood:* Barbara Welter, "The Cult of True Womanhood," *American Quarterly* 18, no. 2, pt. 1 (Summer 1966): 15.

7   *Mr. Rogers respects to Mrs. Anne Royall:* "Mr. Morse's Telegraph," *The Huntress,* January 11, 1845.


## CHAPTER ONE: HER MOTHER'S DAUGHTER


8   *Mrs. Royall has again appeared before the public: Centreville (IN) Western Times,* June 27, 1829.

8   *I am genuine backwoods:* Anne Royall, *Mrs. Royall's Pennsylvania; or, Travels Continued in the United States,* 2 vols. (Washington, 1829), Vol. 1, 202.

9   *Ye who have been torn from the haunts of your childhood:* Ibid., 205.

10  *ineffable scorn:* Anne Royall, *Royall's Sketches of History, Life and Manners in the United States* (New Haven, 1826), 383.

10  *fresh from the backwoods, half horse, half alligator:* Davy Crockett, *The Life and Adventures of Colonel David Crockett of Tennessee* (Cincinnati, 1833), 153.

10  *But the beauty inimitable of the scenery arises:* Royall, *Mrs. Royall's Pennsylvania,* Vol. 2, 220.

11  On the history of Hannahstown or Hanna's Town and the Pennsylvanian frontier, see J. B. Richardson III, "The Destruction of Hanna's Town, Part 1," *Western Pennsylvania History* 90, no. 2: 16–25, and "Who Were Those Guys? The Destruction of Hanna's Town Part 2," *Western Pennsylvania History* 90, no. 3: 26–35; Patrick Spero, *Frontier Country: The Politics of War in Early Pennsylvania* (University of Pennsylvania Press, 2016); Thomas Abler, *Cornplanter: Chief Warrior of the Allegany Senecas* (Syracuse University Press, 2007).

12  *The present generation have scarcely any idea of the privations and trouble of settling the country:* Royall, *Mrs. Royall's Pennsylvania,* 223.

12  *Indian captive . . . who remained with the savage tribe until she reached womanhood:* Anne Royall, *Letters from Alabama, 1817–1822,* biographical introduction and notes by Lucille Griffith (University of Alabama Press, 1969), 19.

13  *Sarah Harvey Porter on Royall in Staunton: The Life and Times of Anne Royall* (Torch Press, 1909), 34.

13  *mingled emotions:* Royall, *Royall's Sketches of History, Life and Manners in the United States* (New Haven, 1826), 91.

14  For more history on William Royall, the Royall family, and Colonial Virginia, see John Royall Harris, "The Colonial Royalls of Virginia," *Virginia Magazine of History and Biography,* 33, no. 4 (October 1925): 420–23; Bessie Rowland James, *Anne Royall's U.S.A.* (Rutgers University Press, 1972); Rhys Isaac, *The Transformation of Virginia, 1740–1790* (University of North Carolina Press, 1999); David Hackett Fischer, *Albion's Seed: Four British Folkways in America* (Oxford University Press, 1989); Woody Holton, *Forced*

*Founders: Indians, Debtors, Slaves, and the Making of the American Revolution in Virginia* (University of North Carolina Press, 1999).

15 *Grison Republic:* Royall, *Royall's Sketches of History, Life and Manners in the United States* (New Haven, 1826), 58.

16 *old gray-headed men, and little boys:* Ibid., 90.

16 *marriage market of the South:* Van Wyck Brooks, *The World of Washington Irving* (E. P. Dutton, 1944), 287.

17 *cattle and horses in their natural state; there were neither geldings or steers to be found in the herd:* Porter, *Life and Times*, 34.

17 *wash-woman and menial:* Ibid., 35.

18 *little histories:* Anne Royall, *Letters from Alabama on Various Subjects* (Washington, 1830), 99.

18 *Some pray for riches—riches they obtain:* Ibid., 201.

19 *What a pity this gentleman had not chosen the profession of a preacher:* Royall, *Letters from Alabama on Various Subjects*, 226.

19 *when dogwood was in bloom:* Ibid., 22.

19 *My husband never laughed:* Ibid., 142.

19 *splenetic fits:* Royall, *Royall's Sketches of History, Life and Manners in the United States* (New Haven, 1826), 14.

19 For background history on Elizabeth and James Roane and their Bill of Complaint, see various papers in *Roane v. Royall et al.*, Box 235, Clerk's Office, Augusta County Circuit Court, Staunton, VA.

20 *much intoxicated at the time: Ann Royall v. Jacob Smith*, Circuit Court Record, October 31, 1814, Greenbrier County Courthouse, Lewisburg, WV.

22 *William Royall never did intend to give his property:* Roane Bill of Complaint, *Roane v. Royall et al.*

22 *Untoward circumstances in this his grand climacteric of life, has in some measure already:* Pension application of William Royall, November 29, 1812.

23 For background history on Royall debts, see various papers in *Roane v. Royall et al.*

24 *One learns more in a day by mixing with mankind:* Royall, *Letters from Alabama on Various Subjects*, 33.

24 *I have little partiality for the mountains:* Royall, *Royall's Sketches of History, Life and Manners in the United States* (New Haven, 1826), 20.

25 *Mrs. Royall was for several years a resident of our (Kanawha) county:* Philip M. Conley, *West Virginia Review* 11 (1934): 284.

25 *Were you not present when the news of the unfortunate——was announced?:* Royall, *Letters from Alabama on Various Subjects*, 27.

26 *at this time, debtors went to prison:* James, *Anne Royall's U.S.A.*, 83.

26 *was next heard of as being confined in the jail of Greenbrier County for debt:* Conley, *West Virginia Review*, 284.

26 *handsomest face in the world for his age:* Anne Royall, *Mrs. Royall's Southern Tour, or Second Series of the Black Book* (Washington, 1830), 39.

27 *Well, never, never, did I expect to see you again:* Anne Royall, *Mrs. Royall's Southern Tour, or, Second Series of the Black Book*, Vol. 3 (Washington, 1830–31), 208.

27 *I had met with a sad reverse of my fortune since I last saw my mother:* Anne Royall, Ibid.

## CHAPTER TWO: FLAYING THE SAUCY ROGUES

28  *I have some notion of turning author some of these days:* Anne Royall, *Letters from Alabama on Various Subjects* (Washington, 1830), 141.

29  For more on "Alabama Fever" and early Alabama historical background, see William Warren Rogers, *Alabama: The History of a Deep South State* (University of Alabama Press, 2010); David J. Libby, *Slavery and Frontier Mississippi, 1720–1835* (University Press of Mississippi, 2008); Virginia Van der Veer Hamilton, *Alabama: A History* (W. W. Norton, 1984); Edwin Bridges, *Alabama: The Making of an American State* (University of Alabama Press, 2016); Lucille Griffith's biographical introduction and notes in Royall, *Letters from Alabama on Various Subjects.*

29  *Mr. L. and myself are both sitting at one table, and trying to write:* Royall, *Letters from Alabama on Various Subjects,* 5.

30  *Colomba root has several broad leaves near the ground:* Ibid., 138.

30  *convey a just idea of the characteristics of men:* Ibid., 116.

31  *America is now wholly given over to a damned mob of scribbling women:* Quoted in Susan Williams, *Reclaiming Authorship: Literary Women in America, 1850–1900* (University of Pennsylvania Press, 2006), 27.

32  *corrupt the morals of our females:* Royall, *Letters from Alabama on Various Subjects,* 90.

33  *This work will long remain a standing evidence of that towering genius which knows no sex:* Ibid., 89.

33  *Bad taste, Bombast and Nonsense, Blunders, Ignorance of the French Language and Manners:* "France. Lady Morgan," *London Quarterly Review* (1817): 375.

33  *humpback old woman, absurdly attired, rouged and wigged:* "Our Survey of Literature and Science," *Cornhill Magazine* Vol. 1 (1863): 132.

34  *worst members of the community:* Frances Wright, *Views of Society and Manners in America* (Longman, Hurst, Rees, Orme, and Brown, 1821), 397. For more reading on Frances Wright, see Celia Morris Eckhardt, *Fanny Wright: Rebel in America* (Harvard University Press, 1984), and Susan S. Adams's introduction to Frances Wright, *Reason, Religion, and Morals* (Humanity Books, 2004); Lori Ginzberg, "The Hearts of Your Readers Will Shudder: Fannie Wright, Infidelity and American Freethought," *American Quarterly* 46 (1994).

34  *Mrs. Wright goes farther than I do:* Anne Royall, *Mrs. Royall's Pennsylvania; or, Travels Continued in the United States,* Vol. 2. (Washington, 1829), 174.

34  *If I admired him as a writer:* Anne Royall, *Royall's Sketches of History, Life and Manners in the United States* (New Haven, 1826), 264.

35  *frontier fights:* James Justus, *Fetching the Old Southwest: Humorous Writing from Longstreet to Twain* (University of Missouri, 2004), 445.

35  *is not always of the most refined nature, and his satirical attacks are perhaps more vigorous than witty:* Henry Roscoe, *Specimens of the American Poets* (T. and J. Allman, 1822), 72.

35  *I also fully believed that the people were a bundling:* James Kirke Paulding, *John Bull in America, or, The New Munchausen* (Charles Wiley, 1825), 2. For more on Paulding, see Ralph M. Aderman and Wayne R. Kime, *Advocate for America: The Life of James Kirke Paulding* (Susquehanna University Press, 2003); James Kirke Paulding, *The Backwoodsman, A Poem* (M. Thomas, 1818); James Kirke Paulding, *The Lion of the West* (Stanford University Press, 1954).

36  *But there is one thing which puzzled me at first:* Paulding, *John Bull in America,* 144.

37  *A more ill-looking, frightened, chagrined, fatigued, be-drabbled, and be-drown set of miserables:* Royall, *Letters from Alabama on Various Subjects*, 76.

37  *I came to recollect that considerably more than three-fourths:* Paulding, *John Bull in America*, 149.

38  *and the poor, penniless, Teague:* Royall, *Mrs. Royall's Pennsylvania*, Vol. 2, 4.

38  *As we stopped at the door:* Ibid., 2:7.

39  *Whatever they told the people of the house:* Ibid., 2:9.

40  *One door was at the foot of my bed:* Ibid., 2:12.

41  *I will not give up my seat to the President of the United States:* Anne Royall, *Mrs. Royall's Southern Tour, or, Second Series of the Black Book*, Vol. 1 (Washington, 1830–31), 77.

42  *His face had assumed all the colors of the rainbow:* Ibid., 79.

42  *He was outrageous, and to convince me he had courage:* Ibid., 80.

43  *But the best is yet to come:* Ibid., 80.

44  *a coarse, boisterous, high-tempered critter:* Frances Whitcher, "Aunt Magwire Continues Her Account of the Sewing Society," *Godey's Lady's Book* 38 (1849). For more on Whitcher and Parton, see Lori Landsay, *Madcaps, Screwballs, and Con Women: The Female Trickster in American Culture* (University of Pennsylvania Press, 1998); Nancy Walker, *A Very Serious Thing: Women's Humor and American Culture* (University of Minnesota Press, 1988).

44  *Hearing of your arrival in Cambridge but a few hours since we:* quoted in Sarah Harvey Porter, *The Life and Times of Anne Royall* (Torch Press, 1909), 108.

46  *the incidents of whose life is a complete novel:* Royall, *Letters from Alabama on Various Subjects*, 107.

47  *I spend most of my time with the Tennessean:* Ibid., 111.

47  *novel "founded on facts":* Hannah Webster Foster, *The Coquette* (Columbia University Press, 1939).

47  *Founded upon a well-known fact:* Anne Royall, *The Tennessean* (New Haven, 1827).

48  *the common room, the jollity, the fire, the grog, the fiddling and the gossip:* Van Wyck Brooks, *Makers and Finders: A History of the Writer in America, 1800–1915*, Vol. 1 (Dutton, 1950), 288.

48  *In a happy republic, like ours, where for the prize of Fame and Fortune:* Quoted on the cover of Lewis Gaston Leary, *The Book-Peddling Parson: An Account of the Life and Works of Mason Locke Weems, Patriot, Pitchman, Author, and Purveyor of Morality to the Citizenry of the Early United States of America* (Algonquin Books, 1984), 144.

48  *His very eccentricities, for failings they could not be called, were the eccentricities of genius and benevolence:* quoted in Leonard Marcus, *Minders of Make-Believe: Idealists, Entrepreneurs, and the Shaping of American Children's Literature* (Houghton Mifflin Harcourt, 2008), 12.

49  *I made a bungling hand of the shipwreck:* Anne Royall to Matthew Carey, February 12, 1824, quoted in Bessie Rowland James, *Anne Royall's U.S.A* (Rutgers University Press, 1972), 93.

49  *All this I liked:* Anne Royall, *Mrs. Royall's Southern Tour, or, Second Series of the Black Book*, Vol. 3 (Washington, 1830–31), 65.

49  *There is a country for you:* Royall, *Letters from Alabama on Various Subjects*, 163.

51  *A poor and friendless female asks of you to patronise her works as named in the enclosed prospectus:* Anne Royall to Thomas Jefferson, June 20, 1824, The Thomas Jefferson Papers at the Library of Congress.

51 *It will be asked then, what encouragement I have to write:* Royall, *Second Series of the Black Book*, 3:XXX, 209.

51 *Having been advised to try the mineral waters in Virginia for my health:* Royall, *Royall's Sketches of History, Life and Manners in the United States* (New Haven, 1826), 13.

## CHAPTER THREE: A FEMALE OF RESPECTABILITY

52 *The author is a female of respectability:* Advertisement, *Albany Daily Advertiser*, February 12, 1825.

52 *respectable physicians:* Anne Royall, *Letters from Alabama on Various Subjects* (Washington, 1830), 131.

52 *When I first began to write:* Anne Royall, *The Black Book: or, A Continuation of Travels in the United States* (Washington, 1828–29), 110.

53 *the friend of the friendless:* quote in Sarah Harvey Porter, *The Life and Times of Anne Royall* (Torch Press, 1909), 59.

54 *a traveler, I only call from curiosity:* Anne Royall, *Royall's Sketches of History, Life and Manners in the United States* (New Haven, 1826), 109.

55 *little dried up old woman:* Anne Royall, *Mrs. Royall's Southern Tour, or, Second Series of the Black Book*, Vol. 1 (Washington, 1830), 42. For more on Dolley Madison, see Holly Cowan Shulman and David B. Mattern, *Dolley Madison: Her Life, Letters, and Legacy* (Rosen Publishing, 2003).

55 *a vigorous countenance:* Royall, *Second Series of the Black Book*, 1:31.

56 *pleasant party of ladies:* Ibid., 1:3

56 *irresistible grace of her every movement:* Ibid., 1:42.

56 *handkerchief round my neck:* Anne Royall, *Mrs. Royall's Southern Tour, or, Second Series of the Black Book*, Vol. 3 (Washington, 1830), 7.

58 *descend so low:* Royall, *Royall's Sketches of History, Life and Manners in the United States* (New Haven, 1826), 124.

59 *eighth wonder of the world:* Ibid., 130.

60 *Every feature in his face shows genius:* Ibid., 166.

60 *wretched establishment which only exists to disgrace Washington:* Ibid., 143.

61 *and cast on me a look which I shall never forget:* Ibid., 195.

61 *an awkward backwoods country person:* Ibid., 188.

61 *I cannot, however, depart without one more remark which forms a link in the long chain of human depravity:* Ibid., 201.

62 *An execution of a negro took place the next day:* Ibid., 201.

62 *He received me with an air worthy of Chesterfield:* Ibid., 199.

62 *American works do not pay the expense of publishing:* Ibid., 201.

63 *great deal of valuable information:* "Darby's Emigrant Guide," *North-American Review and Miscellaneous Journal* 7, no. 20 (July 1818): 268–69.

63 *society appeared in a different light:* Royall, *Sketches*, 236.

64 *independence of manners:* Ibid., 241.

64 *Broadway, Chatham, Pearl and Division Streets:* Ibid., 243. For more background on New York City in this period, see Patricia Cline Cohen, *The Murder of Helen Jewett: The Life and Death of a Prostitute in Nineteenth-Century New York* (Knopf, 1998); Tyler Anbinder, *Five Points: The 19th-Century New York City Neighborhood That Invented Tap Dance, Stole*

*Elections, and Became the World's Most Notorious Slum* (Plume, 2002); Edwin Burrows and Mike Wallace, *Gotham: A History of New York City to 1898* (Oxford University Press, 2000).

65 *To see such a vast number of children:* Royall, *Sketches*, 256.

65 *To see a friendless female in a gloomy prison:* Ibid., 251.

66 *Mr. P. is in height about five feet ten inches:* Ibid., 264. For more on Paulding and New York City, see Andrew Burstein, *The Original Knickerbocker: The Life of Washington Irving* (Basic Books, 2008), and Washington Irving, *A History of New York* (Penguin Classics, 2008).

67 *While others are debating the questions of right and wrong:* Royall, *Sketches*, 261.

67 For more on Mordecai Noah and James Bennett and the era of journalism in that period, see Mathew Goodman, *The Sun and the Moon: The Remarkable True Account of Hoaxers, Showmen, Dueling Journalists, and Lunar Man-Bats in Nineteenth-Century New York* (Basic Books, 2010).

67 *The letters (from Alabama) are a miscellaneous production embracing strictures on Manners:* *Albany Daily Advertiser*, February 12, 1825.

68 *Everything now must pass the fiery ordeal of criticism:* Quoted in Royall, *Sketches*, 372, from *Rhode-Island Literary Review*, "The Corsair, A Tale by Lord Byron," Vol. 1, 1814, 109.

69 *On my way thither I fell in with two of the citizens:* Ibid., 339.

69 *To cure the errors imbibed in our youth, traveling is indispensable:* Ibid., 364.

70 *My country is my home:* Anne Royall, *Black Book*, Vol. 1 (Washington, 1828), 276.

71 *the most liberal, humane, and enlightened citizens we have:* Royall, *Black Book*, Vol. 2, 94.

71 *no other crime in the period attracted as much attention in the northern press:* William Preston Vaughn, *The Anti-Masonic Party in the United States: 1826–1843* (University of Kentucky Press, 2009), 1.

72 *common man and evangelical Christianity:* David G. Hackett, *That Religion in Which All Men Agree: Anti-Masonry and the Public Sphere, 1826–1850* (University of California Press, 2014), 13.

72 *precisely like the witches of Salem:* Royall, *Black Book*, 1:12.

72 *engaged in this farce:* Ibid.

73 *Before the outbreak there were five hundred lodges in New York alone:* Richard Wright, *Forgotten Ladies* (J. B. Lippincott, 1928), 176.

73 *indefatigable literary being of which our country has the honor to toast:* American Masonic *Record and Albany Saturday Magazine* 1 (April 21, 1827).

73 *She marches on, speaking her mind freely:* quoted in *Connecticut Herald*, reprinted in *Boston Commercial Gazette*, June 20, 1826.

74 *a more contemptible book was never palmed upon any community:* New York Commercial *Advertiser*, July 28, 1826.

74 *biographer for nine-tenths of the great men of the Union:* Salem Gazette, December 15, 1826.

75 *We have had the honor of a visit from Mrs. Royall:* "Mrs. Royall," *Northampton Post*, 1827.

75 *modest and delectable lady, and a distinguished traveler:* Hallowell Gazette, September 12, 1827.

76 *We stop the press to announce to our readers:* Portland Argus, 1827.

76 *We are exceedingly vexed at this:* Philadelphia Album and Ladies' Literary Port Folio 5 (January 8, 1831).

76 *A New York lady will not look at a book, unless it has a red cover:* Royall, quoted in Porter, *Life and Times*, 68.

77  *I shall leave this city in the morning: Reformer: A Religious Work* 8–9 (February 7, 1828).

77  *more anxious for notoriety: The Philadelphia Album and Ladies' Literary Portfolio* 5 (January 8, 1831).

77  *silly old hag: Hampden Journal,* July 18, 1827.

77  *Of all the works I have published:* Royall, *Second Series of the Black Book,* Vol. 2, 209.

78  *worst American novel of all time:* Helen Beal Woodward, *The Bold Women* (Books for Libraries Press, 1971), 19.

78  *If it were not ungallant to apply terms of disapprobation to the production of a female: Boston Commercial Gazette,* March 8, 1827.

78  *The best mead of praise we can bestow: Boston Lyceum* 1, no. 3 (1827): 160.

78  *Almost since I can remember to have read a newspaper:* Royall, *Black Book,* 1:315. For more on Duane, see Kim Tousley Phillips, *William Duane: Radical Journalist in the Age of Jefferson* (Garland Publishing, 1989).

79  *We are informed by various papers and by a letter from Mrs. Royall: Reformer: A Religious Work* 8–9 (February 7, 1828).

79  *What think you, Matt, of the Christian religion:* Royall, *Letters from Alabama on Various Subjects,* 136.

## CHAPTER FOUR: THE BLACK BOOK

80  *Am I black enough, think you:* Thomas Middletown, *The Black Book (1604), Collected Works* (Oxford University Press, 2008).

80  *I have always heard widows were jealous of each other:* Anne Royall, *Letters from Alabama on Various Subjects* (Washington, 1830), 96.

81  *A lady asked me one day:* Ibid., 97.

81  *Hence arises all our mistakes in religion, morals, and politics:* Ibid., 97.

82  *This is to be the downfall of our country some day:* Ibid., 98.

82  *Thomas Paine's* Age of Reason . . . *Theophilus Gates'* Reformer, *and Madam Royall's* Black Book: Quoted in *Reformer: A Religious Work* 10–11 (1828).

82  *This attempt to caricature the expression of public opinion on a question deeply affecting its interest: Christian Baptist* 7 (1828): 259.

82  *That if said E. S. Ely, D.D. should refuse publicly to sign this reasonable recantation:* quoted in *Reformer: A Religious Work* 10–11 (1828).

83  *But I have something else to do besides aiding Dr. Ely:* Anne Royall, *Mrs. Royall's Pennsylvania; or, Travels Continued in the United States,* 2 vols. (Washington, 1829), Vol. 1, 83.

83  *Next morning the shoes, stockings, and feet:* Ibid., 87.

84  *The big door was open, and in a splendid passage:* Ibid., 89.

85  *The Duty of Christian Freemen to Elect Christian Rulers:* Ezra Stiles Ely, *The Duty of Christian Freemen to Elect Christian Rulers* (William Geddes, 1828). For more background on Ely, see Ezra Stiles Ely Papers, Presbyterian Historical Society, Philadelphia, PA; Curtis Dahl, "The Clergyman, the Hussy, and Old Hickory: Ezra Stiles Ely and the Peggy Eaton Affair," *Journal of Presbyterian History* 52, no. 2, "Women and the Presbyterian Church" (Summer 1974): 137–55.

86  *I propose, fellow-citizens, a new sort of union:* Ely, *Duty of Christian Freemen,* 8.

87  *Beware of those who come to you in sheeps' clothing:* reprinted in *Hartford Religious Inquirer,* September 19, 1835, 195.

87  *We may bid a final farewell to our religious liberties and the right to enjoy our own faith:* Reformer: A Religious Work 8–9 (1827): 137.

87  *Royall's behavior would not have stood out as extraordinary:* Elizabeth J. Clapp, "'A Virago-Errant in Enchanted Armor?' Anne Royall's 1829 Trial as a Common Scold," *Journal of the Early Republic* 23, no. 2 (Summer 2003): 229.

88  *seek the opinions of the great men in their works:* Frances Wright, quoted in *Unitarian* 1 (Boston, 1834): 227.

88  *class of mankind then:* Lawrence Greatrake, *The Harp of Zion* (Johnston and Stockton, 1827), 72–73.

89  *Anti-Missionism reached its slanderous nadir in the writings of Royall:* Byron C. Lambert, *Rise of the Anti-mission Baptists* (Arno Press, 1980), 227.

89  *Were a foreigner, immediately upon landing, to take up a newspaper:* Frances Wright, *Views of Society and Manners in America* (Longman, Hurst, Rees, Orme, and Brown, 1821), 405.

90  *modern evangelism—protracted meetings, missionary and tract societies:* Bertram Wyatt-Brown, "The Antimission Movement in the Jacksonian South: A Study in Regional Folk Culture," *Journal of Southern History* 36, no. 4 (November 1970): 501–29.

90  *I spurn the narrow mind which is attached to a sect or a part, to the exclusion of the rest of mankind:* Royall, *Letters from Alabama on Various Subjects*, 33.

90  *political power of our country would be in the hands of men whose character had been formed under the influence of sabbath schools:* Ely, *Duty of Christian Freemen*, 21.

91  *tracts, magazines, religious newspapers, etc.:* Eric R. Schlereth, *An Age of Infidels: The Politics of Religious Controversy in the Early United States* (University of Pennsylvania Press, 2013).

91  *It is needless to say that under this economy the destinies of the Church:* Lyman Beecher, *Quarterly Journal of the American Education Society*, no. 3 (January 1828).

91  *Antimasons felt they had translated Ely's dream into reality:* Leslie Griffen, "The Antimasonic Persuasion" (PhD diss., Cornell University, 1951), 19, quoted in Lee Benson, *The Concept of Jacksonian Democracy: New York as a Test Case* (Princeton University Press, 1961).

91  *May the arms of the first member of Congress, who proposes a national religion, drop powerless from his shoulder:* Anne Royall, *Black Book*, Vol. 1 (Washington, 1828), 194.

92  *A great many got religion that day:* Royall, *Letters from Alabama on Various Subjects*, 126.

92  *As to the* Reformer, *and other Editors and myself:* Royall, *Black Book*, 1:193.

92  *risk her talents:* Ibid., 1:110.

93  *They became more and more hostile:* Anne Royall, quoted in *Reformer: A Religious Work* 8–9 (February 7, 1828): 43.

93  *The house had high steps before the door:* Royall, *Black Book*, 1:33. Royall describes the incident in Vermont on pages 33–39.

96  *Let this missionary scheme be called madness:* Ibid., 1:36.

96  *Which is the worse crime:* Ibid., 1:38.

96  *We almost flayed Judge Peters of Hartford, a good sound Presbyterian whom every body knows:* Ibid., 1:85.

97  *a compilation of extremely unflattering portraits of anti-Masons:* Porter, *Life and Times*, 104.

98  *Mrs. Royall's rude sketches convince us of one fact:* New York Enquirer, May 23, 1828.

98  *cloistered:* For more on Alexis de Tocqueville, see Sheldon S. Wolin, *Tocqueville between Two Worlds: The Making of a Political and Theoretical Life* (Princeton University Press,

2003); Jill Locke and Eileen Hunt Botting, *Feminist Interpretations of Alexis de Tocqueville* (Penn State University Press, 2010).

99  *full detail of the corruptions and abuses in the English Church: Reformer: A Religious Work* 5 (1824): 73.

99  *expose that ulcerous concretion, that foul and unformed mass of rapacity:* John Wade, *The Black Book; or, Corruption Unmasked!* (Fairburn, 1820), 274.

99  *Write who will against me:* Stanley Wells, ed., *Thomas Nashe, Selected Works* (Routledge Revivals, 2015), 25.

99  *Now comes the black page, which gives name to the book, and terror to the evil doer:* Royall, *Black Book*, 1:3.

100  *From Maine to Georgia—from the Atlantic to Missouri:* Ibid., 163.

100  *In all countries, and in all ages, from the Druids down to brother Beecher:* Ibid., 165.

101  *brigades, battalions, regiments, companies and platoons:* Ibid., 167.

101  *atrocious acts:* Ibid., 205.

102  *What is it? Nothing but trash:* Ibid., 212.

103  *The friends of virtue and religious liberty:* Ibid., 225.

104  *But Mr. Presbyterians, I know a little scripture too:* Ibid., 227.

104  *Glory to the Pennsylvania Legislature:* Anne Royall, *Mrs. Royall's Southern Tour, or, Second Series of the Black Book* (Washington, 1830), Vol. 2, appendix.

105  *Sunday Mail men and Anti-Masons entirely failed with Congress this season:* Ibid., Vol. 2, 211.

105  *The works of Madam Royall are we grant an exception: Boston Commercial Gazette,* March 8, 1827.

105  *Mrs. Royall is traveling through the interior of the state, circulating her* Black Book, *and annoying the Missionaries: Reformer: A Religious Work* 10–11 (1829).

105  *The cloth I wear is sufficient apology for addressing you:* Quoted in Porter, *Life and Times,* 122.

106  *Sir: I have the honor to acknowledge the receipt of your letter of yesterday:* Quoted in Ibid., 123.

109  *The queen of literature: Philadelphia Album and Ladies Literary Port Folio* (June 3, 1830), Vol. 8, 172.

110  *A lady in New York observed to me once:* Royall, *Black Book*, 1:236.

110  *I am advancing on the missionaries:* Anne Royall, *Black Book*, Vol. 2 (Washington, 1828), 296.

## CHAPTER FIVE: THE LAST AMERICAN WITCH TRIAL

111  *[T]he indictment, trial, and the condemnation of Mrs. Royall: Reformer: A Religious Work,* September 1829.

112  *whereof fail not, at your peril, and have you then and there this writ: US v. Royall,* Box 158, Circuit Court District of Columbia Case Papers 1802–1863, Mat Term 1829, Washington, DC.

112  *I had them front, rear, right and left:* Anne Royall, *Black Book*, Vol. 1 (Washington, 1829), 197.

113  *I'll be another Joan of Arc:* Ibid., 140.

113   *a fit subject for the jail, if not the insane asylum:* quoted in *The Bookman* 33 (March 1911): 526.

113   *new low mark for vulgarity, gimmickry:* Robert Remini, *The Jacksonian Era* (Wiley, 1996), 20. For more on the election of 1828 and Andrew Jackson, see Jon Meacham, *American Lion: Andrew Jackson in the White House* (Random House, 2009); Lynn Hudson Parson, *The Birth of Modern Politics: Andrew Jackson, John Quincy Adams, and the Election of 1828* (Oxford University Press, 2011); Arthur Schlesinger Jr., *The Age of Jackson* (Little, Brown and Company, 1945).

114   *May both their heads be severed from their shoulders:* Anne Royall, *Mrs. Royall's Pennsylvania; or, Travels Continued in the United States,* 2 vols. (Washington, 1829), Vol. 2, 254.

114   *I fear that the time is not far distant:* Royall, *Black Book,* 1:235.

115   *abodes of wretchedness:* Ibid., 1:185. For more background on Washington, DC, during this period, see J. D. Dickey, *Empire of Mud: The Secret History of Washington, DC* (Lyons Press, 2015); Jefferson Morley, *Snow-Storm in August: Washington City, Francis Scott Key, and the Forgotten Race Riot of 1835* (Nan Talese, 2012); Tom Lewis, *Washington: A History of Our National City* (Basic Books, 2015).

115   *Her countenance was humorous and pleasant:* Thomas Davis, *Footloose in Jacksonian America: Robert W. Scott and His Agrarian World* (University Press of Kentucky, 2001), 78.

115   *Ridicule is the only weapon which can be used against unintelligible propositions:* Thomas Jefferson to Francis Adrian Van der Kemp, July 30, 1816, Jefferson Papers, National Archives, Washington, DC.

116   *You say you are a Calvinist:* Thomas Jefferson to Ezra Stiles Ely, June 25, 1819, Papers of Thomas Jefferson, Founders Early Access, University of Virginia Press.

116   *Flinging stones is the daily employment of the children on Capitol Hill:* Royall, *Black Book,* 1:200.

116   *There is Rev. Peter Post:* Royall, *Black Book,* 1:197.

117   *wandering scribblers who infest the land:* Frederick William Shelton, *The Trollopiad: Or, Travelling Gentlemen in America; a Satire* (C. Shepard, 1837), 33.

117   *I don't like argumentative ladies:* Salmon Chase, *The Salmon P. Chase Papers* (Kent State University Press, 1994), Vol. 1, 39.

117   *were guarded by a seven-fold shield of habitual insignificance:* Frances Trollope, *Domestic Manners of the Americans* (Whittaker, 1832), 72. For more on Trollope and women writers in this period, see Rosemarie Zagarri, *Revolutionary Backlash: Women and Politics in the Early American Republic* (University of Pennsylvania Press, 2011); Helen Heineman, *Mrs. Trollope: The Triumphant Feminine in the Nineteenth Century* (Ohio University Press, 1979); Brenda Ayres, *Frances Trollope and the Novel of Social Change* (Greenwood Press, 2002).

117   *One enjoyed famous associates, the other fought cruelty and contempt:* Louis Filler, *Appointment at Armageddon: Muckraking and Progressivism in the American Tradition* (Greenwood Press, 1976), 42.

118   *affected a retreat:* New York Commercial Advertiser, July 6, 1829.

118   *a scheme had been laid amongst the godly of the Capitol:* Royall, *Mrs. Royall's Pennsylvania,* Vol. 2, appendix.

118   *an evil-disposed person:* US v. Royall, Box 158, Circuit Court District of Columbia Case Papers 1802–1863, Mat Term 1829, Washington, DC.

119 *for our law-latin confines it to the feminine gender:* William Cranch, *Reports of Cases Civil and Criminal in the United States Circuit Court of (District of Columbia)* (Little, Brown, 1852–53), 623.

119 *old hag: New England Religious Weekly,* quoted in Porter, *Life and Times,* 167.

119 *virago errant in enchanted armor:* John Adams, diary entry, August 9, 1827, in Charles Francis Adams, ed., *Memoirs of John Quincy Adams, Comprising Portions of his Diary from 1795 to 1848,* 12 vols. (Philadelphia, 1874–77), Vol. 7, 321.

119 *grandmother of the muckrakers:* "The Grandma of the Muckrakers," *American Mercury* (September 1927), 87.

119 *refinement and good breeding: Charleston Western Virginian,* September 20, 1826.

120 *The good pious people of Capitol Hill:* Royall, *Mrs. Royall's Pennsylvania,* Vol. 2, appendix.

120 *new era of political invisibility:* Zagarri, *Revolutionary Backlash,* 181.

120 *the truth being conceded that no women: Sartain's Union Magazine of Literature and Art* 8–9 (1851): 194.

121 *About this time a council:* Royall, *Mrs. Royall's Pennsylvania,* Vol. 2, appendix.

122 *troublesome and angry woman: US v. Royall,* Box 158, Circuit Court District of Columbia Case Papers 1802–1863, Mat Term 1829, Washington, DC; Cranch, *Reports of Cases,* 618, quoting Bishop on the definition of a scold.

123 *quaking in his boots: New York Enquirer,* July 18, 1829.

123 *Many of the respectable citizens who reside on Capitol Hill: Washington National Journal,* July 20, 1829.

124 *Thus it is with great geniuses in all ages: Morning Courier,* June 18, 1829.

124 *blessed with friends, dreaded by foes, above want:* Royall, *Black Book,* 1:150.

124 *ducking car:* Royall, *Mrs. Royall's Pennsylvania,* Vol. 2, 14, appendix.

125 *adjudge any other punishment to a common scold than the ducking stool: Washington Daily National Intelligencer,* July 18, 1829.

125 *Sir William Blackstone, in using the word "shall" in the passage cited: Niles' Weekly Register,* August 8, 1829.

125 *She is destined to immortalize the Tiber: New England Galaxy,* July 31, 1829.

125 *eleven to fifteen feet in length:* Royall, *Mrs. Royall's Pennsylvania,* Vol. 2, 21, appendix.

126 *should enjoy the benefit of a cold bath with as much privacy as possible: Washington Daily National Intelligencer,* July 31, 1829.

126 *lovers of the ludicrous: Boston Patriot,* July 30, 1829.

126 *the gentle captive smile upon her persecutors: New York Enquirer,* July 17, 1829.

126 *the appearance of the prisoner: Boston Patriot,* July 25, 1829.

127 *a longer face, with a good deal of the pumpkin:* Royall, *Mrs. Royall's Pennsylvania,* Vol. 2, 10, appendix.

128 *vernal morning, bright with sunny smiles: Bedford Gazette,* July 17, 1828, quoted in Reid Paul, "In the Publick Streets," master's thesis, University of Wisconsin–Madison, 1998.

128 *I shall make a proposition to my friends in Congress:* Royall, *Mrs. Royall's Pennsylvania,* 12, appendix.

128 *Jacobs* [sic], *in his law dictionary, says "scolds": Niles' Weekly Register,* August 8, 1829.

129 *They place the woman in this chair:* Alice Morse Earle, *Curious Punishments of Bygone Days* (H. S. Stone, 1896), 13.

129 *offender will hold her tongue: American Register* 2 (1817): 328.

130 *The trial was excessively amusing, from the variety of the testimony: New York Commercial*

*Advertiser*, reprinted in *Rambler's Magazine; or, Fashionable Emporium of Polite Literature* 1 (September 8, 1822).

130  *barbarity:* Caleb Cushing, *North American Review*, April 1828.

131  *It destroys all personal respect—the women thus punished:* Pennsylvania Supreme Court, *Reports of Cases Adjudged in the Supreme Court of Pennsylvania, [1814–1828]*, Vol. 12 (Kay & Brother, 1872).

132  *Our ungallant fathers of the common law provided a peculiar punishment for common scolds:* Cushing, *North American Review*, April 1828.

133  *We authors must always bleed for those fellows:* New York *Enquirer*, 1829.

133  *One who writes as much as I do:* Royall, *Mrs. Royall's Pennsylvania*, 19, appendix.

133  *The more I scold them, the better they like me:* Anne Royall, *The Black Book: or, A Continuation of Travels in the United States*, Vol. 2 (Washington, 1828–29), 92.

133  *Richard Wallach, the 13-year-old who acted like an "affectionate son" to Anne:* Royall, *Mrs. Royall's Pennsylvania*, 22, appendix.

134  *opprobrious and indecent language:* Plaintiff's Complaint, *US v. Royall*, Box 158, Circuit Court District of Columbia Case Papers 1802–1863, Mat Term 1829, Washington, DC.

134  *far famed and much maltreated personage:* Philadelphia *Album, and Ladies' Literary Gazette*, Vol. 4 (1830), 215.

134  *According to some of the witnesses, Mrs. Royall, although frequent in her verbal exhilarations, was not always loud, but on the contrary:* Daily Commercial *Gazette*, July 29, 1829.

135  *style of feeling, energy and pathos:* Royall, *Mrs. Royall's Pennsylvania*, Vol. 2, 20, appendix.

135  *was not her blasphemy or her politics, but her public displays of inappropriate behavior:* Paul, "In the Publick Streets," 16.

136  *coolly and deliberately turn the misfortunes and distress of suffering humanity:* Royall, *Black Book*, 2:9.

136  *Holy Willy:* Royall, *Black Book*, 1:203.

137  *She called me a damned old bald headed son of a bitch:* Royall, *Mrs. Royall's Pennsylvania*, Vol. 2, 12, appendix.

137  *none of the family had done aught to provoke:* New England *Galaxy*, July 31, 1829.

138  *This old one C [referring to Coyle] is always around:* Anne Royall, note, July 31, 1829, *US v. Royall*, Box 158, Circuit Court District of Columbia Case Papers 1802–1863, Mat Term 1829, Washington, DC.

138  *Is it not astonishing that those abominable defamers:* Royall, *Black Book*, Vol. 2, 232.

138  *It is also well known that these people made the first attack on me:* Reformer: *A Religious Work* 8–9 (1828): 44.

139  *A great beast like him:* Royall, *Mrs. Royall's Pennsylvania*, Vol. 2, 21, appendix.

139  *looked like Satan's walking staff:* Ibid., 13, appendix.

139  *sundry wicked sayings of their tormentor:* Daily Commercial *Gazette*, July 29, 1829.

139  *Her deportment and her book:* Charles Francis Adams, ed., *Memoirs of John Quincy Adams, Comprising Portions of His Diary from 1795 to 1848*, 12 vols. (Philadelphia, 1874–77), Vol. 7, 321.

140  *He was a good natured simpleton:* Royall, *Mrs. Royall's Pennsylvania*, Vol. 2, 13, appendix.

141  *Those who have the laugh upon their side, have the victory:* Ibid.

141  *abounds with humour, incident and sense:* Anne Royall, *Royall's Sketches of History, Life and Manners in the United States* (New Haven, 1826), 150.

141  *No squaw had ever sold her king for a groat:* Royall, *Mrs. Royall's Pennsylvania*, Vol. 1, 216.

142　*I have delivered to Mr. Coyle the Sunday:* George Watterston to Edward Everett, January 26, 1829, Papers of George Watterston, 1815–1835, Library of Congress, Washington, DC.

142　*traitor in the service of Doctor Ely:* Royall, *Mrs. Royall's Pennsylvania*, 67.

143　*The poor wretch trembles like a leaf whenever he sees me:* Anne Royall, *The Black Book: or, A Continuation of Travels in the United States*, Vol. 3 (Washington, 1829), 213.

143　*little knot of corrupt aristocrats:* Duff Green, Daniel Feller (Editor), Harold D. Moser (Editor), Laura-Eve Moss (Editor), Thomas Coens (Editor), *The Papers of Andrew Jackson*, Vol. 7, 1829 (University of Tennessee Press, 2007), 172.

143　*Presbyterians as cutthroats:* Royall, *Mrs. Royall's Pennsylvania*, Vol. 2, 12, appendix.

143　*long-faced hypocritical sanctification about him:* Royall, *Black Book*, Vol. 3, 213.

143　*Mrs. Royall, as it is well known in her writings and speech: Reformer: A Religious Work* 10–11 (1829): 139.

144　*he never wore coif or wig:* "Life and Times of William Cranch," records, Vols. 4–5, Columbia Historical Society (Washington, DC, 1901), 309. For more on Cranch, see Neil S. Kramer, "Half a Century Past Midnight: The Life and Times of Judge William Cranch," PhD diss., Claremont Graduate University, Claremont, CA, 1978; United States Reports: Cases Adjudged in the Supreme Court, Vol. 74, by United States, Supreme Court, William Cranch, Washington, District of Columbia: U.S. Govt. Printing Office.

145　*Without any reference to the guilt or the innocence: United States Gazette,* July 14, 1829.

146　*The widow of a revolutionary soldier: Morning Courier and New York Enquirer,* July 24, 1829.

146　*Judge Cranch presided with dignity but Mrs. Royall:* "Life and Times of William Cranch," 302.

146　*in the broadest accent of the turf: New York Commercial Advertiser,* July 23, 1829.

147　*Their testimony was clear and unequivocal:* Royall, *Mrs. Royall's Pennsylvania*, Vol. 2, 12, appendix.

147　*His maniken shape, his red picked snuffy nose: New York Commercial Advertiser,* July 23, 1829.

149　*Unfortunately for Mrs. Royall: Reformer: A Religious Work* 10–11 (1829): 139.

149　*"noble and commanding":* Royall, *Black Book,* 1:112.

149　*It requires no ordinary share of animal: United States Gazette,* July 10, 1829.

150　*General Jackson, General Jackson comes:* Anne Royall, *Letters from Alabama on Various Subjects* (Washington, 1830), 69.

150　*Jackson had met Rachel in 1788:* Books on Jackson and his wife, Rachel, abound. See Robert Remini, *The Life of Andrew Jackson* (Harper, 2011); Steve Inskeep, *Jacksonland: President Andrew Jackson, Cherokee Chief John Ross, and a Great American Land Grab* (Penguin, 2016).

151　*Ought a convicted adulteress:* Charles Hammond, pamphlet, quoted in W. David Sloan and Lisa Mullikin Parcell, *American Journalism: History, Principles, Practices* (McFarland, 2002), 182.

151　*In the presence of this dear saint, I can and do forgive all my enemies: Tennessee Historical Quarterly* 10–11 (1951): 27.

152　*particularly in those of a penal character:* Andrew Jackson, *Annual Messages, Veto Messages, Protest, &c. of Andrew Jackson, President of the United States* (E. J. Coale & Co., 1835), 67.

152  *any man who would have not done so, must have had the heart of a beast:* Royall, *Mrs. Royall's Pennsylvania*, Vol. 2, 19, appendix.

152  *in short metre, with no appearance of delight: Boston Patriot*, July 30, 1829.

152  *discovering Secretary E. was not a brute like themselves:* Royall, *Mrs. Royall's Pennsylvania*, Vol. 2, 19, appendix.

153  *has made an honest woman of his mistress:* Charles Hammond, quoted in John F. Marszalek, *The Petticoat Affair: Manners, Mutiny, and Sex in Andrew Jackson's White House* (LSU Press, 200), 48.

153  *perfect nose, of almost Grecian proportions:* Jon Meacham, *American Lion: Andrew Jackson in the White House* (Random House, 2009), 67.

154  *If you love the woman:* Daniel Feller (Editor), Harold D. Moser (Editor), Laura-Eve Moss (Editor), Thomas Coens (Editor), *Papers of Andrew Jackson*, 7:101.

154  *Tonight Gen'l. Eaton, the bosom friend:* Margaret Bayard Smith, *The First Forty Years of Washington Society* (Charles Scribner's Sons, 1906), 252.

155  *ill famed:* Ezra Stiles Ely, quoted in Daniel Feller (Editor), Harold D. Moser (Editor), Laura-Eve Moss (Editor), Thomas Coens (Editor), *Papers of Andrew Jackson*, 7:101.

155  *elegant figure:* Anne Royall, *Mrs. Royall's Southern Tour, or, Second Series of the Black Book* (Washington, 1830), Vol. 1, 20.

156  *a very fine man:* Royall, *Letters from Alabama on Various Subjects*, 212.

156  *I would resign the Presidency sooner than desert my friend Eaton:* Quoted in Charles Sellers, *James K. Polk*, Vol. 1, *Jacksonian, 1795–1843* (Princeton University Press, 2015), 147.

157  *In the midst of your important national affairs:* Ezra Stiles Ely, quoted in Daniel Feller (Editor), Harold D. Moser (Editor), Laura-Eve Moss (Editor), Thomas Coens (Editor), *Papers of Andrew Jackson*, 7:322.

157  *such as truth and justice required, and respect for the memory of my dear wife demanded:* Daniel Feller (Editor), Harold D. Moser (Editor), Laura-Eve Moss (Editor), Thomas Coens (Editor), *Papers of Andrew Jackson*, 7:325.

158  *Do you suppose that I have been sent here by the people to consult the ladies of Washington:* Quoted in Marszalek, *Petticoat Affair*, 65.

158  *The political history of the United States, for the past thirty years:* Quoted in Daniel Walker Howe, *What Hath God Wrought: The Transformation of America, 1815–1848* (Oxford University Press, 2007), 339.

158  *I had rather have live vermin on my back than the tongue:* Quoted in Jill Locke and Eileen Hunt Botting, *Feminist Interpretations of Alexis de Tocqueville* (Penn State University Press, 2010), 136.

159  *Ladies of the Georgetown aristocracy:* Samuel Hopkins Adams, *The Gorgeous Hussy* (Houghton, 1934), 183.

159  *never fails to shower the pearls of her eloquence: London and Paris Observer or Chronicle of Literature, Science* 5 (1829): 639.

160  *May it please the court, and you gentlemen of the jury: New York Commercial Advertiser*, August 4, 1829.

162  *may be rude, very rude—she may be deeply skeptical:* Lawrence Greatrake, *The Harp of Zion* (Johnston and Stockton, 1827), 72–73.

162  *most remarkable woman of her time:* H. S. Boutrell, "United States vs Ann Royal," *Georgetown Law Journal* 9 (1912): 43.

162 *consequence of an erratic career: The Philadelphia Album and Ladies' Literary Port Folio* 5 (January 8, 1831): 12.

162 *flop-bordered cap so exactly:* Royall, *Mrs. Royall's Pennsylvania,* Vol. 1, 217.

163 *driven from Alexandria by the threat of being carted:* New York Commercial Advertiser, August 4, 1829.

163 *It would be advisable before the next session of Congress:* Charleston Gazette, July 28, 1829.

163 *This is a pretty country to live in:* Records of the Columbia Historical Society, Washington, Vol. 23, 1989, 110.

164 *who have fallen into the current against an unprotected female, and chimed in to the same tune of her enemies: Reformer: A Religious Work* 10–11 (1829): 139.

164 *This verdict was pumpkin pie to Judge Cranch:* Royall, *Mrs. Royall's Pennsylvania,* Vol. 2, 16, appendix.

164 *the punishment of common scolds is quite obsolete in England: Niles' Weekly Register* 36, August 8, 1829, 390.

165 *may be dealt with in a lenient way: Morning Courier,* July 24, 1829.

165 *The Court is therefore of opinion: Niles' Weekly Register* 36, August 8, 1829, 392.

166 *I have no peace in my life from the whole gang:* Royall, complaint, *US v. Royall,* Box 158, Circuit Court District of Columbia Case Papers 1802–1863, Mat Term 1829, Washington, DC.

167 *Though these gentlemen have done themselves and the noble fraternity to which they belong:* Royall, *Mrs. Royall's Pennsylvania,* 17, appendix.

167 *the vituperative powers of this giantess of literature:* New York Observer, July 11, 1829.

167 *Still praying to convert me:* Royall, *Mrs. Royall's Pennsylvania,* 17, appendix.


## CHAPTER SIX: THE HUNTRESS IN THE DEN OF VIPERS

168 *There is many a journalist now languishing in poverty: The Huntress,* April 15, 1837.

169 *The excitement in this and the neighboring towns is very great:* Quoted in A. H. Saxon, *P. T. Barnum: The Legend and the Man* (Columbia University Press, 1995), 43.

170 *She strongly sympathized with me in my persecutions:* Phineas Taylor Barnum, *The Life of P. T. Barnum, Written by Himself* (Sampson Low, 1855), 128.

170 SOMETHING MYSTERIOUS: *United States Gazette,* August 6, 1829.

172 *"exceptions" to the pro-slavery Southern writers of their age: Journal of Negro History* 14 (1929): 404. Royall is singled out with abolitionist David Walker as "two exceptions" to other mild opposition to slavery in the press, "both of whom made very bitter attacks."

172 *Health to the sick, wealth to the brave:* Anne Royall, *Letters from Alabama on Various Subjects* (Washington, 1830), 151.

173 *Strange that a nation who extol so much:* Anne Royall, *Royall's Sketches of History, Life and Manners in the United States* (New Haven, 1826), 101.

173 *unspeakably gratified:* Anne Royall, *Mrs. Royall's Southern Tour, or, Second Series of the Black Book* (Washington, 1830), 90.

174 *The ruffians thundered at the door to break it open:* Ibid., 91.

174　*The annals of Camden will hereafter show 1830: Camden Journal*, March 27, 1830.

174　*We have very gloom advices from Fayetteville: Fayetteville Weekly Observer*, March 18, 1830.

176　*The only reputable people:* Royall, *Second Series of the Black Book*, 4.

176　*When I left the western country some years back:* Ibid., 6, appendix.

177　*My Dear Friends: What is the reason: Morning Courier and New York Enquirer*, March 1830.

178　*band of pirates in his name:* Royall, *Second Series of the Black Book*, 81.

178　*The lead trade, the Santa Fe trade:* Ibid., 82.

178　*From Orleans, arrived the eccentric and no less strange Woman:* William Clark, diary entry, quoted in *Kansas Historical Quarterly* 4 (1948): 395.

179　*cow skin, followed the complainant downstairs and inflicted the assault and battery: Pittsburgh Statesman*, reprinted in Louisville *Courier-Journal*, November 26, 1830.

179　*gazetted in every press, and he should be punished by the frowns of every petticoat in the Union: United States Telegraph*, November 26, 1830.

179　*To this end, let it be understood that we are of no party: Paul Pry*, December 3, 1831.

179　*Let all pious general, colonels and commandants of our army:* Ibid.

180　*There is no press in Washington to combat those traitors:* Anne Royall, *Black Book*, Vol. 1 (Washington, 1828), 197.

181　On Duff Green, Joseph Gales, William Winston Seaton, and early journalism in Washington, DC, see Carolyn Eastman, *A Nation of Speechifiers: Making an American Public after the Revolution* (University of Chicago Press, 2009); Maurine Hoffman Beasley, *The First Women Washington Correspondents* (George Washington University, 1976); Donald A. Ritchie, *Press Gallery: Congress and the Washington Correspondents* (Harvard University Press, 1991); Maurine H. Beasley, *Women of the Washington Press: Politics, Prejudice, and Persistence* (Northwestern University Press, 2012).

181　*The time has arrived when we have to make our* congee *to the public: Paul Pry*, December 3, 1831.

182　*An old lady of a perpetual liveliness, no property but a printery: American Mercury*, September 1927.

182　*65 women editors and printers took the reins prior to 1820:* Jonathan Wells, *Women Writers and Journalists in the 19th Century* (Cambridge University Press, 2011).

183　*She was the terror of the politicians:* John Forney, quoted in John Seely Hart, *A Manual of American Literature* (Eldridge and Brother, 1873), 308.

184　*A squat old woman, with a green calash:* William Price, *Clement Falconer, or The Memoirs of a Young Whig* (N. Hickman, 1838), 94.

185　*completely destitute of intellectual ability:* Mary Chase Barney, "General Jackson," *National Magazine* (July 2, 1831): 210.

185　*The natural timidity of my sex vanishes before the necessity of my situation:* Quoted in Wells, *Women Writers and Journalists*, 98.

185　*I have to set type—learn Grammar—and spell words for Mrs. Royall: The Huntress*, October 9, 1852.

186　*Her fidelity, industry, and dispatch of business have never been surpassed:* Quoted in Sarah Harvey Porter, *The Life and Times of Anne Royall* (Torch Press, 1909), 151.

186　*Should there be any shortcoming in the present number of our paper: Paul Pry*, February 4, 1832.

187　*We leave party questions in better hands, to our friends of the Union and Intelligencer: The Huntress*, quoted in Porter, *Life and Times*, 180.

188  *a greater influence on the souls of men:* Alexis de Tocqueville, *Democracy in America* (Edward Walker, 1847), 382.

188  *We have just been through the U.S., and with the exception of Louisiana and Georgia:* Paul Pry, December 31, 1831.

188  *defend the rights of people against tyranny and corruption:* Paul Pry, December, 31, 1831.

190  *lest the report might injure the bank-men, who own property in the city:* Paul Pry, June 20, 1835.

190  *These unions will form an era in the history of the world:* Paul Pry, April 26, 1834.

191  *fearlessness of spirit:* Thomas Dowling, *Political Observer*, printed in *Paul Pry*, July 27, 1833.

192  *powers of observation and description:* New York Commercial Advertiser, printed in *Paul Pry*, December 31, 1831.

192  *all the scum, billingsgate and filth extant:* New England Religious Weekly, reprinted in Porter, *Life and Times*, 167.

192  *Wonder in what part of the Bible:* Paul Pry, April 28, 1832.

192  *Me to inspire ye sacred nine:* Quoted in Porter, *Life and Times*, 166.

193  *the Second Bank of the United States played an oversized role in financial concerns:* For more on the Second Bank crisis, see Daniel Howe, *What Hath God Wrought: The Transformation of America, 1815–1848* (Oxford University Press, 2007), 379; Robert Remini, *Andrew Jackson and the Bank War: A Study in the Growth of Presidential Power* (Norton, 1967).

193  *the strikes of Hydra:* See Robert V. Remini, *Andrew Jackson: The Course of American Democracy, 1833–1845* (HarperCollins, 1984).

194  *I paid little attention to the US Bank until my last tour:* Royall, *Second Series of the Black Book*, 6, appendix.

194  *something negative about the Bank:* Jeffrey Bourdon, "Compassionate Protector of America: The Symbolism of Old Hickory in a Jackson Woman's Mind," *American Nineteenth Century History* 12, no. 2 (June 2011): 177.

195  *reputation and honor:* Sean Wilentz, *Andrew Jackson: The American Presidents Series: The 7th President, 1829–1837* (Times Books, 2007), 75.

195  *the fiery, female editor:* Bourdon, "Compassionate Protector," 192.

196  *You are a den of vipers:* Bourdon cites Stan V. Henkels, *Andrew Jackson and the Bank of the United States* (Gollifox Press 1928), which published the memo from 1834.

196  *a lady of great literary eminence:* Thomas Benton, *Thirty Years' View; or, A History of the Working of the American Government for Thirty Years, from 1820 to 1850* (Appleton and Co., 1886), 263. Chiefly taken from the Congress debates, the private papers of General Jackson and the speeches of ex-senator Benton, with his actual view of men and affairs; contains historical notes and illustrations and some notices of eminent deceased contemporaries.

196  *frankly and fearlessly:* Howe, *What Hath God Wrought*, 379.

196  *The rich and powerful too often bend the acts of government to their selfish purposes:* Quoted in Thomas M. Leonard, *James K. Polk: A Clear and Unquestionable Destiny* (Rowman and Littlefield, 200), 21.

197  *ushered in a new mode of investigative reporting:* Doris Kearns Goodwin, *The Bully Pulpit: Theodore Roosevelt, William Howard Taft, and the Golden Age of Journalism* (Simon and Schuster, 2013).

197  *Having silenced the anties:* Paul Pry, February 4, 1832.

NOTES TO PAGES 197-212

197   Hon. Aaron V. Brown is a new member from Tennessee: The Huntress, June 13, 1846.

198   The fulsome flattery bespattered: Georgetown (KY) Herald, quoted in The Huntress,
        June 13, 1846.

198   Mrs. Royall has a rare knack of castigating the enemy: Montgomery (AL) Journal quoted in
        Porter, The Life and Times of Anne Royall, 128.

199   to slander a whole nation: Maria Weston Chapman, Harriet Martineau's Autobiography
        (Osgood and Co., 1877), 240.

199   I do not like their principles; I do not like their manners, I do not like their opinions: Frances
        Trollope, Domestic Manners of the Americans (Whittaker, 1832), 321.

200   Were it not for the churches, indeed, I think there might be a general bonfire of best bonnets:
        Ibid., 75.

200   Many of these wretched creatures were beautiful young females: Ibid., 144.

201   expose the hypocrisy and impositions of the clergy in general: The Huntress, June 17, 1837.

202   will be open to any and every party or sect, who may consider themselves aggrieved: Ibid.

202   Our paper is small, the weather is cold: Paul Pry, December 31, 1831.

202   I always have a bad opinion of women: Royall, Second Series of the Black Book, 133. For
        more on women, travel writing, and respectability, see Elizabeth J. Clapp, "Black
        Books and Southern Tours: Tone and Perspective in the Travel Writing of Mrs. Anne
        Royall," Yearbook of English Studies 34, Nineteenth-Century Travel Writing (2004): 61;
        Karen Ramsay Johnson, "Anne Royall's Apocalyptic Rhetoric: Politics and the Role
        of Women," Women's Studies (October 2010); Anne Scott, Unheard Voices: The First
        Historians of Southern Women (University of Virginia Press, 1993).

203   A friend, now present member of Congress, says, "Mrs. R": Royall, Second Series of the
        Black Book, 105.

203   Were I a man, this fallacious argument ought to have no weight: Royall, Mrs. Royall's Penn-
        sylvania, 185.

204   If ever the liberty of America is overturned: Paul Pry, April 5, 1834.

204   We do not oppose abolition: Paul Pry, June 4, 1836.

205   The poor abolitionists are not the prime movers of these appalling principles: Quoted in
        Porter, Life and Times, 189.

206   plot to make this place the seat of MONARCHY: Paul Pry, July 12, 1834.

207   cannot be blinded by these rotten-hearted pretenders: Paul Pry, March 21, 1835.

207   van of the editorial corps, attacking the enemies of the country: Paul Pry, November 19,
        1836.

208   There could not exist a greater evidence of unbounded avarice and ambition which distin-
        guished the Christian world: Royall, Letters from Alabama on Various Subjects, 56.

208   While we advocate equal rights: Paul Pry, 1832.

209   The name is not inappropriate: The Huntress, December 2, 1836.

210   Mrs. Royall owes an apology to her friends for the very limited editorial matter: The Huntress,
        May 12, 1837.

210   Our country is an asylum for foreigners, and long may it be so: The Huntress, February 8,
        1840.

211   under the pretence of fighting battles of the lord: The Huntress, October 21, 1848.

211   There is nothing more unpleasant to us than political controversy: The Huntress, June 17, 1837.

212   Those who feel an interest in the lonely and suffering condition of the widow: The Huntress,
        October 21, 1843.

212   Three years later, a congressional bill: Royall's actual pension was granted via RG 217:

A Bill for the Relief of the Widow and Heirs of Captain William Royall Deceased, April 25, 1834, Public Statutes at Large, 6:595.

212 *El Republicano:* Corydon Donnavan, *Adventures in Mexico* (Robinson & Jones, 1847), 69.

213 *What a wonderful woman you are:* Ann Gordon, *The Selected Papers of Elizabeth Cady Stanton and Susan B. Anthony: In the School of Anti-Slavery, 1840 to 1866* (Rutgers University Press, 1997), 265.

214 *trust in heaven for three things: The Huntress,* July 24, 1854.

## EPILOGUE: THE TRIAL OF PUBLIC OPINION

215 *I shall be told that historians confine themselves to great females:* Anne Royall, *Mrs. Royall's Pennsylvania; or, Travels Continued in the United States,* 2 vols. (Washington, 1829), 186.

216 *Anne Royall made her way from frontier obscurity:* Shirley Graham Du Bois, "An Explanation" (summary of *The Woman in the Case,* her biography of Anne Royall), September 1962, Shirley Graham Du Bois Papers.

216 *Does she know I'm a criminal:* Shirley Graham Du Bois, *There Was Once a Slave: The Heroic Story* (J. Messner, 1947), 111.

218 *Anne knew that she was overstaying her time:* Shirley Graham Du Bois, *The Woman in the Case,* unpublished manuscript.

219 *As a radical woman writer of color:* See Gerald Horne, *Race Woman: The Lives of Shirley Graham Du Bois* (New York University Press, 2000); Shirley Graham Du Bois, *His Day Is Marching On: A Memoir of W. E. B. Du Bois* (J. B. Lippincott, 1971).

220 *beggar, blackmailer and common scold:* "The Life and Times of Anne Royall," *New York Times,* March 27, 1909.

221 *This eccentric woman whose death we noticed yesterday was aged ninety-two years: Washington Evening Star,* October 3, 1854.

222 *bow down in fear:* "She Was a Holy Terror: Her Pen Was as Venomous as a Rattlesnake's Fangs; Former Washington Editress: How Ann Royall Made Life a Burden to the Public Men of Her Day," *Washington Post,* February 22, 1891.

222 *wandering piper: New Yorker,* August 27, 1836.

222 *Obituaries that mostly stressed her satirical gifts missed the main point:* Paul Krugman, *New York Times,* February 2, 2007.

223 *One kind that makes us chuckle about our foibles:* Molly Ivins, "The Mouth of Texas," *People Weekly,* December 9, 1991.

223 *This Amazon would have been more appropriately employed: Gowan's Catalogue of American Books* (W. Gowans, 1860).

224 *Female irreligion:* Barbara Welter, "The Cult of True Womanhood," *American Quarterly* 18, no. 2, pt. 1 (Summer 1966): 15.

224 *ethos of a politicized American womanhood:* Karen Ramsay Johnson, "Anne Royall's Apocalyptic Rhetoric: Politics and the Role of Women," *Women's Studies* 31, no. 5 (October 2002).

224 *that she published* The Huntress *for a quarter of a century:* Elizabeth C. Stanton, Susan B. Anthony, *History of Woman Suffrage* (Fowler & Wells, 1881).

224 *special pest of Washington city:* John Seely Hart, *A Manual of American Literature,* (Eldridge and Brother, 1873), 308.

225 *voice, a strident voice, crying out for national righteousness:* Sarah Harvey Porter, *The Life and Times of Anne Royall* (Torch Press, 1909), 229.

225 *brought tears to the eyes of some of the listeners: New Age Magazine* 15 (1911): 199.

226 *People laughed at Anne Royall: Cavalcade of America Radio,* "The Printer Was a Lady," May 4, 1942.

226 *pioneer woman journalist:* "Common Scold," *Ms. Magazine*, 1974.

226 *Royall's apocryphal tale of her dalliance with John Quincy Adams:* Cokie Roberts, *We Are Our Mothers' Daughters* (Harper Perennial, 2010), 165.

227 *Anne Royall's stone:* "TO SAVE HISTORIC STONE; Protest Over Removal of Anne Royall Rock from Park," *New York Times*, August 1913.

227 *practically non-existent:* Margaret Truman, *The President's House: 1800 to the Present*, (Ballantine Reprint, 2007).

227 *America's first nationally recognized gossip columnist:* Nancy Isenberg, "The Infamous Anne Royall: Jacksonian Gossip, Scribbler, and Scold," in Kathleen Feeley and Jennifer Frost, eds., *When Private Talk Goes Public: Gossip in American History* (Palgrave Macmillan, 2014).

228 *I feel that if this were a crime today:* Cokie Roberts, address to the Commonwealth Club, San Francisco, California, May 11, 1998.

229 *common vengeance writes the law:* Arthur Miller, *The Crucible* (Penguin Books, 2003), 51.

230 *Mad Anne, the Huntress:* Anne Royall, *Royall's Sketches* (New Haven, 1826), 50.

# Bibliography

I first encountered Anne Royall during the research for my book *The United States of Appalachia* (Counterpoint Press, 2006) and began my research from primary and secondary sources at archives and courthouses in Monroe County, West Virginia; Staunton, Virginia; and Washington, DC. Over the past decade, I have been indebted to librarians and researchers at numerous archives, including the *Schlesinger Library* at the Radcliffe Institute for Advanced Study at Harvard University, which houses the Shirley Graham Du Bois Papers; the Anne Newport Royall Collection; the Library of Congress Manuscript Division, where I had access to the George Watterston Papers and the Thomas Jefferson Papers; the National Archives and Records Administration in Washington, DC; the University of Virginia, where the Anne Royall Papers and the Thomas Jefferson Papers are kept; the Pennsylvania State Archives; the Presbyterian Historical Society in Philadelphia; and the University of Iowa.

As a prolific writer and newspaper publisher, Anne Royall left behind a treasury of written documents, much of which has received scant historical attention or analysis.

## ANNE ROYALL SOURCES

*Paul Pry* newspaper, 1831–36, Washington, DC.
*The Huntress* newspaper, 1836–54, Washington, DC.
Royall, Anne. *The Black Book; or, a Continuation of Travels in the United States.* 3 vols.
  Washington, DC, 1828–29.

*Letters from Alabama on Various Subjects: To Which Is Added an Appendix Containing Remarks on Sundry Members of the 20th and 21st Congress and Other High Characters, etc. etc. at the Seat of Government.* Washington, DC, 1830.

*Mrs. Royall's Pennsylvania; or Travels Continued in the United States.* 2 vols. Washington, DC, 1829.

*Mrs. Royall's Southern Tour; or Second Series of the Black Book.* 3 vols. Washington, DC, 1830–31.

*Sketches of History, Life and Manners in the United States. By a Traveller.* New Haven, Connecticut, 1826.

*The Tennessean; A Novel Founded on Fact.* New Haven, Connecticut, 1827.

*United States v. Royall,* Box 158, Circuit Court District of Columbia Case Papers 1802–1863, May Term, 1829.

## NEWSPAPERS AND PERIODICALS

*Albany Daily Advertiser*
*American Masonic Record and Albany Saturday Magazine*
*American Mercury*
*American Quarterly*
*American Register*
*Baltimore Patriot*
*Baltimore Sun*
*Bedford Gazette*
*Bookman*
*Boston Daily Commercial Gazette*
*Charleston Gazette*
*Cincinnati Gazette*
*Columbia Historical Society*
*Christian Baptist*
*Cornhill Magazine*
*Fayetteville Weekly Observer*
*Georgetown Law Journal*
*Godey's Lady's Book (Magazine)*
*Hallowell Gazette*
*Hampden Journal*
*Hartford Religious Inquirer*
*Journal of Negro History*
*Journal of Presbyterian History*
*Journal of Southern History*
*Kansas Historical Quarterly*
*Literary Port Folio*
*London and Paris Observer or Chronicle of Literature, Science*
*London Quarterly Review*
*Louisville Courier Journal*
*Morning Courier and New York Enquirer*
*National Intelligencer*

*National Journal*
*New England Galaxy*
*New England Weekly Review*
*New Hampshire Gazette*
*New Hampshire Patriot*
*New York American*
*New York Commercial Advertiser*
*New York Enquirer*
*New York Spectator*
*New York Times*
*New Yorker*
*Niles' Weekly Register*
*North American and United States Gazette*
*North American Review*
*North-American Review and Miscellaneous Journal*
*Northampton Post*
*Ohio Statesman*
*Philadelphia Album and Ladies' Literary Port Folio*
*Portland Argus*
*Quarterly Journal of the American Education Society*
*Rambler's Magazine; or, Fashionable Emporium of Polite Literature*
*Reformer: A Religious Work*
*Salem Gazette*
*Sartain's Union Magazine of Literature and Art*
*Tennessee Historical Quarterly*
*Unitarian*
*United States Gazette*
*United States Telegraph*
*Virginia Magazine of History and Biography*
*Washington Post*
*West Virginia and Kenawha County Gazette*
*West Virginia Monthly Review*
*West Virginia Review*
*Western Pennsylvania History*
*Western Times*

## PRIMARY SOURCES

Adams, John Quincy. *Memoirs of John Quincy Adams, Comprising Portions of His Diary from 1795 to 1848.* Edited by Charles Francis. Philadelphia, 1874–77.

Adams, Samuel Hopkins. *The Gorgeous Hussy.* Boston: Houghton, 1934.

Barnum, Phineas Taylor. *The Life of P. T. Barnum, Written by Himself.* London: Sampson Low, 1855.

Benton, Thomas. *Thirty Years' View; or, A History of the Working of the American Government for Thirty Years, from 1820 to 1850.* New York: Appleton and Co., 1886.

Bowlan, Elizabeth. *Trial of a Scold: The Trial of Mrs. Elizabeth Bowlan, Who Was Indicted for*

*Being a Common Barrator, and also a Noisy, Turbulent Brawler and Common Scold.* Boston: Nathaniel Coverly, 1813.

*Cavalcade of America Radio.* "The Printer Was a Lady." May 4, 1942.

Chase, Salmon. *The Salmon P. Chase Papers.* 5 vols. Kent, OH: Kent State University Press, 1994.

Cranch, William. United States Reports: Cases Adjudged in the Supreme Court, Volume 74, By United States. Supreme Court, William Cranch, Washington, District of Columbia: U.S. Govt. Printing Office.

Crockett, David. *The Life and Adventures of Colonel David Crockett of Tennessee.* Cincinnati, OH: 1833.

Donnavan, Corydon. *Adventures in Mexico.* Cincinnati, OH: Robinson & Jones, 1847.

Du Bois, Shirley Graham. "An Explanation." Summary of *The Woman in the Case,* her biography of Anne Royall. September 1962. Shirley Graham Du Bois Papers, Schlesinger Library, Radcliffe Institute for Advanced Study, Harvard University.

———. *There Was Once a Slave: The Heroic Story.* New York: J. Messner, 1947.

Ely, Ezra Stiles. *The Duty of Christian Freemen to Elect Christian Rulers.* Philadelphia: William Geddes, 1828.

Foster, Hannah Webster. *The Coquette.* New York: Columbia University Press, 1939.

Greatrake, Lawrence. *The Harp of Zion.* Pittsburgh: Johnston and Stockton, 1827.

Irving, Washington. *A History of New York.* New York: Penguin Classics, 2008.

Jackson, Andrew. *Annual Messages, Veto Messages, Protest, &c. of Andrew Jackson, President of the United States.* Washington, DC: E. J. Coale & Co., 1835.

———. *The Papers of Andrew Jackson.* Vol. 7: 1829. Knoxville: University of Tennessee Press, 2007.

Jefferson, Thomas. Thomas Jefferson to Ezra Stiles Ely, June 25, 1819. Papers of Thomas Jefferson, Founders Early Access, The University of Virginia Press. http://rotunda .upress.virginia.edu/founders/default.xqy?keys=FOEA-print-04-02-02-0542.

Middletown, Thomas. *The Black Book (1604), Collected Works.* Oxford: Oxford University Press, 2008.

Miller, Arthur. *The Crucible.* New York: Penguin Books, 2003.

Nashe, Thomas. *Selected Works.* New York: Routledge Revivals, 2015.

Paulding, James Kirke. *The Backwoodsman, A Poem.* New York: M. Thomas, 1818.

———. *John Bull in America, or, The New Munchausen.* New York: Charles Wiley, 1825.

———. *The Lion of the West.* Palo Alto, CA: Stanford University Press, 1954.

Pennsylvania Supreme Court, *Reports of Cases Adjudged in the Supreme Court of Pennsylvania, [1814–1828],* vol. 12 (Kay & Brother, 1872–75).

Price, William. *Clement Falconer, or The Memoirs of a Young Whig.* Baltimore: N. Hickman, 1838.

Reagan, Ronald. Public Papers of the Presidents of the United States: Ronald Reagan, 1988–89, Washington, DC: U.S. Govt. Printing Office, 1990.

Roberts, Cokie. Address to the Commonwealth Club, San Francisco, California, May 11, 1998. http://gos.sbc.edu/r/roberts.html.

Roosevelt, Theodore. Address at U.S. House of Representatives, Washington, DC, April 14, 1906.

Shelton, Frederick William. *The Trolliopiad: Or, Travelling Gentlemen in America; a Satire.* New York: C. Shepard, 1837.

Smith, Margaret Bayard. *The First Forty Years of Washington Society.* New York: Charles Scribner's Sons, 1906.

Stanton, Elizabeth C., and Susan B. Anthony. *History of Woman Suffrage*. New York: Fowler & Wells, 1881.

Tocqueville, Alexis de. *Democracy in America*. New York: Edward Walker, 1847.

Trollope, Frances. *Domestic Manners of the Americans*. London: Whittaker, 1832.

Wade, John. *The Black Book; or, Corruption Unmasked!* London: Fairburn, 1820.

Wright, Frances. *Views of Society and Manners in America*. London: Longman, Hurst, Rees, Orme, and Brown, 1821.


## SECONDARY SOURCES


Abler, Thomas. *Cornplanter: Chief Warrior of the Allegany Senecas*. Syracuse, NY: Syracuse University Press, 2007.

Aderman, Ralph M., and Wayne R. Kime. *Advocate for America: The Life of James Kirke Paulding*. Plainsboro, PA: Susquehanna University Press, 2003.

Anbinder, Tyler. *Five Points: The 19th-Century New York City Neighborhood That Invented Tap Dance, Stole Elections, and Became the World's Most Notorious Slum*. New York: Plume, 2002.

Beasley, Maurine Hoffman. *The First Women Washington Correspondents*. Washington, DC: George Washington University, 1976.

———. *Women of the Washington Press: Politics, Prejudice, and Persistence*. Evanston, IL: Northwestern University Press, 2012.

Bourdon, Jeffrey. "Compassionate Protector of America: The Symbolism of Old Hickory in a Jackson Woman's Mind," *American Nineteenth Century History* 12, no. 2 (June 2011).

Botting, Eileen Hunt. *Feminist Interpretations of Alexis de Tocqueville*. Harrisburg, PA: Penn State University Press, 2010.

Bradley, Patricia. *Women and the Press*. Evanston, IL: Northwestern University Press, 2005.

Bridges, Edwin. *Alabama: The Making of an American State*. Tuscaloosa: University of Alabama Press, 2016.

Brooks, Van Wyck. *Makers and Finders: A History of the Writer in America, 1800–1915*. Vol. 1. New York: E. P. Dutton, 1950.

———. *The World of Washington Irving*. New York: E. P. Dutton, 1944.

Burrows, Edwin. *Gotham: A History of New York City to 1898*. Oxford: Oxford University Press, 2000.

Burstein, Andrew. *The Original Knickerbocker: The Life of Washington Irving*. New York: Basic Books, 2008.

Chapman, Maria Weston. *Harriet Martineau's Autobiography*. Boston: Osgood and Co., 1877.

Clapp, Elizabeth J. "Black Books and Southern Tours: Tone and Perspective in the Travel Writing of Mrs. Anne Royall." *Yearbook of English Studies* 34, Nineteenth-Century Travel Writing (2004).

———. "A Virago-Errant in Enchanted Armor? Anne Royall's 1829 Trial as a Common Scold." *Journal of the Early Republic* 23, no. 2 (Summer 2003).

Cohen, Patricia. *The Murder of Helen Jewett: The Life and Death of a Prostitute in Nineteenth-Century New York*. New York: Knopf, 1998.

Davis, Thomas. *Footloose in Jacksonian America: Robert W. Scott and His Agrarian World*. Lexington: University Press of Kentucky, 2001.

Dickey, J. D. *Empire of Mud Washington*. Guilford, CT: Lyons Press, 2015.

Du Bois, Shirley Graham. *His Day Is Marching On: A Memoir of W. E. B. Du Bois.* New York: J. B. Lippincott, 1971.

Earle, Alice Morse. *Curious Punishments of Bygone Days.* Chicago: H. S. Stone, 1896.

Eastman, Carolyn. *A Nation of Speechifiers: Making an American Public after the Revolution,* Chicago: University of Chicago Press, 2009.

Eckhardt, Celia Morris. *Fanny Wright: Rebel in America.* Cambridge, MA: Harvard University Press, 1984.

Filler, Louis. *Appointment at Armageddon: Muckraking and Progressivism in the American Tradition.* Westport, CT: Greenwood Press, 1976.

Griffen, Leslie. "The Antimasonic Persuasion." PhD diss., Cornell University, 1951. Quoted in Lee Benson, *The Concept of Jacksonian Democracy: New York as a Test Case.* Princeton, NJ: Princeton University Press, 1961.

Griffith, Lucille. Biographical introduction and notes, *Letters from Alabama, 1817–1822, by Anne Royall.* Tuscaloosa: University of Alabama Press, 1969.

Goodman, Mathew. *The Sun and the Moon: The Remarkable True Account of Hoaxers, Showmen, Dueling Journalists, and Lunar Man-Bats in Nineteenth-Century New York.* New York: Basic Books, 2010.

Goodwin, Doris Kearns. *The Bully Pulpit: Theodore Roosevelt, William Howard Taft, and the Golden Age of Journalism.* New York: Simon and Schuster, 2013.

Hackett, David G. *That Religion in Which All Men Agree: Anti-Masonry and the Public Sphere, 1826–1850.* Oakland: University of California Press, 2014.

Hackett Fischer, David. *Albion's Seed: Four British Folkways in America.* Oxford: Oxford University Press, 1989.

Hart, John Seely. *A Manual of American Literature.* Philadelphia: Eldridge and Brother, 1873.

Heineman, Helen. *Mrs. Trollope: The Triumphant Feminine in the Nineteenth Century.* Athens: Ohio University Press, 1979.

Holton, Woody. *Forced Founders: Indians, Debtors, Slaves, and the Making of the American Revolution in Virginia.* Chapel Hill: University of North Carolina Press, 1999.

Howe, Daniel Walker. *What Hath God Wrought: The Transformation of America, 1815–1848.* Oxford: Oxford University Press, 2007.

Inskeep, Steve. *Jacksonland: President Andrew Jackson, Cherokee Chief John Ross, and a Great American Land Grab.* New York: Penguin, 2016.

Isaac, Rhys. *The Transformation of Virginia, 1740–1790.* Chapel Hill: University of North Carolina Press, 1999.

Isenberg, Nancy. "The Infamous Anne Royall: Jacksonian Gossip, Scribbler, and Scold." In Kathleen Feeley and Jennifer Frost, eds., *When Private Talk Goes Public: Gossip in American History.* New York: Palgrave Macmillan, 2014.

Jackson, George Stuyvesant. *Uncommon Scold: The Story of Anne Royall.* New York: B. Humphries, 1937.

James, Bessie Rowland. *Anne Royall's U.S.A.* New Brunswick, NJ: Rutgers University Press, 1972.

Johnson, Karen Ramsay. "Anne Royall's Apocalyptic Rhetoric: Politics and the Role of Women." *Women's Studies* (October 2010).

Justus, James. *Fetching the Old Southwest: Humorous Writing from Longstreet to Twain.* Columbia: University of Missouri, 2004.

Kramer, Neil S. "Half a Century Past Midnight: The Life and Times of Judge William Cranch." PhD diss., Claremont Graduate School, Claremont, CA, 1978.

Lambert, Byron C. *Rise of the Anti-mission Baptists*. New York: Arno Press, 1980.

Landsay, Lori. *Madcaps, Screwballs, and Con Women: The Female Trickster in American Culture*. Philadelphia: University of Pennsylvania Press, 1998.

Leary, Lewis Gaston. *The Book-Peddling Parson: An Account of the Life and Works of Mason Locke Weems, Patriot, Pitchman, Author, and Purveyor of Morality to the Citizenry of the Early United States of America*. Chapel Hill, NC: Algonquin Books, 1984.

Leonard, Thomas M. *James K. Polk: A Clear and Unquestionable Destiny*. Lanham, MD: Rowman and Littlefield, 2000.

Lewis, Tom. *Washington: A History of Our National City*. New York: Basic Books, 2015.

Libby, David J. *Slavery and Frontier Mississippi, 1720–1835*. Oxford: University Press of Mississippi, 2008.

Marcus, Leonard. *Minders of Make-Believe: Idealists, Entrepreneurs, and the Shaping of American Children's Literature*. Boston: Houghton Mifflin Harcourt, 2008.

Marszalek, John F. *The Petticoat Affair: Manners, Mutiny, and Sex in Andrew Jackson's White House*. Baton Rouge: Louisiana State University Press, 2000.

Maxwell, Alice, and Marion Dunlevy. *Virago! The Story of Anne Newport Royall*. Jefferson, NC: McFarland, 1985.

McDonald, Linda. "Anne Royall: Social Critic." Master's thesis, University of Washington, 1967.

Meacham, Jon. *American Lion: Andrew Jackson in the White House*. New York: Random House, 2009.

Morley, Jefferson. *Snow-Storm in August: Washington City, Francis Scott Key, and the Forgotten Race Riot of 1835*. New York: Nan Talese, 2012.

Parson, Lynn Hudson. *The Birth of Modern Politics: Andrew Jackson, John Quincy Adams, and the Election of 1828*. Oxford: Oxford University Press, 2011.

Paul, Reid. "In the Publick Streets." Master's thesis. University of Wisconsin–Madison, 1998.

Phillips, Kim Tousley. *William Duane, Radical Journalist in the Age of Jefferson*. New York: Garland Publishing, 1989.

Porter, Sarah Harvey. *The Life and Times of Anne Royall*. Cedar Rapids, IA: Torch Press, 1909.

Remini, Robert. *Andrew Jackson and the Bank War: A Study in the Growth of Presidential Power*. New York: W. W. Norton, 1967.

———. *The Jacksonian Era*. New York: Wiley, 1996.

———. *The Life of Andrew Jackson*. New York: Harper, 2011.

Ritchie, Donald A. *Press Gallery: Congress and the Washington Correspondents*. Cambridge, MA: Harvard University Press, 1991.

Roberts, Cokie. *We Are Our Mothers' Daughters*. New York: Harper Perennial, 2010.

Rogers, William Warren. *Alabama: The History of a Deep South State*. Tuscaloosa: University of Alabama Press, 2010.

Roscoe, Henry. *Specimens of the American Poets*. London: T. and J. Allman, 1822.

Saxon, A. H. *P. T. Barnum: The Legend and the Man*. New York: Columbia University Press, 1995.

Schlereth, Eric R. *An Age of Infidels: The Politics of Religious Controversy in the Early United States*. Philadelphia: University of Pennsylvania Press, 2013.

Schlesinger, Arthur, Jr. *The Age of Jackson*. New York: Little Brown and Co., 1945.

Scott, Anne. *Unheard Voices: The First Historians of Southern Women*. Charlottesville: University of Virginia Press, 1993.

Sellers, Charles. *James K. Polk. Vol. 1: Jacksonian, 1795–1843*. Princeton, NJ: Princeton University Press, 2015.

Sherwood, Grace. "Grace Sherwood, The One Virginia Witch." *Harper's Magazine* 69 (1884).

Shulman, Holly Cowan, and David B. Mattern. *Dolley Madison: Her Life, Letters, and Legacy*. New York: Rosen Publishing, 2003.

Sloan, W. David, and Lisa Mullikin Parcell. *American Journalism: History, Principles, Practices*. Jefferson, NC: McFarland, 2002.

Spero, Patrick. *Frontier Country: The Politics of War in Early Pennsylvania*. Philadelphia: University of Pennsylvania Press, 2016.

Steadman, Jennifer. *Traveling Economics: American Women's Travel Writing*. Columbus: Ohio State University Press, 2007.

Sterling, Dorothy. *Ahead of Her Time: Abby Kelley and the Politics of Antislavery*. New York: W. W. Norton, 1994.

Truman, Margaret. *The President's House: 1800 to the Present*. New York: Ballantine Reprint, 2007.

Van der Veer Hamilton, Virginia. *Alabama: A History*. New York: W. W. Norton, 1984.

Vaughn, William Preston. *The Anti-Masonic Party in the United States: 1826–1843*. Lexington: University of Kentucky Press, 2009.

Walker, Nancy. *A Very Serious Thing: Women's Humor and American Culture*. Minneapolis: University of Minnesota Press, 1988.

Wells, Jonathan. *Women Writers and Journalists in the 19th Century*. Cambridge: Cambridge University Press, 2011.

Welter, Barbara. "The Cult of True Womanhood." *American Quarterly* 18, no. 2, pt. 1 (Summer 1966).

Wilentz, Sean. *Andrew Jackson: The American Presidents Series: The 7th President, 1829–1837*. New York: Times Book, 2007.

Williams, Benjamin. *A Literary History of Alabama: The Nineteenth Century*. Rutherford, NJ: Fairleigh Dickenson University Press, 1979.

Williams, Susan. *Reclaiming Authorship: Literary Women in America, 1850–1900*. Philadelphia: University of Pennsylvania Press, 2006.

Wolin, Sheldon S. *Tocqueville between Two Worlds: The Making of a Political and Theoretical Life*. Princeton, NJ: Princeton University Press, 2003.

Woodward, Helen Beal. *The Bold Women*. Freeport, NY: Books for Libraries Press, 1971.

Wright, Richard. *Forgotten Ladies*. New York: J. B. Lippincott Company, 1928.

Zagarri, Rosemarie. *Revolutionary Backlash: Women and Politics in the Early American Republic*. Philadelphia: University of Pennsylvania Press, 2011.